The Micro-Society School

The Micro-Society School

A REAL WORLD IN MINIATURE

GEORGE RICHMOND

HARPER & ROW, PUBLISHERS
New York, Evanston, San Francisco, London

 For information address Harper & Row, Publishers, Inc., 10 East 53rd Street, New York, N.Y. 10022. Published simultaneously in Canada by Fitzhenry & Whiteside Limited, Toronto.

FIRST EDITION

Designed by Sidney Feinberg

Library of Congress Cataloguing in Publication Data

Richmond, George H.
The micro-society school.
1. Education—Simulation methods. 2. Economics—Study and teaching. 3. Role playing. I. Title.
LB1029.S53R52 372.1'3 73–4119
ISBN 0–06–013548–4

To
Jill and Riva
and to
Richard B. Sewall

Contents

Part III. Theory

Acknowledgments

I have learned that a book is the product of many people, not just one. In various places in the text I have acknowledged my indebtedness to the giants of social philosophy, of psychological theory, and of education practice. This section of a book is usually set aside to thank the people who had a direct hand in making the manuscript and the projects described herein happen.

First, let me thank Bill Watman, who years ago shared with me the dream of the Society School. Thanks next to Mrs. Brooke Astor and Robert Bickford of the Vincent Astor Foundation, Martha Wallace and Robert Armstrong of the Henry Luce Foundation, William Beinecke and Edward Hynes of the Beinecke Foundation, Neil M'Connell and Douglas Williamson of the M'Connell Foundation, and the Harvard–M.I.T. Joint Center for Urban Studies. Their support and vision in my hour of need made it possible to continue what we had started.

I am also grateful to Francis Keppel, former U.S. Commissioner of Education, Christopher Jencks, Donald Oliver, Lawrence Kohlberg, Robert Dentler, and Thomas Edwards. I owe debts to Barbara Leondar, Mary Allison, Dan Waddell, and Leslie Orear for helping me learn to write, to my wife and daughter for standing the obsession of writing, and to Sarah and Fred Dubin for their unflinching loyalty and help. I owe more than I can say to the staffs of Broad Jump and

P.S. 126 but for whom there would be nothing to say. I owe a special debt to Jeannette Hopkins. She saw possibilities in this manuscript that others did not, and did more than anyone else to see that they bloomed. Thanks, thanks, thanks, but most of all thanks to the children for sharing experiences with me and to Doug Booth for typing them.

Foreword

Five years ago, I expected to say whatever I might have to say in oils, or in pen and ink. Suddenly, I found myself in a classroom struggling to remain sane in an unhealthy place. That struggle necessitated a certain amount of shifting, experimenting, and inventing, so much so that I have not picked up a brush since. And yet when I examine what I've done, it seems to me to be an extension of a quest to put imagination at the center of my life. That's the vocation of a poet, not of an educator.

For me, then, this volume is a poem about being in a difficult place, and about inventing a fiction and, thus, changing that place. In a sense, this book for me is a poem about a poem that took place in the physical world in such a way that those touched by it became poets themselves. A book that is a poem attempts to rub out outworn and existing conceptions of things, to see things freshly without evasion by a single metaphor. The events that make the poem, however, are something different. They are a Supreme Quest. In the final analysis, it may turn out to be nothing more than a journey into a sort of Divine Purgatory. If this particular quest is also seen as an attempt to break with education romantics, it will please me to be read that way despite an occasional desperate feeling that the venture, the quest, and the poetry along the way may be every bit as quixotic as the romantics I have put off.

NOTE: In order to protect their privacy, the names of all persons except for George Richmond, Sarah Dubin, and Tom Edwards have been changed. Any similarity to the names of real individuals other than the above is coincidental. P.S. 484 and P.S. 452 are not the real names of the schools referred to.

PART I

The Experience

1. The War Game

Rita looked up at me from her desk in the front row. "You ain't Mrs. Rouse."

"That's right. I'm not."

They stared at me. Something in the atmosphere of the class struck me as impenetrable, as a trifle chilling. One by one I took the measure of the thirty fifth-graders squeezed into the room.

"We want Mrs. Rouse!" Rita led the chorus.

"What's your name?"

"Rita Ramirez. You call me Rita, spelled R-I-T-A. You remember it 'cause you betta spell it right."

"Well, Rita, I understand that Mrs. Rouse is teaching the first grade this year."

"She was supposed to have this class. How come she ain't here?"

"She chicken." Pablo made clucking sounds in his throat that delighted his classmates.

Class 5–308 expected a veteran teacher, an experienced opponent who could carry on the classroom war near their level of refinement. Instead, they had drawn a beginner. Looking back, I understand their sense of loss, a loss that comes from over-matching the competition.

"Who are you?" someone asked.

"I'm Mr. Richmond. In Spanish, it's Ricomundo."

"You speak Spanish?"

"Some. Un poco."

"Que bueno!" said a child in the second row.

The bell rang as two latecomers dashed to their seats.

"Everyone stand. That includes you, Rita."

A recording of the pledge of allegiance came over the loudspeaker. The class stared vacantly at the brown box above the blackboard. The flag in the corner of the room might as well have not been there. They'd said the pledge so many times that they no longer listened to what they were saying. Chairs creaked throughout the ceremony. Only about half the class stood up. The other half slouched over their desks. Rosa leaned one knee on her seat. Another child stood up, but then set his elbows on his desk for support throughout "America the Beautiful."

Rita remained seated. I motioned to her to stand. She didn't budge. I moved toward her, attempting a more subtle pressure. "What's the matter?" Rita, two years older than the rest, on the verge of puberty, looked at me brazenly, caught the eye of Rosa, one of her followers, and motioned to her to come over to take a message. Rosa did so obediently. After receiving a whispered explanation, Rosa turned to me. In a whisper, she said, "Rita has something she can tell no man."

For a moment I was baffled by the mystery in her tone. Then it dawned on me what she was talking about.

"For God's sake! Rita, go see the nurse."

The tone in my voice startled the class. The leaners, benders, elbowers during the anthem came to their feet, not, as I was convinced then, as a sign of respect for my teacherly authority, but to watch what would happen. They heard it for what it was, the signal to do battle.

Before I could solve that encounter, shouts came from another corner of the room. I whirled to find two boys wrestling over a chair. I quickly slid between the combatants. By a process of addition and division, I surmised that Carlos had left his seat to go to the clothes closet. By the time he returned, Felipe had taken his place, and the pair squared off.

"Never mind the chair. You're both supposed to be standing."

"You creep, you motherfucker!" Felipe muttered at Carlos through clenched teeth.

Carlos spat on the floor. "See you at three, baby."

"Be seated! All of you!"

They obeyed. I'm not sure why.

So this was what it was going to be like. It was going to be a game of power politics complete with territorial struggles, alliances, and misalliances. I had a secret foreboding that the incidents that had already occurred were only a warm-up. The next few hours, the first few days would determine the entire year, and I hadn't the slightest idea about what I could do so it would be different.

I spent what remained of the morning parceling out a desk and a chair to each student. My desire to placate the combatants with a solution that would save face for everyone prompted me to fix the seating arrangement. I also hoped that by defining each student's territory, a repetition of the seating squabble might be avoided. What I didn't know, but soon learned, was that my students had an inexhaustible repertoire of petty contentions, any one of which was calculated to inflame tempers and to disrupt whatever had been planned for the day. I began getting a clearer understanding of what I was up against later that morning when, still in civilian habit, I mumbled the word "damn" out loud.

"Ooooo-oooo, what you said," they sang in chorus.

I discovered instantly I'd fallen into a trap. It was thirty against one—only a matter of time before they got me on a technicality.

"Damnation!" I said, intending to wriggle free. But they had me. Chalk up a point for them—they'd caught Teacher swearing.

Real soldiers, I thought to myself. Despite our differences, it was becoming increasingly clear as the day passed that when they weren't sniping at me they were sniping at each other; all too often sniping was too mild a word. I had successfully settled the chair incident, saving face, pride, and honor for everyone. That must be my model from now on. Either that, or I would have to spend myself quelling the violence that was an integral part of their eleven-year-old diplomacy.

Several days later I met Mrs. Rouse in the teachers' cafeteria.

"I'm Mrs. Rouse. I was supposed to have your class this year. But by a stroke of luck I pulled 1–1. They're so alert, so innocent, such a pleasure."

1–1 is the "brightest" first-grade class in the school. Mrs. Rouse looked so pleased with her fortune that I was tempted to withhold my morning's miseries.

"Alert! My children are alert too, Mrs. Rouse. That's not their problem. They just don't happen to be alert to what I've been told to teach them. Why am I given a fifth-grade curriculum guide when they can't read even a second-grade primer?"

I was to hear a rumor later that Mrs. Rouse's "lucky" assignment to 1–1 may not have been altogether a matter of chance. As chapter chairman of the United Federation of Teachers, she was a power in the school.

"You've got quite a bunch," said Mrs. Rouse. "Isn't Pablo DeSoto in your class?"

"I don't think he's introduced himself yet," I replied.

"No surprise. If he was there you'd know him by now. He's probably absent. He's a truant. When he comes to school, he's a perfect terror. Last year, in the first week, he took apart his teacher's desk, broke a window, cut two students, and fell down a flight of stairs. All in one week. It must have been some kind of record, so he was expelled. Anyway, he's back here now on probation. They had to bring him back. He's escaped from the institution they put him in. Some kid. A tough customer. I was sure he was in that class."

Mrs. Rouse looked at me with a look that was a perfect marriage of sympathy, guilt, and relief.

"I have my lesson plans from last year. Would you like them? They're not for the kids. They're for the AP."

"AP?"

"Assistant Principal. Mr. Herman checks them every week. If they're not perfect, he makes you redo them.

"You don't mean to say teachers get graded for penmanship!"

"Oh, I know what you mean. It sounds silly, doesn't it? But if you take them, they'll save you trouble. Anyway, those plans are vague enough to work for any class. When I wrote them, I expected to have 5–308 the next year and I had no intention of playing the game again. The AP doesn't care so long as they are neat and follow the guide books. Also, be neat with your attendance book. The AP checks that too. A couple of mistakes and you start copying."

My first few days took a heavy toll. Every minute seemed to be filled with petty quarrels, fights, acrimony of almost every imaginable proportion, and I felt revulsion, fatigue, anger at being caught, self-hatred for what I saw myself becoming. To get the children to concentrate on reading, writing, or arithmetic for even two minutes seemed outside the realm of possibility. I felt as if I had been locked into a room with madmen, and that their madness was a cancer eroding my humanity. I climbed the stairs to 308 very much as they did, feeling condemned.

If a chance existed of terminating the thousands of skirmishes and miserable little battles I would have to either fight or arbitrate, then I would take it. Instead of battles, forays, incidents, alarms, I would launch a war. At that point, I accepted wholly the idea that I was being tested by the children. Paralleling the rationale elder statesmen give for their policies, "I launched my war to win a peace."

Down the Up Staircase

At 2:30 P.M. several days later I set the trap. "How many of you want to go home now?"

The children in the room looked at the clock. Raoul Rodriguez approvingly said, "I'm beginning to like this teacha."

"It's now two thirty. I'm willing to let you go home a half-hour early IF you can get from this room to the schoolyard in line and without a sound. If anyone says a word, we turn back and start from the beginning."

"Okay, Mr. Richmond," shouted Rita exuberantly.

"Girls stand." Every student in the class rose obediently. "I see we have more girls than my class register shows. Are there any boys in this room?" The girls snickered. The boys, who had already begun slouching back into their seats, grew sullen at my challenge. I was going to insist they do it perfectly. Now they knew I was serious.

"I didn't stand, Mr. Richmond. I ain't no girl." Raoul laughed victoriously.

"Return to your seats. Raoul broke the silence."

The class grew quiet.

I made a second offer. "Shall we try again? Girls stand."

This time only girls left their seats.

"Boys stand. Put seats up."

I watched. Three or four students made a special effort to do this chore as noisily as possible.

"Do it again, this time quietly."

Repetition began to test their patience. Again the chairs went up and came down, but this time silently.

"Okay, line up," I said.

This was a simple instruction, one they had followed maybe eight times a day for four years. Notwithstanding, they began to push each other. Books tumbled to the floor. Tempers flared. Two chairs on the front desk crashed to the floor as three boys jockeyed for position on line.

Carlos shouted at Felipe, "You creep, I'm ahead of you!" Felipe angrily lunged for Carlos.

"Return to your seats!" I showed my own exasperation by pacing around the room. Angry hisses were directed at Felipe and Carlos. Several children, feeling English obscenities were too polite, spoke them in Spanish. After they were all seated, I told them the time. It was a quarter to three.

"Look how much time you've wasted. You all could have been out of here fifteen minutes ago. Try again. We can do this all night," I warned.

On the fourth attempt, 5–308 made it all the way to the second floor. We turned back when Garcia dropped his books on someone's head.

It was five minutes to three. Children in the first two grades were being dismissed. They filled the yard with their screaming laughter. The sound of this easily won freedom brought my students to the brink of despair. An exchange of shoves between Enrico and Rosa caused another about-face. This time they stomped back to our third-floor room. Montrose Avenue was no nearer at 3:10 than it had been at 2:30.

By the time the whole class was back in the room and seated, I thought we'd need strait-jackets to control the anger. Rita, looking haggard, whispered threats to everyone. But something was different. The tide had turned. Their anger with each other had begun to make me its object. They sat there. I stood silently in my mantle of petty tyranny. So many children were now responsible for the group's failure that they ceased blaming each other.

"I hate you, Mr. Richmond!" Rosa screamed.

"You better let me out!" Elizabeta, a quiet and shy girl, judging by our week together, burst into tears.

This time they removed their chairs from the tables with all the racket they could muster. The whines, groans, and catcalls grew and, infectious as they were, spread.

Rita made a dash for the door. "I've got to take my baby brother home! I'm goin'!"

But there was to be no escape. I had wedged the door closed with my shoe. I announced that no one would leave 308 until we were all ready. Elizabeta's tears caused the affliction elsewhere in the room. Even Rita feigned tears. Meanwhile, the boys started pacing around the room. Some stopped to watch tears stream down the faces of their classmates. A half-puzzled look passed over the faces of the others.

"Mr. Richmond is the worse teacher I ever had, worse even than Mrs. Cox. You'll see, Mr. Richmond. I'm gonna transfer out of this class so fast. I'm gonna bring my mother, my father, my uncle, and my brother tomorrow and they're gonna get me outa your class," steamed Rita.

"Me too-ooo-oooo!" they chimed in chorus.

"I look forward to meeting them."

They had been pushed as far as they could go. In another minute they might make a shambles of the room, of each other, of me.

"If you take your seats, I will let you go one at a time, quietest first."

A hush fell over the class as each child, now to be judged on his own merits, took his seat. Fingers locked. Backs stiffened. Arms extended rigidly in the perennial posture of student supplication. Everyone seemed to hold his breath. One by one, I called their names. One by one, they rose and hurriedly escaped. Some looked back gleefully at those who remained my captives.

As I walked to the subway, I took a careful look at the tenements along Montrose Avenue. The buildings, almost a century old, reminded me of the Lower East Side of Manhattan, where I, in similar circumstances, spent my boyhood. Williamsburg, like the Lower East Side, hosted an influx of new settlers from Puerto Rico. With few exceptions, these most recent immigrants were poor. A few had managed to get into the public housing in the area, but even public housing was too expensive for most. Renters in these "projects" usually had enough money to send their sons and daughters to the Catholic school situated on the corner opposite P.S. 250.

The walk brought back memories of my first seventeen years. So much the same. Bathtub in the kitchen. Three-by-two toilet out in the hall. Six-legged armies surfacing nightly from mattresses and floorboards to attack us, their human prey. I felt chilled just remembering drafts that made the journey to the hall latrine a time-and-motion study. Every room in the apartment served as a hallway into the next. There was no door on any room. What privacy we had was obtained by a blanket. Not many extra blankets when the radiators failed.

Rows of slums line the main thoroughfares and the side streets.

Their high stoops, leading to second-floor entries, jut halfway to the curb and are usually filled with sitting, standing, loving, smoking, and drinking tenants. North of the school, towering above this squat barrio, are five twenty-story red brick structures put up by the Public Housing Authority. The Lower East Side and Williamsburg had much in common. Both have traditionally made room for generation after generation of immigrants. If the hearth has not been too warm, well, whose fault was it? At any rate, most of the immigrant groups that have lived in these rat-infested and roach-swarming flats eventually escape into the suburbs, making room for the next wave of immigrants to be similarly assimilated and digested.

And as on the Lower East Side, the students of 5–308 came to straight-walled, tube-lighted classrooms to which we teachers from Middle America commute to socialize the new immigrants. I tried to remember what it felt like to leave my six-story walk-up for school, but couldn't. There are things one just doesn't remember. The barrio was the same. I was someone who had left and come back. It was no longer the same for me. Men stood around the bodegas sipping beer as they had always done. Women sat in their living rooms looking out windows. Corner grocery stores sold beer on credit. The poor spent next week's check, making it theoretically possible to die in debt and therefore ahead. The streets felt the same: living, vital, difficult, and—on some corners and in some classrooms—frightening.

Escalation of Warfare

Two months passed. My strategy of war to end all war proved bankrupt. Every defense I devised to limit combat simply escalated it. If I took gym privileges away, students responded with disruptions for the hour they were kept from play in the schoolyard. If I devised other ways to pacify them, like ordering a child who was being abusive to stand quietly in front of the room (on the theory that the subtraction of one of the parties to a conflict leads to a collapse of the problem), students eventually refused to acknowledge the order.

The logic of the opposition seemed simple: anything that promised a cut in the action would be eliminated by common consent.

If classroom warfare is to end, everyone must first want peace. In 308, I was alone. All the others were making war because they loved to. I was alone in insisting that they were in school to learn to read as expertly as they fought. From the standpoint of the students, reading was a bore or, worse, a confirmation of their failure. If they could not write, that inability to manufacture words was more than compensated by turning pencil and paper into missiles that could crush enemy batteries across the room. Success in classroom combat anesthetized academic failure; so it alone awoke enthusiasm in my students.

We spent day after day wearing each other down. What if "Teecha" had different expectations? If it gets too hot, get out. Each morning we came to class alive, awake, refreshed for the day's engagement. Each evening we slouched homeward exhausted, tallying our hits and misses and licking our wounds. By the third month, I was tired of grinding out concessions, bribes, compromises, payoffs, and of granting every other form of largess. Yet patronage, vengeance, alliances, and interpersonal treason kept us going. War was the curriculum, and not a hidden curriculum at that. The fact that the war couldn't be won by military means did not depress me half so much as did my failure to get students to cooperate in my aspirations for them.

As conflict persisted, and as issues that had seemed resolved were repeated, my patience withered. I saw myself becoming tyrannical, oppressive, unbending, at moments cruel.

I decided to try negotiating a truce. I had tried everything but surrender. Somehow I had to cut away the trappings of authority and the rituals of warfare that they associated with teachers. We had to begin discovering each other as people.

The next morning, after the pledge to the flag, I spoke plainly.

"Look, I am tired of ordering you around. I'm weary of threatening, weary of punishing you. Our fights, your fights among yourselves, get you nowhere. If I stop a fight in the front of the room, another starts in the rear. If I didn't stop you, you'd beat each other to death over desks and chairs. Sometimes I think you believe they belong to you. They don't. Look, they're stamped 'Board of Education.' You spill each other's blood over the smallest things: pencils, pens, paper, books, chairs, getting on line, being first to the closet, over anything else you define as your territory and then are obliged to defend.

"If spitballs could kill, you'd all be dead. If spray paint didn't wash off, you'd all be different colors. Girls and boys fight each other like married couples. You complain about each other so much that when you have a real gripe no one listens to you. Do you really want to go on like this? Don't you see how pointless it is? Can't we find some better way to be together?"

"We'll be good, Mr. Richmond," Rita called. She was responding to the appeal in my voice.

"You've told me that before. Really, how can we go on like this? I care about you. You don't read any better today than you did two months ago. I'm beginning to lose hope. I don't know why I'm here."

Their eyes glittered with something near the compassion of the hunter for the hunted just before the kill. Although they were visibly moved, I was unsure whether the show of tenderness demonstrated grief at the loss of a worthy opponent or compassion for a victim brought to his knees.

"I had a teecha who wuz a nun. She used to pull a hair out of ya head every time you wuz bad. We wuz afraid of gettin' bald. She useta tell us that if someone pulled your hair out, it would never grow back. Why don't you do that to us?" offered Rosa.

"I know!" said Raoul. "You should make us stand in a corner with our arms out and then put heavy books in our hands. Maybe even for a whole day. Then we'd be good."

"Send us to Mrs. Swartz when we're bad," suggested Rita.

Bendito made another suggestion. "I had a teecha who wouldn't let you go to the bathroom if ya wuz bad. Ya hada stand in the back of the room, and if you wiz in ya pants, everyone said you wuz a baby."

Everyone laughed.

"Maybe you should make us write 'I'll be good' a thousand times," proposed Hector.

"I've tried that, Hector. *You* ought to know better than anyone else that it doesn't work."

He nodded sheepishly. "Yah, I guess you're right."

"How about locking us up in the closet?" offered Pablo.

And so it went. They hadn't understood. Their solution was to give military aid to me so I could continue to fight. Public punishment and physical pain, especially if endured by others, held the same lure for these children as it did for Roman crowds who jammed stadiums to watch Christians being thrown to the lions. Nothing excited them as much as blood except a fight, providing it led to blood. Even now I shudder when I recall how eagerly my children supplied me with ways to inflict pain—on them!

2. The Micro-Economy Game

If I was to avoid becoming a complete despot, then it was up to me to chart a course that would allow conflict to kindle intellect. Riding home on the subway one afternoon, I searched my mind for a comparison that might shed some light on my situation and found one that amused me. The traditional schoolroom was a feudal society. Teachers were fiefholders to whom the principal parceled out authority. The patronage which I in turn dispensed to students took the same form, and monitors who accepted the largess bathed for a time in advantage over their peers; they were my petty vassals. Weren't my students tied to the land—to Room 308? Even their most precious liberties required my permission. Private property, private wealth, and political competitors did not exist in the classroom. Trade among citizens and between 308 and other classrooms was nonexistent. It fitted. It fitted well enough. The tenant of the classroom identifies with a social caste determined by his physical and political prowess. Arms make the man. The mixture of authority roles that summed up my role in the classroom—lord, judge, lawmaker, policeman, and cleric—added a final touch.

The next morning I arrived in 308 with a plan, and with some materials. I immediately began a discussion that eventually altered everything.

"How many of you are poor?"

There was no response.

"How many of you are poor or come from poor families?"

Still no response. It occurred to me that my question might have pierced the boundary between schooling and the real world. They looked uneasy. They were trying to figure out what I was up to. They were poverty cases by any American standard, and all of us knew it. Nearly every student in the class was from a family that depended on public assistance to survive. Yet, asking for an admission of their condition violated the social and economic anonymity fostered for so long in school. I knew what I was doing. I wanted to strike a blow against the unreality of the kind of education that taught children the world was ordered on merit. Children don't begin the race to abundance from the same starting gate. Some children start at the finish line and most of those kids go to private schools. Somewhere along the track poor kids learn to accept their lot: worse, they learn to deserve their lot.

The silence forced me to take another tack.

"Well, how many of you are rich?"

Raoul and Rita inched their hands into the air.

"Are you rich, Rita?"

"No, but my father works, so I'm richer than everybody here except you."

"Rich people don't work, Rita. At least, they don't become rich because they work. How many of you knew that?"

They thought I was playing some trick on them. No one answered. They were incredibly attentive, trying to discover the sermon attached.

"How many of you want to know how the rich get rich?"

Everyone raised a hand. No one had ever told them.

"How many of you know what real estate is?"

Several students responded by raising their hands. I called on Juan.

"It's a business where you buy and sell land."

"That's right. Before we discuss land business, I want you to answer some questions. How much money do you want to earn when you grow up and get a job? Bendito, how much for you?"

"Sixty dollars a week," he replied.

"And what do you want to be?"

"A cop."

"Why a cop?"

" 'Cause a cop's got a stick and a gun and nobody can mess with him. Also, 'cause when you're a cop you can go into any store and they'll give you a hamburger for nothin'. You never have to pay for nothin'."

"And you, Elizabeta? What do you want to be and how much money do you want to earn?"

Her answer, as usual, was inaudible, so Rita took it upon herself to amplify it. "She says she wants to earn fifty dollars a week. She says she wants to be a maid in a rich lady's house like her aunt."

"And, Rita, what do you want to be?" I asked.

"A secretary. And I won't take no fifty pesos. I want eighty dollars a week."

"That's too much," chortled Rosa. "Ain't nobody gonna pay you eighty pesos a week."

I broke in. "What does eighty dollars buy for a family of four? Wait. First figure this. At eighty dollars a week, how much will you earn in four weeks?"

"Three hundred and twenty dollars," Ramon offered.

"Okay, Rita. How much do your parents pay in rent a month?"

"A hundred dollars a month," she replied.

"Subtract a hundred dollars from three hundred and twenty. How much do you have left?"

Rita puzzled over the subtraction, but again was saved by Ramon. "Two-twenty."

"Take another fifty dollars away for taxes, and you've got a hundred seventy dollars left to spend. Food costs about forty dollars a week for a family of four, so take away another hundred and sixty dollars. Carfare from home to work costs another ten or so a month, and that takes care of the rest. Rita, if you earn only eighty dollars a week, you'll have to go to work naked because you won't have enough money left to buy any clothes."

The class laughed.

"You make a fool of me, Mr. Richmond," Rita said warningly.

"You couldn't afford to go to the movies, to have a phone, to have electricity, or to buy furniture, or even gas to cook with. Rita, do you really think you'd be rich?"

"Then they're gonna pay me more. Maybe a hundred. Maybe even two hundred."

Rosa made a face and then shook her head in disbelief. "Ain't nobody gonna pay her two hundred pesos."

"Class, how long did it take Rita to earn three hundred and twenty dollars?"

"A month," someone answered.

"Rich people earn three hundred and twenty dollars a minute. It doesn't take a month."

"How do they do it?" asked Bendito.

"One way is in real estate. For example, I buy a piece of land for two hundred dollars. I build a house on it which costs me a thousand dollars. How much have I spent so far?"

"Twelve hundred," Ramon faithfully called.

"Then I go over to Ramon and say: 'Ramon, how would you like to buy a house? I'll sell it to you for five thousand dollars.' Ramon says, 'Okay.' "

"Aw, I wouldn't give you no five thousand for no house," Rita said contemptuously.

"What if you had ten families each willing to rent apartments in that house for a hundred dollars a month?" I countered. "That means you would get all your money back in five months and make seven thousand dollars profit by the end of the year.

"I'd do it!" Rita said, sure now she wasn't being cheated.

"So Ramon buys my house for five thousand dollars. Remember, I spent twelve hundred to build it. How much profit did I make?"

Bendito raised his hand. "Thirty-eight hundred."

"Good. And how long did it take me to earn it?" I asked.

"A minute," responded Hector, who had gotten the point.

"And how much work did I do? I paid someone else to do the work. That's what I spent twelve hundred dollars for. All I had to do was find a buyer. So you see, rich people get rich from other people's labor."

From the silence, I concluded that they were still listening. I doubted that they had heard anything like it in school before.

"Another way to get rich is to use other people's money. Say that we got together and opened a bank. People, convinced we were honest and had a safe place for their savings, put their money into our bank. In return we paid them what is called 'interest.' "

"I know what that is," Rosa broke in. "If you put a hundred dollars in a bank, they add five more dollars to it during the year."

"Right. The interest rate on your hundred dollars is five percent in that bank. Say that you offer that rate to your bank customers. How much interest would we have to pay a thousand customers each of whom had put a thousand dollars in our bank? First, how much money has been deposited in our bank?"

"A thousand times a thousand?" asked Ramon. I nodded. "One million dollars!" he said after scribbling furiously on a scrap of paper.

"Good," I said encouragingly. "You can find how much interest we'll pay the first year by finding out how many hundreds there are in a million dollars. In other words, *divide*. How many are there, Rosa?"

"A thousand," she guessed.

"Ten thousand," someone called.

"The last answer's the right one," I said. "Now someone multiply ten thousand by five dollars, and we'll know how much we'll have to pay our customers in interest."

"Fifty grand!" said Raoul, proud to have won the race to the answer.

"Right. Besides holding people's money, banks lend it to people or businesses who need it, to people they are sure will pay them back. Banks charge borrowers rent for the use of the money. Usually the rent is two or three times the interest they pay savers. If we take in a hundred and fifty thousand in interest from lenders and pay out fifty thousand in interest to savers, how much profit will we make?"

"Another hundred grand," Bendito said, his eyes nearly popping out. "That's loan-sharking, Mr. Richmond."

I laughed. "So you see, you can get rich using other people's money just as you can get rich using other people's labor in real estate. What's more, it's legal."

Interruption

I looked to see if they were still with me. Until then, their interest span on any given subject had rarely exceeded two minutes, and we had been talking on this subject for nearly half an hour. The bell rang. "What's that for?"

"Today's assembly, Mr. Richmond," Rosa said. Her tone implied that I should feel some shame for having forgotten.

"Oh, it is?" I did not welcome the interruption. "Okay, when we return I'm going to teach you a game. Girls line up." They followed obediently. "Now boys." They also obeyed. Only four of the young men found a person in front of them moving slow enough to be pushed from behind. With a few loving shoves we made our way out of the room.

All thirty of us marched through the corridor to a stairwell appointed for our descent. At the bottom we proceeded to assigned seats in the assembly. On prior occasions, the auditorium had vibrated with giggling, whispering children. Teachers' commands got lost in the clamor. Assemblies were usually happy: we all welcomed the release from our cells if only because it meant we would see unfamiliar faces.

But today was different. We had come to assembly to practice discipline. Children sat stiffly in rows. There was an atmosphere of tense order. Not a head turned. No seats creaked. The usual enjoyment had fled with the noise. Teachers gave no commands. Four hundred children and a dozen adults sat as if waiting to be memorialized in a photograph. As customary, a teacher was in charge of the assembly. She stood in front of the audience glaring at the last students entering the hall.

"*That girl!*" the teacher screamed. "*Out!* Get out of this assembly at once! Yes! You! You in the pink dress! Out! Mrs. Hopper, would you see that she's removed. I want her name. Get me her name. That young lady is going to spend this afternoon in my room. Miserable! I'll teach her. I've never seen such insolence! What's your name?"

The frightened child mumbled her name. The teacher could not hear it. "What is it? Well, whatever it is, didn't you hear me say that you are not to talk to your neighbor in *my* assembly? Are you *deaf* or *retarded?* Never mind. Just get out this minute! Your deafness will certainly earn you trouble this afternoon. Is there anyone else here who wants to keep her company?"

Children strained to go unnoticed. For the moment, I forgot that my position in the school exempted me from her rage. I too shared the horror of being visible. Pressed against the hard wood seats to avoid detection, everybody stiffened in an effort to remain unseen. Four hundred people in a room, all trying to be overlooked . . . that is, all but one.

It happened too quickly. A child in the seventh row turned his head. Perhaps he said something to the girl next to him, oblivious of the danger. The teacher's voice raged at him. A minute later a frail black child climbed four steps to the stage, stood on the top stair, and, dazed, followed the teacher's finger to the center of the platform.

That morning when that child dressed himself in an immaculate white shirt, red tie, and blue pants, had he known that his patriotic dress, against the backdrop of other children similarly uniformed, would not ensure his invisibility? Now he stood on the stage. His head dropped to his chest to avoid the hundreds of eyes fixed on him. His posture was perfect: his body controlled.

"Look at him! He doesn't understand that I mean what I say. That's because he doesn't have a thing in his head, not an ounce of brain. All *mouth!*"

We all stared at him, too dazed to intervene.

"Get to your knees! On your knees!"

The child's legs shook beneath his frail black body. His knees touched the floor where his shoes had been. His lids closed over his eyes.

"Beg forgiveness for delaying this assembly," the teacher ordered, pointing to the audience. She growled the command again, loud enough so the children in the back rows wouldn't have to strain to hear.

The child fumbled, "Forgive me for—"

The teacher was upon him before he finished. *"Louder!* They *can't* hear you!"

"Forgive me for delaying this assembly." The child's voice broke.

"Get up and get out!" she ordered. "Who's his teacher?" She turned to the audience.

Someone on the side aisle beckoned the child down from the stage. Free of the altar, the eight-year-old fled from the stage, ran down the aisle to the exit.

"Walk!" the teacher called after him. She meant to say crawl.

The Poor Get Rich

My students returned from the assembly in an ugly temper. The hour of harsh discipline had pressed them to the limits of endurance. They buzzed with stories about this teacher, stories that terrified and fascinated them. I saw immediately from the manner in which they took their seats that they had to release their horror. A half-hour remained before lunch. In the first ten minutes of that interval, I broke up three fights. Concluding that a continuation of our economics discussion was unfeasible, I invited everyone to stand for Simple Simon Says. After a few minutes of matching wits with their teacher, their tempers thinned with laughter.

As was customary, we met in the yard at the end of the noon hour and headed in two irregular files up the stairs to 308. Coats were put away. Students strolled to their seats for the afternoon attendance check. Compared with that morning, they were relaxed. Most of them had engaged in a game of tag in the schoolyard and had returned to the room exhausted. Two months in the classroom had taught me to make the most of their exhaustion, so I began immediately.

"How many of you have played Monopoly?"

Seven students responded with raised hands.

"That's very few. I'll have to start from the beginning. Remember this morning before assembly—do you recall what we said about rich people getting rich?"

"Yeah, you use what belongs to somebody else. Ain't that right, Mr. Rich?"

"Good, Hector. Monopoly is a game that teaches us how to get rich buying and selling property. Our version of that game has a different name, Micro-Economy. One difference between the two is that thirty or even a hundred people can play Micro-Economy at once, but only four or five can play Monopoly together. Another difference is that Monopoly takes only a few hours to play. Micro-Economy takes a whole year."

"When can we play?" asked Barbara.

"We will play two afternoons a week, probably Tuesday and Thursday, for about an hour and a half."

"That word you said, *Micomony,* whasit mean?"

"Micro-Economy. Micro means small. You've heard of a micro-mini, haven't you?"

Raoul whistled. "Wooowееее! My brother's girl got one. You can see right under it when she bend down and tie her shoes."

The girls blushed.

"Micro-mini is a small skirt. Whenever *micro* is put in front of any other word, it makes the second word mean something small. An economy is a system of stores, jobs, goods, things you wear, eat, or drive, houses, factories, movies, everything. An economy makes it possible for you to be housed, fed, go to school, find a job, and be entertained. Micro-Economy means small economy. We are going to make a small economy in this room."

"Shooooe, I thought you wuz gonna give us mini-comic books."

"Sorry, Juan. If it makes you feel any better, Micro-Economy may turn out to be more fun than a comic book. I've got an idea. If you write your own comic book, I'll buy it from you."

"How much you pay?"

"Four hundred *soul* dollars."

"Soul dollars? Whatsa soul dollar?"

"Do you want to learn to play or not?" Rosa said, impatient with Juan.

"Sit down, Juan. Don't you see Mr. Richmond wanna talk?" seconded Rita, who never let a cheap opportunity to build up credit get by.

"We gonna get rich, Mr. Rich?"

"Hector, if you'll wait with that question for half an hour, I'll answer it, okay?"

"Okay, Mr. Rich."

"From now on, I'm going to buy compositions with this." I held up a bundle of paper money that I had mimeographed the day before. "These are soul dollars. They come in ones, fives, twenties, hundreds, and five hundreds. You'll also get a dollar for each point that you score on a spelling or a math test."

"You mean ya gotta be smart to get that money?"

"You'll have to work hard, Rosa."

"Then a lotta kids in this class is gonna be poor. They stupid and they lazy. Get rich? Ain't no way possible. You got welfare in this game?"

"Not yet, Rosa. Do you think we should?"

"You better. Not for me or for Rita. But the others is gonna need welfare to play."

Angered by this superior attitude, Rosa's classmates commenced firing.

"You the only one gonna be on welfare, dumpy! You empty up here and full down here. Hah!" Raoul tapped her head and then poked her belly.

"Get your filthy hands off me." Rosa turned on Raoul threateningly. Rita scowled at Raoul in support of Rosa.

"Hey, Mr. Richmond," Sandoval called. "You expect us to get rich off that phony stuff? Man, if I take that phony-baloney down to the candy store, all it gonna buy me is a kick in the ass."

Everyone laughed. The tension between Raoul and Rita evaporated.

"Patience, Sandoval, patience. You want to know what you get for this money, right?"

"Yeah," they chorused.

"At the end of each month, I'm going to bring books, brownies, cookies, soda, and other things to school and auction them off to the highest bidder. That means that the people with the most of this phony-baloney get what they want."

"You mean this money buys things, real things?"

"Yes."

"Then you can count on me to win that stuff, Mr. Richmond." Raoul massaged his stomach and smiled pityingly at Rosa.

"Shiii . . ." Rita hissed. "Raoul's gonna be so poor we gonna have to give him charity. Gotta get him a caseworker."

"Oh, yeah!"

Rita's eyes renewed the invitation to do battle. Of all the students in the classroom, Rita alone dared brave Raoul in a fight. The outcome of such a contest was anything but clear, so the two contestants usually avoided an actual showdown. Today, however, Rita was itching for a fight—Raoul's arrogance made her mad, and, anyway, she was helping Rosa. Raoul stuck his chest toward Rita, who flashed her nails. The likelihood of a struggle did not diminish until Rosa's next question conveniently changed the subject.

"Whatsa auction? Teechas don't give away that stuff for a few scraps of mimeo paper unless they crazy. I know you ain't that crazy, Mr. Richmond."

"No, Rosa, I ain't crazy. My job is to let you in on how the world does business. I tell you the facts. You judge them for yourself. You don't have to listen if you don't want. But if you shut your ears, somebody's gonna shake you down someday and you won't even know it's happening to you. You asked me what an auction is. It's a marketplace. It's a place where you buy and sell things. Your parents work, right?"

A couple of kids shook their heads.

"Well, some of them do. They trade their work for dollars. Then they trade their dollars for food that somebody else's work produced. Well, you work too, but in school. And I'm going to pay you for your work because it's valuable to me. Then I'm going to bring stuff —candy, soda, and other things—and you'll trade your work for food just the way your parents do."

"Man, this is cool. How come we never got paid for work before?"

"They gave you grades in payment."

"Grades don't get you nuthin'," said Raoul.

"I know what grades get you," called out Barbara. "Grades get you a whupping." Half the class reacted by clapping, but the other half looked solemn.

"I promised to tell you what auctions are. There are several kinds. One kind is a place where I sell you cake, but there's a second kind of auction in Micro-Economy. Instead of buying refreshments, you buy land."

"What land? You gonna bring land to sell too?"

"The actual land is located on those shelves and tables and on top of that clothing closet. When you build houses, we'll put them on the land you buy. Do you see these pieces of paper? These are deeds to the land. When you buy and sell land, you use these pieces of paper to do it, to exchange land for money. After all, land is too big to put in your pocket."

Sandoval raised his hand. "What good is this land? It just wood. Can't grow nothin' on it."

"Once you own land, anyone who lands on it pays you rent. If there is nothin' on the land but dust, the tenant pays the owner very little. But if you put up an apartment house, then your tenants pay you rent—a hundred dollars, two hundred, sometimes even a thousand dollars."

"Wow!"

"Do we throw dice like in Monopoly?" asked Barbara, who wanted people to know that she was an expert Monopoly player.

"No, a transportation manager moves you."

"What's that?" three or four children demanded in unison.

"It's a job and I'll hire two people for it."

Ten hands went up indicating there were volunteers. I heard muffled squeals. "Me, me, me."

"What does it pay?" asked Rosa, who was already beginning to carve out a reputation as a hardheaded businesswoman.

"Fifty dollars a week."

Ten more hands shot up.

"I only need two people for the job. Those of you who are not chosen today will be offered other jobs in a week or two, so don't worry about finding work. Since there are so many of you, I'll have to choose the two transportation managers by lottery. I am writing two numbers on this piece of paper. Whoever guesses the numbers get the jobs."

Sandoval and Hector won.

"What do we do?" inquired Sandoval immediately after congratulating Hector for being the other lucky one.

"If you stay fifteen minutes after school today, I will tell you what your duties are."

"What job do I get?" asked someone who was disappointed.

"There are two jobs for real-estate managers which pay fifty dollars a week to start. I have four sanitation jobs, one job for a gardener, two jobs as cashier, and some others, but I only need real-estate managers now. The others can wait until next week."

Again hands were raised. I went through the same selection procedure as before. Rita got the first number.

Before I could continue, Rita stood up. "Two boys got jobs, right? Now two girls."

"I'll tell you what. Let's vote. If the class thinks both real-estate managers should be girls, then it's okay with me. How many of you think I should choose a girl for the second job?

Rita looked around the room; as she did, hands went up. The resolution passed. I limited the lottery to girls. Rosa chose the second number. Rita was pleased with the outcome. It was like handing out patronage.

"If you girls come to class fifteen minutes early tomorrow, I'll tell you what you do."

"Okay, Mr. Richmond."

"Well, how do you play?" Rita's exuberance had obviously been heightened by her prestigious job.

"Okay, listen carefully. Every move has four parts: assessment, transportation, marketplace, and auction. During assessment you bring me your houses and anything else you want to put on your property to make it more valuable. I'll assess it. That means I'll tell you how much it's worth."

"How can you tell?" asked Juan.

"Well, I look at what you've built. If you make a beautiful house, it's worth more than an ugly one. If you put a lot of work in—build furniture, make windows, hang curtains, put in wallpaper, anything—it will be worth more. The second step is transportation. Everyone finds out where he's landed during transportation. It only takes a minute. Then comes marketplace. During marketplace, you may walk around the room, talk to whomever you please, make deals, borrow money, sell land, buy houses, form partnerships, visit the bank, or pay and collect rent you owe or are owed."

"How do you know how much to collect?" asked Raoul.

"You certainly have all the questions. Rent is ten percent of the assessed value. That means if the property is worth a hundred dollars, the landlord collects ten dollars from anyone who lands on it. Now, remember how the property gets assessed. You bring me the house or whatever you build, and I'll tell you how much it's worth. If your land is worth two hundred dollars and the house you build is worth another two hundred, then how much are the land and house worth together?"

"Four hundred dollars," said Rosa.

"Let me teach you a trick for figuring the rent when your property rents for ten percent of its assessed value. To get ten percent of four hundred dollars, all you do is cross out the last number." I went through several examples until they all had the idea. When they seemed satisfied with the rules, I explained the final step of the sequence.

"The last step in each move is called auction. I've already explained what an auction is. When you hear me say 'Auction,' I will count to five. Anyone out of his seat at the end of the count gets fined."

"What if you get stalled?" Hector had decided to test just how serious I was going to be about this rule.

"Hector, do you know what a traffic ticket is?"

"Yeah, Teacher. Cops give em to ya when you speed."

"They also give them to you if you park illegally. Anyone who is not back in his seat and quiet by the count of five gets a parking ticket. That means you pay five dollars. If you are noisy when you get to your seats, it's another five dollars for disorderly conduct. Are there any questions? Okay, let's practice. *Marketplace!*"

Students rose slowly from their chairs. They were unsure of what to do.

"Wander around," I urged. "Talk to your friends."

When they were finally moving freely, I called, *"Auction!"* and counted to five. Every student returned to his seat in time. We tried this exercise a second time. On the second try Raoul got back to his seat late.

"Raoul, you owe me five."

"I ain't got no dough, Teach."

"That's all right. I'll take it out of your pay at the end of the week."

Raoul swallowed. He had miscalculated.

Turning to the class, I went on with the instructions. "Those people who listen carefully now have the best chance of getting rich." There was instant silence except for Juan, who was wagging his tongue in the back of the room. "Class, you see Juan. He's not listening. Remember that, because he's going to be somebody's pigeon."

"We just figgerin' how to build a model house. What you build it with?"

"You build houses out of anything you can find. Cardboard, wood, plastic, paper, shoeboxes, anything. Go to your bodega and get cartons, or buy some from students in this classroom who want to sell them. Cut holes in the side for windows and doors. Paint it. Fix it up inside. Some of you might be interested in making the roof come off, or even the front of the house. Then you'd be able to put furniture inside."

Raoul rubbed his hands together. "Man, I'm gonna be stinkin' rich."

"You said it," grumbled Rita in a tone calculated to shame him.

"If you ain't got no land, can you build a house?" asked Raoul, ignoring her.

"You can build, but if you have no place to put the building, you can't collect rent. But you can sell your house to someone else or sell it at auction. Model builders have a very good chance of becoming millionaires in this game."

"This is gonna be cool!" said Mannie, " 'cause I love makin' models."

"Try to figure out an answer to this question. Say you landed on property number five. Say it costs four hundred dollars. You have two hundred and need another two hundred dollars to buy it. How do you get the rest of the money?"

Mannie thought for a moment and then looked at me with a winning smile. "Geez, Teach, I couldn't buy it, could I? Maybe you would let me have the property on credit. You know, I could pay you maybe next week when I get some more money."

"Sorry, Mannie, I don't give credit."

"Teach, you got no heart. You hard like a rock." Mannie groaned and hammed. "Hey, Sandoval, baby, you got soul and money, right? You make me a loan of two hundred, won't you?"

"Sure, anything for a friend."

Mannie smiled triumphantly.

"Sandoval, would you charge Mannie interest for the use of your money?"

"No, Mr. Richmond, Mannie's my best friend."

"Shoooe, I wouldn't let him get away with payin' nothin'," Rosa broke in. "I'd make him pay me twenty pesos to use *my* money. I don't care what kind of friend he is. If a bank can loan-shark ten dollars on every hundred you borrow, then why not me? Answer me that. I ain't rich like no bank. Man, I would even charge you more. I ain't stupid like Sandoval."

Rosa's words were having their effect on Sandoval. He looked at Raoul. I read both their faces.

"If Raoul were in his shoes, would Raoul do the same for him?"

If it was the first moral dilemma raised in the Micro-Economy, it would not be the last. A curtain was being drawn aside, admitting the world to the classroom. For those who regard the classroom as a haven against a social order fragmented by racial differences and segregated by wealth, drawing the curtain would not be especially pleasant. Nevertheless, admitting society to the classroom seemed charged with potential.

The next day we began actual play. After what seemed an awkward introductory period, the game ran smoothly. The pace continued to pick up as more and more currency was pumped into circulation. Every student who wanted a job found one. Those who took jobs performed enthusiastically. Students doubled their academic output. A week later I began teaching the students in 308 the fundamentals of accounting. They kept records of income and expenditure, and these records provided them with ample arithmetic exercises. A month and a half later, several students began showing signs of leaving their comrades behind in the race to acquire consumer goods I was supplying. Two or three students refused to have anything to do with what we were doing. But that was nothing new—they usually sat in the back of the room watching those who were active. A few of these inactivists, however, fell under the spell of the revamped classroom war that I called Micro-Economy.*

The Rise of Ramon

Ramon waved Raoul to the end of the line of people waiting to see him. "You have to wait your turn like the rest. Can't you see the people ahead of you?" Seven or eight of Ramon's classmates stood on line to see him about their financial problems. Ramon was talking to Hector.

"How much do you need?"

"Two hundred."

"For how long?" asked Ramon.

Hector measured Ramon and began a bargaining pantomime. "How about a month?"

"A month! You kidding! Two weeks is the most I can let you have." Ramon met Hector's scowl with a blank look.

Then, in a most conciliatory tone, Hector said, "Let's make a deal. Three weeks, okay?"

"Okay," said Ramon, "but the interest is fifty dollars on the two hundred." Ramon looked ready to peel the skin off a lemon.

"Fifty dollars! Man, you must think I'm some kind of sucker."

But Ramon, having already conceded a point in the bargain over the term of the loan, was intent on extracting a concession of his own. "Then get it from someone else." To emphasize this suggestion and his impatience with Hector's quibbling, Ramon threw his hands into the air. I was almost certain he would follow this gesture by getting up and leaving, but they were closer to agreement than I had guessed. "If I give you the money for less than that, I'm going to lose out. I could use the money myself. I'm probably stupid lending the dough to you at all."

Other students waiting to see Ramon began to show their impa-

* The materials for Micro-Economy have been published by Harcourt Brace Jovanovich, New York.

tience. Hector could no longer withstand the moans of those on line to do business with Ramon.

"Okay, fifty pesos. You're a bloodsucker, Ramon."

Hector signed the promisory note Ramon handed him, and took his soul dollars. Rosa stepped up to the table from her place next in line. The haggling began anew. Hector, who had finished his business with Ramon, came over to me.

"Did you get your loan?"

"You call that a loan? I gotta pay back in blood, Mr. Richmond. That Ramon is getting rich on the loans he makes me. I take the risks! He takes my money." Hector wrung his hands like a sixty-year-old merchant.

"Why do you do it, then?"

Hector looked at me. I could tell that he was deciding whether he should share one of his secrets. He motioned to me to bend over and whispered into my ear. "I gotta deal going that's gonna make me a thousand from this two hundred. Hah!" With my ear ringing, Hector walked into the marketplace without looking back.

"Capitalist!" I said, not sure whether to feel proud or saddened.

Ramon became 308's banker. From his dickering with Hector he must seem a natural for the position. Frankly, I would never have predicted that Ramon, of all people, would get the job. When I first began teaching in P.S. 484, he caused me so little trouble that I barely knew him. Ramon was quiet, well mannered, but uncoordinated; he played only a nominal role in the daily skirmishes that claimed our energies. In the order of selection for a punchball team, Ramon was often the last to be chosen. Sometimes team captains refused to let him play.

Sometimes I intervened, threatening to end the gym period then and there unless everybody played. It was usually enough to crush the resistance. Ramon struck out with a consistency no one else could match. His teammates cheered if he even so much as tipped the ball, and if he fouled it off they made great ado about nothing and turned him into some kind of hero.

In one respect, Ramon's passivity was an effective strategy for survival. As every hack in the schoolhouse knows, if you keep to yourself and take few gambles, teachers and other students don't bother you. No one was threatened by Ramon. He made no challenges, so few calls were made for him to defend himself in the brutal infighting that went on in 308. At least, this description fitted Ramon until we started playing Micro-Economy.

After I introduced money to the classroom, all that multiplying, adding, and subtracting began to make sense, and Ramon's life began to change. He was unanimously chosen to be banker, not for his popularity, only possibly for his anonymity or his prosperity, but chiefly because he could add, subtract, and multiply better than anyone else. He became rich by getting a hundred on his math tests, and after I began paying for points on spelling tests, he scored perfectly there too.

Yet his climb to the throne of finance went unheralded. Bombast was not part of Ramon's style. He shied away from the recognition his fellow students sought in ever increasing doses. In a homogeneous society of illiterates, it did not matter that Ramon could barely read. Ramon was the best in arithmetic, and the class had a growing need for adders, subtracters, and dividers. Instinctively entrepreneurial, Ramon turned a part of his cash holdings into property; the rest he loaned to his classmates. Both investments earned him enviable returns.

As Ramon got richer and richer, he began to pay a price for his success. The cloak of anonymity came off; he became important and powerful; his advice, previously ignored, was now sought by other children. At first he continued a policy of avoiding conflict, but he found himself inevitably at the center of things. Choices were inescapable. His natural business head and his common sense were important ingredients in the new social order. The fiefdom was breaking down in favor of commercial baronies, and whether he liked it or not, Ramon was 5–308's first commercial baron.

Ramon had understood instinctively that pursuing rewards in a feudal system would throw him into conflict with other children. The teacher distributed the spoils, the patronage, the largess to students, who, in turn, distributed portions to their followers. Since Ramon was impoverished where physical resources were concerned, it was only natural that he make no claims on the spoils and avoid being muscled out by his peers. As banker, however, he had his own largess to distribute. He had emerged as a figure on whom the fortunes of others depended. Intellect was now competing with muscle for dominance. It came as no great shock to anyone when Ramon hired Raoul, the strongest kid in the class, to protect his interests, to collect his debts, to run his errands. No one but me saw the significance of that seemingly inconsequential reversal of the student hierarchy. Muscle had surrendered to commerce. Soon after this development I persuaded Raoul and Ramon that it might be better for everyone if Raoul performed police duties for the whole class, and I began paying Raoul to protect and to enforce the as-yet-unwritten laws. There were other signs of change. The first indication of Ramon's emergence had been a line of children waiting to see him with their financial problems. The second sign, however, shook me just a little. Ramon was now among the first to be chosen for punchball.

Parents' Day

Late in November, P.S. 484 held its Parents' Day. It began at seven P.M. and was to end at nine. The entire teaching staff returned to the classrooms for the evening. Mrs. Winthrop, the teacher in the room adjoining mine, followed a simple plan with parents. During the lunch hour she had said, "Every time you tell them something bad about their child, mix it with something good. That way they go away less depressed. You have to give them hope or they won't come." As she finished giving advice, she shrugged. There wasn't any hope, not for Williamsburg youngsters. For Mrs. Winthrop and for many others, Parents' Day was a ritual of community involvement.

Mrs. Donna, my first visitor, arrived at 7:30 P.M. She was the first of three parents who would appear that evening. Mrs. Donna was the mother of one of three black children in the classroom.

Both parents were employed. Barbara was the only child in my class who lived in the housing project adjacent to the school. Mr. Donna followed Mrs. Donna into 308.

"Good evening. You are?"

"We are Mr. and Mrs. Donna. Barbara is our daughter."

"Oh, yes, is she with you?"

"No, we left her home with the baby."

Mr. Donna got right to the point. "Barbara's been coming home with play money, deeds, and with God knows what else. What's goin' on here? We took her out of Catholic school because they weren't teaching her to read or write. All they cared about was discipline and praying. Now, I agree with discipline. Kids can't always have things their own way, can they? And I don't mind the praying either, but someday Barbara's gonna have to earn a living and she's gonna need a heap more than prayin' to do it."

"We want Barbara to go to college," said Mrs. Donna. "We want her to have what we missed. You can't get into one of them colleges if you can't read."

"Let me explain about the money and deeds, but first let me ask you a question. Has Barbara been writing more lately? Does she do more written work now than she did when she was in Catholic school?"

"Yes, she does," replied Mrs. Donna.

"Do you know why?"

"She tells me you are payin' them to write. What is it? You pay fifty dollars a composition, right?"

"The amount I pay depends on the quality and the length of the work. Some students only earn ten dollars. That's because I think they can do better. Others earn as much as fifty dollars. I usually pay that amount for something really original." I dipped into Barbara's folder. "Here are some samples of her work in class and at home." I handed Barbara's papers to her parents. "I think it's important for children to write. It helps them a lot with their reading, and it is something they must become less afraid to do. I don't correct every mistake. If I did, they would probably put their pencils down forever. They're working on spelling this month. Next month we'll concentrate on simple sentences."

"So you get more work outa them with this money."

I nodded. "I also pay them for every book they finish, no matter what it is."

"Makes sense." Mr. Donna turned to Mrs. Donna. "Don't it? If I work for money, why not Barbara? The more she reads, the better."

"What do they do in math?" asked Mrs. Donna.

"Barbara gets the regular fifth-grade math course," I answered. "We are supposed to teach the New Math, and I do, but it is also important for Barbara to get some computation experience. I'll say this for Barbara. She's good in arithmetic. In fact, her job in the game is to check the financial records of her classmates for errors. If she finds any, she keeps the difference. So in addition to her weekly salary for the job, Barbara earns extra money finding other people's errors."

"That's right. Barbara said she was the class accountant. She likes the job." Mrs. Donna turned to her husband. "She's learning double-entry bookkeeping."

"That's good," said Mr. Donna. "She oughta learn things she can use when she gets out of school."

After looking at some of their daughter's artwork, Mr. and Mrs. Donna put their coats on. Mrs. Donna shrugged. "You a new teacher, Mr. Richmond. I hope you teach her to read better."

"I'll do my best."

My next visitor appeared at 8:30 P.M.

"How do you do?"

"I am Ramon's aunt. His mother didn't come because she don't speak English so good. So I came in her place. That all right?"

"Oh, yes. Have a seat. I'm glad to meet you. Ramon is a favorite topic."

She smiled, glad I'd be doing the talking.

"When Ramon came to this class, he was very shy. He kept to himself. He's still very much that way, but in the last few weeks he's begun to use his talent. Your nephew's got a lot. Lately, he's been important in transforming the values of his classmates. We used to measure a person's importance by how many people he could beat up, but, thanks to Ramon and some others, brains count too. Ramon lacks fists, but has his wits about him."

Miss Hernandez smiled, amused by my fervor. "That's good to hear. Ramon likes school better this year than before. When he comes home, he spends time working on his accounts or doin' math and compositions. His mother thinks he's crazy workin' so hard, but I tell her he does good."

"Ramon handed me five compositions yesterday. It's overwhelming. My wife has to help me correct them. I've been receiving forty or fifty a week for the last three weeks. Some students would never lift a pencil before I started paying them."

"It's good. I never learn to write. I even hate to write letters," said Miss Hernandez.

"Do you know about Ramon's business exploits?"

"He tells me. He wants to be a banker when he grows up. I never heard a kid wanting that before. A Puerto Rican banker! My boyfriend broke up when I told him about my nephew."

"He's got the head for it. If his reading improves, he might just do it."

Transfer

Early in December I learned that I would be leaving P.S. 484. The news came through a grapevine in the teachers' cafeteria. A week later Mr. Herman confirmed the gossip, explaining that a group of teachers with permanent certification had been assigned to the school. Teachers holding conditional licenses would have to accept new assignments. Since I was one of those, I would be leaving.

"How can you interrupt a year like this?" I had asked. But the assistant principal only shrugged.

In January I began dismantling the game. My students turned

their cash holdings into consumer goods proportional to their holdings.

I had one conference with the principal. I indicated a desire to remain with 5–308 and described what I'd been doing with my students. She repeated the assistant principal's explanation. It wasn't until the day I was replaced that the shape of the purge took a somewhat different character. Of the eight conditional licensees that had been assigned to the school through the Intensive Teacher Training Program the previous summer, six were male. All six were being reassigned. The two women teachers from ITTP were to stay. An older teacher explained that the principal regarded female teachers as more suitable for elementary grades. The teachers who replaced us were recent graduates of the School of Education at St. John's. They had even less experience in the classroom than the ITTP people who'd been in classrooms for half the year.

I felt a mixture of bitterness and relief: bitterness because I could not finish what had been started, and relief because I could start again with a little experience behind me. I announced my departure to the children a day before it took effect. Perhaps I should have shared the news earlier, but I wanted as little commotion as possible; it seemed to be the best way.

"Why you leaving? Don't you like us?"

"I like you all very much. I'm being transferred by the Board of Education. I've asked them not to. They won't listen."

They did not understand. When Miss Jump, my replacement, showed up the next day, they directed their anger against her. She seemed frightened; she had every right to be. Rita was more infuriated than I'd ever seen her. "Why didn't they ask us! They take away everything they give us that's good." Referring to Miss Jump, they screamed, "We don't want that tomato." Miss Jump, sunburned a Bermuda pink, was visibly trembling at this reception. I tried to cool them, but to no avail. A screaming mob of children escorted me to the subway. One of the boys said, "I want a man teacher. I ain't coming to school." It was Pablo the Truant.

3. Police Power

I was reassigned to P.S. 452 in Astoria, about six miles upriver from Montrose Avenue. P.S. 452 isn't a ghetto school. The seven-block walk from the subway to the schoolhouse takes one past peaked roofs and beneath oaks and elms. It's the country, after Brooklyn. Williamsburg's gamut of four- to six-story tenements doesn't compare with Astoria's red brick two- and three-family houses. The neighborhood surrounding P.S. 452 is composed mainly of a stable population of Greek and Italian Catholic working people. Many hold two or more jobs to maintain their tenuous hold on New York City's version of Middle America. Class 5–319 comes to school from these houses: their parents are renters, not owners. Twenty years ago most of the houses in this section of Queens were parceled into apartments by their original owners, who then fled into the suburbs. What they left behind is habitable. People in Astoria are not rich, but they are not poor either. Children come to school scented with detergent, with creases in their trousers, and with hair plastered down with Vitalis. Astoria children have a just-washed look that Williamsburg youngsters would be hard put to imitate.

The moment I entered 5–319, I noticed the difference. Instead of thirty fifth-graders, there were only twenty-five. When Mr. Smith, the school principal, entered the class with me, to do the introductions, the class stood at respectful attention. Our appearance interrupted a penmanship lesson left behind on the blackboard by my predecessor in anticipation of my arrival. The orderliness nearly overcame me after Williamsburg. These children were disciplined soldiers compared with the guerrillas I'd left behind. In the quiet of 5–319, I could hear Rita, Raoul, Rosa, Pablo, my whole Williamsburg crew, rattling in my memory.

At noon that first day I made my way to the teachers' lunchroom with Amy Vladeck, my next-door neighbor and the school's art teacher.

"You've got two real problems: Robert Howard and Tammy Bunting. They gave Miss Kroll, your predecessor, a fit."

"Two? And only twenty-five students. Where I've come from, that's a gifted class."

"Where have you been?" asked Miss Vladeck, who could not see how anyone could be ecstatic over my legacy.

"I've been in Vietnam, Miss Vladeck—Vietnam, Brooklyn. I probably had ten or fifteen Roberts and Tammys. Two seems healthy. A little dose of rebellion."

I began eating my lunch, and tuned into the conversations buzzing around me.

"Jose hit his teacher. That boy is headed for big trouble someday. . . ."

"Andrea—you know my Andrea, don't you? I caught her in the closet cleaning out coat pockets. I've never heard of such a thing in the fourth grade. . . ."

"Ethel left school without permission. She didn't say a word—just walked out. Not a word. . . ."

As I listened, Astoria and Williamsburg merged in my mind. I remembered the figure on school crime that I'd seen in the morning paper: "7000% Rise In One Year!" If true, it meant that schools were doing more to breed criminals than any other institution except possibly a prison. It made one wonder about Dewey's educational aphorism connecting experience with education. From my own experience, I guessed that every form of crime encountered in the street was previewed in a classroom.

"I can't get that child to leave Hester alone. . . ."

"Steve was caught smoking in the bathroom."

"At least it wasn't dope. In Harlem nine-year-olds smoke dope regularly. It's only a matter of time before our kids turn their tobacco in for heroin."

"Just when my lesson was going so well, he threw his shoe across the room. The lesson went with it."

The lesson, I thought. A teacher's prescription against boredom. I felt disgust. Lesson or no, all too often what's going on in the classroom amounts to nothing more than a simulated failure of law enforcement. I accept the responsibility, but what can that possibly mean? Nothing we teachers do in the classroom is half as interesting as classroom war. A regular saga of crime and punishment. Only problem is too many crimes to solve any, too many criminals to punish. By the time a teacher investigates an offense, accuses someone of misbehavior, hears the conflicting stories, resolves the case and punishes whoever is guilty, why there's another crime; it never concludes. The game's got a name: Perpetual Cops and Robbers.

More sounds from the lunchroom filtered through my thoughts.

"You know Herman, don't you? He's the Puerto Rican boy in Beth's class. Beth says he's having an affair with Roberta. Can you believe it? At their age? Roberta's in *my* class! What am I going to do?"

Again I thought of the lesson. At some point a teacher must admit the failure of her prescriptions; scandal infects schooling to the point where classroom troubles immunize themselves to remedies. All that's left is perpetual police duties, and at best they're a recipe for the failure of police power.

The Extortionist

Class 5–319's leading underworld figure was Robert Howard. Robert specialized in extortion. He was very good at it. The extent of his dealings came to light by accident—well, not quite by accident. Two dozen children, half in my class, half in the third and fourth grades, were emptying their pockets regularly to fulfill Robert's requests.

Tony, proprietor of Tony's Pizza across the street from the school, gave me the first clue. One noon hour I visited Tony's Pizza just as Robert was leaving. He was in the company of a child I'd never seen before. The pair struck me as an odd match. You don't see a tall, heavy-set, black ten-year-old arm in arm with a seven-year-old every day, not in Astoria. A mixture of fear, discomfort, awkwardness, of being crowded, emanated from Robert's tiny companion: occasionally he squirmed under the arm of his escort.

"Tony, you know them?" I pointed to the pair as they crossed the street.

"Oh, sure. The big kid. Quiet-like. One of my best customers. Buys three or four slices every day. Usually two at lunch and two after school. Wish I had more customers like him. Kids seem to like him. They are always treating him. Hardly ever spends his own money."

You expect extortion in the barrios, but not in Astoria. My Williamsburg crew knew thieves, numbers men, dope pushers, and confidence men. Sometimes they were even friends or relatives. During our current-events hour it wasn't unusual to hear first- or second-hand accounts of the latest expressions of violence on a block or in an apartment house. Now and then someone would cut out a clipping from one of the Spanish dailies or from an English tabloid to verify a story. Since no one read Spanish or English, the reporter stood in front of the class pretending to read the print, all the time embroidering an account of his own. Curiously, these embroideries often turned out to be accurate and colorful reports of what had actually happened. I read the news clippings.

No slum surrounds P.S. 452. The parents of students in 5–319 work. Very few suffer public assistance. Plaster icons of the Nativity and Crucifixion decorate almost every lawn, symbols of an upstanding community intent on steering its children into legitimate channels. In this tight-knit working-class community, parents point to blacks like Robert as the source of trouble, and to the busing program that brings them from city-owned housing projects in the Kingsbridge section of Queens as the real culprit. With clenched fists, they point to the white figurines on their lawns, symbols of their own pious and patriotic way of life, and demand that the number of blacks in the school be kept low.

Miss Vladeck had tried to reason with them at one meeting. "Every classroom has a criminal population, white or black. There has never been a classroom without some bad apples. For that matter, there's never been a group of people anywhere without its bad apples. That's just the way people are. If you get children who cooperate, you're going to get some who don't. If you get a class of thirty children, you pray, 'Lord, just rid me of these three.' Say the Lord answers that prayer and you lose the three who are making your life the most miserable. Well, before you can send their record cards down to the office you find three new rotters on the branch." She'd been right, but it hadn't weakened the rage of parents whose children came home bruised.

During my second month in P.S. 452, complaints about Robert began reaching me regularly. His behavior in class, never something deserving praise, took a sharp turn for the worse. I do not know whether the number of misdemeanors increased or whether I was growing more aware of his activities as I became familiar with the new surroundings.

One week it would be a note from the assistant principal instructing me to confiscate some photographs Robert was selling in the schoolyard. The following week it'd be a note from the principal telling me to keep the boy under constant supervision. I did all I could do. But there was no end to the troubles. One morning Robert was detained for lying down on the stairwell so he could look up a teacher's dress as she descended.

Another morning, a cluster teacher relieved me with a note asking me to come to the front office immediately. When I arrived, Mr. Smith grimly handed me a note from an irate parent.

Dear Mr. Smith,

I give my son lunch money every day and he don't eat lunch. This is because a colored kid named Robert takes his money and makes my son buy him Pizza. I want this stopped. Because if I take off from work to get this bully, he is going to pay for it. You tell him to leave off my son.

Yours,
Bill Anderson

"Mr. Richmond, Mr. Anderson will not be leaving work to rescue his son," I was told. "If I can't guarantee the safety of every child in this school, then . . . I will not remain here as principal. Robert is suspended, effective immediately. Please get in touch with his parents. I want them here tomorrow morning. We won't have a repetition of this incident."

Soon after my return to 5–319 a messenger handed me a note from the main office.

Mrs. Steinitz, the school social worker, has reached Mr. Howard at his place of business. You, Mrs. Steinitz, Robert and his parents will meet in room 327 tomorrow at 11 o'clock to discuss the boy's problem. I'll see to it that Mrs. Price covers your class. And also I want you to keep an anecdotal file on young Mr. Howard. Write down every incident of misconduct. Send me a copy at the end of the week.

Yours,
Art Smith, Principal

The campaign to transfer Robert to another school had been launched.

At any stage of the transfer, a parent, an assistant superintendent, or a principal in the school most likely to receive the transferee may find some procedural defect which will result in the denial of the transfer. So when a veteran like Smith decides to work a transfer, he prepares thoroughly. Parents must be contacted and told where their children are in school. A child must be transferred from class to class within a school before an interschool transfer will even be considered. This is to make sure that the child's problems don't stem from a personality clash with one teacher. His behavior must be consistently destructive. School authorities allow the child to build the case against himself. Adults need only record it, and when there is enough on file to cut off every avenue of escape, the cord is cut and the problem floats into someone else's school. As it turned out, Robert did all he could to aid his eviction, not because he didn't like P.S. 452 but because he couldn't help himself.

Mr. and Mrs. Howard

At eleven o'clock the next day Mr. and Mrs. Howard, Robert, the school social worker, and I met. Robert's parents sat quietly with their son. Every so often Mrs. Howard would shake her head toward him. Robert didn't seem to notice. He just stared at the floor or looked around the room. He was dressed neatly; his dark tie had been tucked carefully under a starched white collar. Looking at him in his adult uniform, I couldn't help feeling that there was no child under that tie—that this scene, this hearing, this trial would be repeated again and again all his life. I imagined the boy's oval face cast in a mug shot in some police line-up: blank, lifeless, impervious to rage. I'd never seen Robert angry. He never blew off steam; his anger oozed through his actions into children around him, and there turned into fear.

Robert's parents were well-dressed upper-proletariat. Mrs. Howard mothered, cooked, and cleaned for five children. Judging from her son's clothes, she took special care with household chores. She saw no reason to do less for her children than for the white folk who employed her. Mr. Howard wore a gray suit. He was a supervisor in the shipping room of a mail-order company. Throughout the meeting Robert's father gave assurances about his son's future conduct; after each one he cast an iron look toward Robert, but his looks were rebuffed. His son, although meek enough, didn't tremble as he was supposed to, so his father eventually gave up.

"It's extortion," said the social worker. "I can't understand how a boy with such fine parents can take money from little children."

"We give him everything, everything," said the father. "This should never have happened. Look at his clothes. His mother works herself to death so he can go to school lookin' decent. We give him spending money. . . ." The father's voice trailed off.

Robert's troubles reflected on his parents; they didn't know whether to close ranks as a family against the attack or to side with the school and participate in shaming their son. The social worker helped them decide. She divided them, first complimenting the parents and then scolding their son, until Mr. and Mrs. Howard joined in his prosecution.

"Why, Robert? Why do you do these things?" Mrs. Howard studied her son until she got the look of remorse she was trying to wring from him. "Don't you get a good lunch in school?" Robert nodded. "Then why did you make that child give you his lunch money? Don't he have a right to eat just like you?"

Robert said nothing during the entire interview, letting his parents do the talking, and nodding when it was required of him. Mr. Howard agreed to the conditions proposed by the social worker for returning Robert to class. There would be a diary. Robert would bring it to me every afternoon for an entry. The entry would be brought home each day for his mother's signature. If Robert's problems continued, there would be a beating—maybe even a 600 school. The meeting ended.

The effects of this conference lasted for about a week and a half. Robert's behavior during that time was flawless. Just as I began to think this change might be lasting, I noted the first signs of decay in his effort. In the second week of the probation period, Robert lost his diary. The loss of the diary followed a morning on which Gregor, a sensitive Greek boy, had accused Robert of stealing his Micro-Economy money; another girl had said he had gone through her purse. My own receiver was dimly aware of his heightened metabolism. Robert couldn't sit still. His limbs carried him aimlessly from one place to another. Whenever my attention wandered to another corner of the room, he would leave his seat. When

I asked him to return to his desk, he dallied and pretended not to hear. The diary entry that day, although it ended on a hopeful note, wasn't very flattering. The following morning he informed me that it had been lost. I asked him to provide himself with another. He did, but that one soon disappeared too.

The next entry went in the anecdotal file. I sent a letter to his mother, but received no reply. I suspected that it had never reached her. Soon after, Robert helped fill a page in the file subtitled "The Projector Incident." Every Thursday afternoon we pulled the shades, sent for a projector, and viewed either a movie or a film strip related to some topic we had studied during the week. On this Thursday the teacher in charge of audio-visual told me of a new strip on Africa that had just arrived from the Board of Education. I made a point, wherever possible, of chipping away at the racial stereotypes planted in the children by their parents. This was especially important for the black children in my class: they had not yet received the "Black Is Beautiful" message. To call someone "black" was to invite trouble. According to the teacher who had recommended it, this new strip attempted to reach black children with a message of African culture and racial pride. It might be a good way to confront the racial attitudes that seethed within this community.

The projector arrived. I threaded the film and agreed to let a student operate the projector. After each strip we discussed what had been screened. During this discussion I took my usual place at my desk and called on children who had something to say. Robert headed for the projector.

"Robert, please return to your seat."

He pretended not to hear. His fingers touched the lamp switch; his nose pushed up against the lens.

"Robert, don't touch the projector." My hand directed him to his seat.

"I'm not touching it." His arms bent into a cradle; his torso coiled over the machine. He wasn't touching it; he was surrounding it.

"Robert!" I was becoming impatient. The discussion was ruined.

His body uncoiled long enough for him to try another tack. His hands took hold of the projector stand and gently propelled it backward and then forward. "This ain't touching," he said, a naïve note in his voice.

I stepped toward him.

Robert began blowing on the lens. "I ain't touching."

By the time I reached the machine, he had retreated to his desk.

"Robert, I will want to see you in this room at three P.M."

Robert frowned. He hated to stay after school.

It was this constant drain on my patience that angered me. He was the master of the technicality, knew every lawyer's trick. If one ever could get one's distance, one might learn to admire the dexterity with which a word like "touch" got stretched or contracted until it covered a whole new set of meanings. We adults treat words as if they were our own special monopoly; we use them to bolster our authority over children and to get them to do what we want. What we sometimes overlook is the ways children have of negating that power by refusing to hear us.

The average teacher believes that conflict can be settled with talk, with words. Children know this and also know that they're licked before they start if they play by those rules. So they play a different game or, at least, by different rules, and their game has one purpose: to find the pressure point, different in every adult, where a teacher or a parent moves from twisting words to twisting arms.

My move toward Robert signaled my readiness to go beyond verbs and nouns; it accomplished what speech could not.

Soon after the projector incident, complaints about Robert began to come from his classmates. One child accused him of removing money from the child's coat. Another said Robert was going to get him after school, but wouldn't say why.

The class had been playing Micro-Economy for less than two months. The game added a dimension to our classroom life that all found very satisfying. As we played I made an effort to teach my students some fundamental economics. We studied the interest formula, commercial banking, real estate, supply-and-demand theory, money, aspects of monetary policy such as inflation, and partnerships. Of course, there were the inevitable squabbles, but these—far from draining my patience—led me to see opportunities for growth.

Since I paid their salaries each week and kept track of their transactions in Micro-Economy, I knew roughly how much money and property each student had. During one game session Robert took out his billfold to pay a debt. In the process, he showed me $3,000 or $4,000 more than my estimates indicated he should have had. My suspicions were aroused.

"Robert, where did you get all that money?"

"You paid me for my spelling test and my compositions."

"How much do you have?"

"Six thousand dollars."

"Six thousand dollars!" echoed Gregor angrily. "He stole it!" I motioned to Gregor to be silent.

"I collect rent on my properties, just like you!" said Robert. But his words were light on conviction. He noticed my dissatisfaction and decided to add something to his explanation. "The rest I got selling pictures after school. They buy 'em from me."

I turned away from him, but as I approached my desk someone whispered: "He takes it off ya."

That afternoon I asked Robert to stay after school for a talk. It was important to try to get through to him. One more try, I thought. I had to penetrate his shell. After I dismissed the class on the first floor, Robert and I turned to ascend the stairs.

"I have to catch the bus, Mr. Richmond."

"When does it leave?"

"Right now."

"Miss it. I'll give you carfare for the city bus."

Robert sighed. His escape had been cut.

"Do you know why I asked you to stay?"

"No."

"Robert, you and I have been fighting each other for two solid months. Why?"

"I ain't been fighting you, Mr. Richmond."

I recited a history of combat. "Look, I've been trying to help you. Do you think I like chasing after you all day? Is that why I took this job? I come to school to teach you how to read and write, and maybe a little about the world you're going to face. And you give me the ho-hum."

For a moment his face was open, then closed, retreating from the possibility that I might be human.

"There must be a dozen children who live in fear of you. They come to school to learn, not to be robbed. Robert, the principal is making me keep a journal where I record everything you do in class. They want to send you to a Six Hundred school. You keep filling that journal with the things that are buying you a one-way ticket there."

"I don't rob nobody." It was a high squeaky denial, weak and unconvincing.

"Then, where did you get the extra three thousand dollars?"

"I told you."

"What about all the kids who tell me you're hustling them?"

He shrugged his shoulders.

"That's not an answer!" I couldn't get through to him, and it was frustrating. "Do you think I have you here because I don't care about you or because I want to frighten you? I *do* care. You have a right to know what you're doing to yourself, and you're heading for a fall."

He hadn't understood. Too abstract. "A fall?"

"A Six Hundred school. A reform school, where they beat you instead of reasoning with you." The explanation was unnecessary; he knew what I meant.

I paused, hoping for the breakthrough, but none came. We'd both lost.

"Dismissed."

Robert escaped down the stairs without looking back.

"Your bus fare."

But he was gone.

The Slambook

The next day Robert did not come to school. At the beginning of our daily writing period, I spoke to the class. "Those of you who are interested in taking a rest from your writing projects may write essays about Robert Howard. Depending on the quality and length, I'm willing to pay up to a hundred dollars ME."

The topic stirred most everyone in the class. I noticed eyes darting over to Robert's desk to make sure it was still empty; others balanced tomorrow's twisted arm against a moment of truth. His empty chair made brave men of those who might otherwise be cowards. The sharpener honed their pencils to a fine point. I noted the way they were turning Robert's undoing into a ritual. They waved their pencils in the air as if their imaginations were working overtime to turn the pencils into swords. Yet one sensed their fear and their elation, fear of Robert when he came back, elation at their courage to expose him. They wrote with steady concentration. They finished, one by one, and each author brought his work to my desk personally. I read some as they came in. Yes, I thought, this is going to be something. When nearly everyone had turned his work in, I invited volunteers to read what they'd written. Gregor usually populated his essays with ghosts, demons, witches, and supernatural events, and he did not fail us this time.

> Robert Howard. By Gregor. Robert Howard is a bad person. He is a monster in the corpse of a human being. . . . He makes me pay him $100 ME if I want to be left alone. He is bigger so I pay. When I don't pay him a $100 a week, he takes my money from my back pocket. Sometimes he goes through my coat. I end up paying more that way. . . .

The rest of the essays told similar stories. Only details differed. Two or three children mentioned Robert's activities in the schoolyard, where he preyed on children in the lower grades, forcing them to surrender their funds. I remembered watching Robert from my classroom window. Were those games of tag innocent? Robert and his seven-year-old companion came to mind.

When the last essay had been read, a feeling filled the room that hadn't been there before. Before, each person had had his private grief with Robert, but now that everyone had been heard, an accumulation of private causes had occurred and it welled into anger. Eight students had been extortion victims. Three quarters of the class traced thefts of their personal property to Robert. Until the beginning of Micro-Economics, Robert had been interested exclusively in U.S. currency and personal property, but the introduction of Micro-Economy money led him to add it to his list of sought-after items. Their essays exposed their fears; the exposure itself was fearful. Only those who were most anxious quieted their anxiety by being openly angry.

"Mr. Richmond, you better keep him off us."

"He ought to be put away," said another.

"You're the teacher! Why don't you do something?"

Their demands for protection from the local fiefholder echoed through the ages. And, like their ancestors, they worried about what would happen if Robert caught them alone. No one disputed that I should be the one to find the solution to the problem of Robert.

"Wait a minute!"

They stopped.

"You'll have to save yourselves from Robert."

"Whadya mean? He'll squash us like flies."

"If you want Robert to stop bothering you, then you're going to have to get together. Aren't ten people stronger than one?"

"Yeah." But a look of surrender overtook them.

"You scared of him yourself, Mr. Richmond, that's why you won't take him on," said Andre.

"You think I should take him on, Andre?"

"I guess not." He smiled. "It's different for teachers."

"What do people do when they don't like something a person's doing to them, or to their property?"

Gregor said, "You call the police. They put him in jail."

"But the police can't arrest a man unless he breaks a law."

"Let's pass a law against Robert!" shouted Anthony. Laughter lessened the tension.

"Don't laugh. *I'm* taking this seriously. Laws are not written for one person. Laws are the same for everybody."

We discussed legislative process. After many questions and answers, I suggested that they try writing a law.

"Say, Mr. Richmond," called out Naomi, "putting some words down on paper isn't going to stop Robert from bothering us. You still got to have police. Why bother with this? We'll just tell you what the law should be; you take care of that baboon."

"All right. What if someone breaks the law? Any suggestions?"

"We could paddle him in the gym," offered Anthony. After snickers and a few bizarre counter-suggestions, our talk took a more serious turn.

"We could all get him if he bothers any one of us," suggested Gregor. "But first we have to give him a trial."

"That might work, but you can't give a guy a stiff sentence for a first offense. The law has to get tougher on the crook if he keeps after people."

The discussion took the better part of the afternoon, but by three o'clock we had a law against extortion. Tammy, one of a handful of children who could give Robert worse than she got, was appointed to read the law to Robert when he returned to school.

Two days later Robert appeared. By the time he arrived in class, he knew everything that had gone on during his absence. Moreover, he knew just who had spoken against him. Later I learned that two students in the class had decided to play both sides of the issue, hedging against a failure of the legal process. Not surprisingly, both had taken active parts in writing the slambook and in drafting the law against extortion. Upon his return, they became his informers. It was not the last time I was to be reminded that children are not the innocents educators make them out to be, but shrewd politicians constantly attuned to the law of survival.

Reports reached me that indicated Robert was threatening to "get" anyone who had written something bad about him. Fortunately for the authors of the slambook, I retained their essays. For a while, at least, they'd be able to fend Robert off with their own versions of what had happened.

He moved cautiously. Something in him must have sensed the danger. He was no longer sure that he was the hunter. Perhaps it was the defiance he saw in the eyes of those who once had feared and deferred to him. It produced a calm in some, but others hesitated. Caution ended when a note arrived from a third-grade teacher accusing Robert of strong-arming one of her nine-year-olds. The note asked me to send Robert to her room.

I acquiesced. During his absence I called for a trial. I felt sure that I could win the cooperation of that third-grade teacher. When he returned he must have known that the trap had closed. He simply nodded when I informed him that he would stand trial for breaking the law against extortion. In the interests of fairness, I informed him that he could count on my help in preparing a defense. The blank expression he always wore lifted. For a moment he seemed to thaw.

We chose a six-man jury by lot. So many children had been his victims that it was impossible to select an unbiased panel; we did the best we could. It turned out that everyone wanted a part in the trial: Robert and the prosecution had three attorneys each, which meant they'd work in teams. Although our primitive legal procedure might not be ideal, I was convinced that the experience might be worth the procedural sacrifices. We relied on common sense to guide the verdict.

Preparations for the trial took two class days and a weekend. It was amazing how much television had taught them about courtroom acting, and how ignorant it had left them about legal preparation. Composing the brief was a writing lesson to remember. I forced them to test their language constantly for clarity. What they learned about writing in those few days was more than ten formal lessons could teach. After a heated discussion about who the judge should be, they decided that I would preside over the first trial, although I insisted that a student should have the job in the future.

That evening my thoughts were monopolized by Robert. What did I want to say to the class about him? It was important that their anger be prevented from inflicting irreparable harm. He was a human being who needed help, not maiming. At the same time, his confusion and his behavior were harming others and required a concerted effort to bring it to a speedy end. The court had to consider what was best for Robert and what was best for the community he seemed willing to offend regularly. Maybe his defense attorneys would discover why he committed these crimes and their discovery would suggest a verdict. I shook my head. That happens only in the movies. There were moral lessons and legal lessons to be drawn from this experience, and I saw it as my responsibility to draw them clearly.

The trial was slated to begin on Monday. When I arrived at school Monday morning I saw a transfer slip in my box. It had Robert's name on it: he was being sent to another fifth-grade class. It seemed that the third-grade teacher had taken her complaint to Mr. Smith. Robert collected his things and left.

The trial didn't take place. One child put our feelings into words: "It's too bad we weren't the ones who transferred him. It's like having a verdict without a trial."

4. Broad Jump

Late in June the Selective Service System ended my work in the New York City schools by assigning me to the Transitional Year Program (TYP) for a stint as a conscientious objector. TYP provided young men and women from minority groups with a thirteenth year to prepare for college, and me with employment in a twenty-four-hour-a-day position as assistant director, instructor, and dormitory resident. TYP was affiliated with Yale. During the course of my first year there, I met Tom Edwards, the dean of one of Yale's colleges, who left to become the director of Broad Jump, and Tom became interested in my ideas. When TYP recessed for the summer he urged me to join his staff at Broad Jump's Trinity campus. I agreed.

Nine months of the year, Trinity School in New York City is a private school for boys. But during the summer, when Trinity's winter occupants take off to vacation lands on the Riviera or to summer houses in Maine, Vermont, or on Cape Cod, Trinity School rents its facility to Broad Jump for a summer program. Every weekday, 130 boys between the ages of nine and thirteen, predominantly black or Puerto Rican, come from the Lower East Side, Harlem, East Harlem, and the South Bronx by subway and by bus to the school. The summer heat that routs the private school's regular clientele from their winter nests drives the less privileged into the chairs, desks, gym, pool, classrooms, and halls vacated by the sons of the wealthy.

Broad Jump is operated in cooperation with the Boys' Clubs of New York and is supported by over a dozen foundations and public agencies. Its link to the Boys' Clubs helps it obtain financial support and provides it with its clientele. Boys are chosen from neighboring schools and from clubs on the recommendation of teachers, parents, and club counselors who believe that these students will benefit from a summer at one of the program's eight campuses. Half the campuses are at New England prep schools outside the city; the other half operate in the city, offering students academic and recreational programs.

The prospect of implementing the Micro-Economy game here excited me. Ramon the banker, Raoul the bill collector, Robert the extorter, the entire experience the year before had kindled a hunger in me for a renewal of the possibilities. Ramon had come to represent a moment of human history, a replay in microcosm of the commercial revolution; the humor, irony, and possibilities gnawed on me. If human history, the play of forces, the relationships between one historical movement and another, could be recreated in a classroom or a school, it might be possible to catch a gleam of an undiscovered land, a different kind of education, one that would provide students with tools, with knowledge, with a desire to make history themselves, and one, finally, that would give them the power to shape the world and its history.

Along with six other teachers, I implemented the real-estate game; we played in the afternoon. The staff also used the currency in the morning academic program to compensate students for their work. It gave the program focus and excitement. And while the impact of the incentives on the students was uneven—some reacted strongly and positively, others only weakly—everyone agreed that on the whole it was positive. One teacher went further: "It's time black kids knew this. It's time they learn how to run institutions. My people have always been run *by* institutions."

Roland Chase, twelve, black, energetic, gifted, smiled at Reggie Mark. "Sell me your option."

Reggie looked suspicious. "How much?"

Roland got real cozy, arm on shoulder, warm brotherly affection oozing out, the whole bit. "Ten dollars."

"Twenty!"

Roland scowled. "Can buy it for fifteen from Tommy over there."

"So why you sweatin' me?" Reggie scowled back.

"Okay. Okay. Here, take twenty."

Reggie nodded. He didn't have enough money to bid anyway, so why not? What he did not know was that Roland had been asking around. None of the people who landed on property 32 had enough money to buy it. It was going to go for a song. All you had to do was get an option to buy and have a little more cash than someone else and the property was yours. Reggie didn't know something else Roland had figured out: the demand for property changed over the course of a week. The closer payday came, the less money circulated, and, consequently, the lower the price of property. On payday, prices skyrocketed. When that happened, Roland sold.

Teachers paid students a week's wages on Friday. Students earned that money in a standard academic program offered in the morning. That program consisted of one hour of reading, one hour of math, and one hour of language-arts development: spelling, phonetics, word games, etc. Each teacher developed a wage scale for the students in her classes. On Friday the teachers filled out a form listing the earnings of each student and sent it to the office to be inscribed in individual student bank accounts. The bank opened four afternoons a week in the school cafeteria. Students were permitted to withdraw their funds twice each week, usually on days on which they were scheduled to attend the City Game in the afternoon.

Students spent their "soul dollars"—scrip—or invested them. Some spent their earnings at two auctions, one held the third and the other held the sixth week. Educational games, books, athletic equipment, photographic equipment, comic books, records, food, and other items attractive to boys between nine and thirteen were offered at these auctions. Others discovered that their soul dollars could be exchanged for commodities on an informal basis. For instance, Emil Jackson reputedly sold Afro-combs for $200 in Broad Jump currency. Tom's announcement that the program would no longer supply students with free pencils but would sell them for two soul dollars each inspired another student to stay after school and collect stray pencils—and then undercut the established price by offering two for $3. On another occasion Broad Jump sold students Trinity tee-shirts for $100 each, two to a customer.

Every teacher paid wages differently. Some teachers paid $5 for attendance. Others refused to pay children for merely being somewhere, insisting that they do something for it. One teacher paid $10 a week for neatness. However, the majority of the staff used the allocation of $100 per student per class to encourage extra work, to reward effort or originality, and to ensure completion of assignments.

The real-estate game provided a focus for other activity. A number of children went to the art class. On afternoons when they were not using the Micro-Economy materials, a number of children went to art class to build and decorate their houses. The buyers and sellers, the wheelers and dealers always seemed to be scratching sums on pieces of paper, negotiating trades, writing contracts, or simply trying to figure out what to do next. Several students spent one afternoon measuring off ten-foot blocks for each of the four real-estate games in the fourth floor attic. So many houses were going up, it had become necessary to find a place to put them. With the help of masking tape, they broke these ten-foot squares into smaller lots and put the completed cardboard houses on them.

By the end of the second week, the Micro-Society approach had permeated every aspect of their program. One teacher who had been somewhat worried that she might be contributing to a "capitalist" mentality stopped me in the hall to tell me she had changed her mind. "I'm sure you didn't mean it, but your system helps people like me to get at moral issues. Now what I tell them about being moral, about ethics, doesn't go in one ear and out the other. When one child does something awful to another child, I ask the second child to tell the first how he feels. Beats preachin' anyhow."

"It's funny, I keep telling people that the Society School is open-ended. No one seems to believe it or hear me. I think you've discovered that for yourself. It's your society to shape as much as anybody's."

The teacher smiled. "Well, I'll say this, I feel differently about it. Not convinced, just different. I mean, I just had one of the most exciting days of teaching in my life."

When an invitation to return to Trinity came the following year, I knew I wanted to continue exploring the possibilities for what I increasingly saw as an effort to put students in touch with experience, in its divine and comic forms. The success of the year before earned me the right to address the teachers on the opening day of the program.

"As simply as I can say it, our job is to create a society in this school! We will start by generating an economy." I looked at the Broad Jump staff sitting in front of me. Some knew what to expect—they had been with the program the year before. "We want to expose students to fundamental economic concepts, to financial operations: check writing, banking, savings, interest, making change, building houses, concepts of capital and investment, contracts, exchanging assets for debt, the functions of money. We also want to integrate each activity in the school with every other—we want to make what happens here a bit closer to the real world. You will determine what happens. You will be sources of employment and, therefore, sources of income. You will decide what kinds of work your students will be paid to do, and how much to pay them for what. You remain autonomous. You may integrate the incentives with your academic program in any way you choose. You can even choose not to."

A hand went up.

"I'm sorry, I don't know your name."

"Priscilla Canyon. You mean we don't have to use the soul dollars if we don't want to?"

"I hope you will use the money. If you don't like using monetary incentives as motivation, just divide what I give you among your students equally. At least they won't be at a complete disadvantage when we sell the loot at the end of the summer."

"It won't damage your game?"

"I don't think so." I was rather afraid that equal distribution of the currency would hurt them more than me. "Last year students refused to work for a teacher who paid students equally. They didn't think it was fair for a kid who did nothing all summer to get paid the same amount as students who worked. If you don't pay your children according to a pay scale they think is fair, then you live with the consequences."

Everyone smiled, including Miss Canyon.

"We are going to build a city out of cardboard, wood, tin cans, milk containers, and anything else we can find. I hope those of you who will be handling the art program will help students design their building projects. We also want students to confront the moral issues that come up. They come up in any society and in any economy: wealth distribution, crime, theft, what society should do about poor people, about contracts. If it can be said that we are programming economic and other kinds of conflict into school, then I think we also want it said that we are not sidestepping the real issues. Face them. Struggle with them. Teach. Think."

The City Game was to be divided into four sections. Each one would meet for an hour and a half two afternoons a week, and slightly more than thirty students would be assigned to each one. Teachers assigned to manage a game would have one assistant. I would attend all the sessions for the first two weeks to teach the game's operations. Then I would work with groups of students on small projects, and the teachers would take over the game.

First the classes would discuss the function of money in the economy as a medium of exchange, store of value, and unit of account. We would introduce the game materials: the deeds, currency, checks, bank ledgers, and the transportation board. We would consider such questions as how the rich get rich, what to do about crime in the classroom, welfare, and the problems that societies face when a few own almost everything and the majority owns very little. By the third session there would be enough money in circulation to begin to play. Management tasks would be delegated to students, who would handle most matters in the game without teacher supervision.

"Would you explain how students get money to buy property in the City Game?" asked Mrs. Randolph.

"Last year I gave each teacher a hundred dollars a week per student. If you have twenty-five students you get twenty-five hundred soul dollars. You decide how you'll use it. You establish a wage list. The list says students get ten dollars for this kind of exercise, twenty for that, and so on. In math, you might pay students for each problem they solve, for extra work, for good questions, for coming up with unique solutions to math puzzles, for tests. We want to encourage writing, so we pay students between ten and fifty dollars for compositions they write. Teachers who work individually with students can attach the incentives to more subjective kinds of behavior, like creativity. We want quality, not just quantity."

"Interesting." Miss Perez looked at me thoughtfully. "We'll always be evaluating what we're doing. Someone said students learn to manage the whole thing?"

"I don't know about you. I want that. I want to do everything that can be done to help students manage their own environment. It's easy to do. One of you will start out as the auctioneer. Teach a student to do it. There's absolutely no reason why students can't auction property themselves. The same is true for transportation, banking, and solving problems that come up. We should help students start their own enterprises. We are giving students opportunities to manage. We no longer expect them to act like they're the under class. If we want them to run the world, then we must give them a world to run."

"Is there a guide with rules, procedures . . .?"

"I'll distribute them to you the next time we meet."

"I'm teaching reading. How do *I* use the money?"

"Tie it to comprehension exercises: answer a set of questions and earn ten dollars. Ask your students to collect words. Pay them to teach these words to the other students in the class. Give your worst readers scholarships so that they can hire better readers to tutor them after school or on a weekend. You could pay students for independent reading projects." I smiled. "You'll think of ways."

One of the counselors who sat in the back of the room called for the floor. "Can you tell us what the City Game accomplished last year?"

"Every time I do this program something different happens. I'm not sure I know why. Perhaps it's personality differences, the size of the class, age, teacher—it isn't clear. When I think of last year the first person who comes to mind is Worthington. A big kid. Muscles in his fingers. Not a tough kid. He did his work. Well, he got excited by the money, the game, got excited by just about everything. In his own quiet way he made an impact on everyone. He stood outside school in the morning making deals and talking to his partners. He invented it—the partnership, that is. That may not seem important to you; it may seem obvious, but it wasn't. Not to anyone. You might say he discovered the principle of cooperation. Within a week everyone else in the school learned it from him —discovered that by joining together in an enterprise, by pooling resources and talents, they could create something very powerful, something more effective than when you work alone. That principle revolutionized everything. One minute everyone's on his own. A week later everyone's in a group. Imagine what happened inside people's heads.

"Was it dramatic? Was it visible? Why did everyone learn Worthington's secret? I think maybe Worthington didn't understand it himself. He certainly didn't get up on his feet and teach a lesson. Students learned by watching him. He and his partners swallowed up property after property. Somebody'd be always paying him rent. His partnership kept outbidding everyone else. They bought what they wanted. They sold what they didn't want. Those who might have missed the significance of collecting resources could not miss seeing them prosper: the wads of bills, the houses, the division of work. It made them winners. It made others want to win.

"In two weeks a dozen cooperative associations formed in his section alone. Instead of struggles between individuals, we had a struggle between groups. What had been simple was now increasingly complex. You don't look astounded. All right, think—what if children learned the principles of cooperation and organization in school? Imagine how different their world might be. Mind, they learned it without sermons.

"Then, there was Fats. Fats refused to pay his rent. Fats said, 'I ain't payin' nothin' nohow.' And I said, 'You landed on Wendall's property and you got to pay him rent.' And Fats said, 'What I got to pay him rent for?' 'Ask your parents why. Don't they have to pay rent the first of every month? That's life. No one likes paying the landlord. You pay or you get an eviction notice. And you're *out*.' "

"What did Fats do?"

"Fats had a friend called Rivero. He came to Fats' side. Fats said to him, 'Man, all I want to do is earn my money, put it in the bank, and take it to the auction at the end and turn it in for a basketball. I don't want no part of this funky game.' Well, Rivero said, 'Better pay, Fats. They gonna charge you double.' In the end, Fats paid."

"Is that all!"

"No. Fats got wise. He took his money and bought every property in sight. He got Rivero to build him houses, and before you know it, Fats is the *funkiest slumlord in the class,* and I'm quoting one of the people he collected from."

We all laughed.

"And you should have seen him come down on his tenants. His eyes would light up just like a flashlight, and he would spread the fingers on his hand just as wide as he could. As each bill got laid in his palm he'd say, 'Gimme five, baby, gimme five,' and he'd jive around the classroom like he was king of soul. 'All I wants to be is a successful landlord. Someday I'm gonna own this whole city!'

"Let me tell you another, about a teacher who had money problems. He decided to use soul dollars to bribe students to be good. For the sake of anonymity, let's call the teacher Mr. Fenton. Now, Fenton is a nice guy. He dressed in suits and ties all summer—you know, the kind of guy who gives cocktail parties in the old prep-school tradition. He teaches in a prep school. Well, public-school kids smelled the high class the moment they set eyes on him. If he told them to do something, they refused, just to see what he'd do. To shorten a long tale of woe, Fenton got desperate and he decided to pay students to be good. At first it got him the results he wanted, but then . . . well, it turned sour. He paid five dollars if you stayed in your seat, ten dollars if you kept quiet. Whenever a crisis came he'd offer to raise the ante. Well, you know public-school children, they've been running lines on teachers for years. It took 'em maybe a week to run the preppie teacher to the liquor closet. Thompson, a kid from Harlem, met me in the hall one afternoon and said, 'Mr. Richmond, you wouldn't believe what we're running on Fenton. It's better than the City Game.' I looked at him curiously. 'We got him so we earn all our money by being bad. I mean, we being real bad. When we done bad stuff on him, Fenton says, "I'll give you five to be good." We shakes our heads—no. Man, then Fenton offers us ten, fifteen, and when he get up high enough we say, "Okay, Teacher, we be good." And then he pays us, and we stay good maybe ten minutes, and then we start the whole act just like before.' "

"How about fining them?" one asked.

"That's almost as bad. A teacher in the City Game last year fined one student five hundred dollars for getting up on a chair. Well, it infuriated the kid. If he paid up, it would have meant that he was knocked out of the game for the rest of the summer. He vowed to wreck the school. He might have done it, too. Don't use a tank to kill a mosquito. Small fines work just as well as large ones. We're not in the business of fining and bribing students, we're trying to get 'em moving, to build their possibilities for action. When incentives are misused, we risk setting the whole thing back."

"One last question," said Judy Perez. "What happens to children who can't pay their bills?"

The others in the group chuckled.

"First, understand we have an inflationary economy. We pump new money into circulation all the time, so everyone usually has some money, but everyone has to continue earning at the same rate to maintain the same relative position in the economy. So it's hard to get and stay very rich or very poor."

"But some children will be poor, won't they? Do they go on welfare? What happens?"

"Last year a teacher in this program proposed a one-percent tax on income to help children who didn't earn enough to pay their bills."

"And?"

"His students refused. Many of them came from very needy circumstances, parents and relatives on public assistance; not one wanted any form of welfare. Their teacher said everything he could think of to get them to reconsider. Nothing doing."

"They hate El Welfare," said Judy. "They hate what it does to them. I'm not surprised. This program allows them to separate themselves from the lot of their parents. You expect them to give that up?"

"No, I don't."

The Bank Robbery

The second summer of the Micro-Economy program came to pass. For the first three weeks the program unfolded predictably. We introduced the currency. We taught everyone the game. Students began learning their roles, and teachers began delegating responsibilities to them.

In the fourth week a worried eleven-year-old sprinted to my desk. "Mr. Richmond, they robbed the bank!" he said in a whisper.

"Who?"

"Them." He looked over his shoulder. Julie Gonzalez and his two buddies, Vincent and Gregany, strutted into the room.

The informer slipped quietly into a nearby seat. Julie, Vincent, and Gregany were fourteen. That not only made them the oldest kids in the program, it also made them the tallest, the strongest, and, in their eyes, the baddest trio imaginable. They saw themselves as foxes among chickens; they liked to think that they were foxes everywhere, but back on the block the big kids still put "little" in front of their names. Except maybe for Julie. Everyone watched his step with Julie. He'd beat on you if you batted an eyelid the wrong way. He'd even take on bigger kids, ones that could whip him, just to prove he was afraid of nothin'. My own observations convinced me he did everything one could do to build on that image.

"The junior mafia is here," announced Julie as he and his followers took seats in the first two rows. Vincent smiled. Gregany looked sullen. Something in their entrance betrayed a caper.

"You ever heard of Cosa Nostra?" asked Julie. "Around my block they training me. When I get out of school, they got a job all lined up for me." He snapped his fingers, stuck a pencil in his mouth, and puffed.

Vincent and Gregany looked at him worshipfully.

"Julie, I heard you robbed the bank."

"Someone squealed, eh? Yeah, the bank got robbed, but I don't take all the credit." He pointed his thumb to Vincent and Gregany, who sat behind him. "They helped."

The two boys smiled, grateful for the recognition, and slightly embarrassed by Julie's confession.

"I want the money back."

Julie's face shifted from arrogance to outrage. "What do you mean! Finders keepers!"

"You didn't find the money. You took it."

"That's too bad. If you don't want it took, don't put such a dummy counselor to guard it. Anyway, what if I did? Ain't no rule you told us against stealin'."

He had a point. The kid played every angle. I decided to respond with the Astoria routine and try to turn the class against the outlaws. Maybe it would work here too.

"Let's ask the class what they think."

"Ask them. None of them gonna mind. No skin off their backs. If you smart like us, you make it on the outside, right? Same inside." Julie's hand spread toward every school in the city.

I turned to the class. Everyone looked away.

"Do you think the boys who robbed the bank should return the money they stole? Or should we let them keep it?"

No one volunteered a reply.

"If they use their money to buy land, everyone is going to end being owned by them. You get nothin' at the auction. They'll take every basketball, every toy—maybe they'll leave you the books."

"It ain't nothing to them. Right?" said Vince, puffing out his chest and showing his biceps. "You're the onliest one that minds, Mr. Richmond. Jus' you, Teacher. No one else. Leave it like it is."

Julie knew where things stood. He had taken on his share of teachers. A thousand times. They knew they would win. I looked for a protest. I met the submissive faces of ten- and eleven-year-olds instead. I knew they were enraged, knew without a tongue having to tell it. They were just scared. Julie had asserted a different law, the law that makes might right. It's law on the street, and it's law in a lot of urban schools. And the weak learn not to trifle with the strong.

One fourth-grader whispered an aside to me: "If they make their money that way, why should I work?" Only I wasn't the only one who heard him.

"Shut your mouth and live!" Julie sneered. The fourth-grader wilted submissively.

No mistake. He had seen into the heart of the dilemma. Only seeing wasn't enough.

I didn't know what to do. My attempt to turn the class against the mob had aborted. Julie held all the cards; there wasn't enough time to force a new deal. I thought of making an ethical appeal, but realized it would accomplish nothing. The thought seemed unspeakably naïve. I finally decided to postpone the decision. I needed time to figure out a response.

"Julie, Gregany, and Vincent, I'd like to see all of you in the director's office after school today. We'll discuss the bank robbery and what should be done about it. After that discussion, I'll decide whether you keep the money or not."

In my mind, I was vacillating between two alternatives. On the one hand, I felt the urge to protect ten-year-olds against older toughs. On the other hand, I knew that if I let Julie and his boys go free and clear, students might learn to organize themselves against such Huns. I wrestled between the choices. If I intervened, wouldn't the ten- and eleven-year-olds I wanted to help have to pay the price? They had to learn to cope with Julies of the world. Where else but in school? My attempt to engineer a struggle between Julie and his mob and the rest of the class had petered out miserably.

As it turned out, matters came to a head more swiftly than I expected. Following my aborted attempt to wrap them in an ethical dilemma, we began playing the City Game. Predictably, Julie, Vincent, and Gregany began using the money they had stolen to buy real estate. They bought everything in sight. At the end of the hour, they had spent all they had. As more and more of the unknown amount of missing funds returned to the bank's possession, I realized that my position vis-à-vis the bank robbers was improving. After all, it was easier to issue new land securities than to wipe out their gains by printing a new currency. Either one could have nullified the effects of the bank robbery. However, it wasn't until they had spent all their money that they realized they had also lost the advantage: namely, knowledge of how much had been taken. They had half plotted to avoid giving up the money by saying they'd spent it. It occurred to them only later that I could just seize their assets. When they realized this, they asked me if I was going to take their property. I repeated what I had said before: "It depends on what happens in the director's office." The boys left disgruntled with their prospects.

At the end of the period, I gathered all the City Game materials together and made my way up to the office where the meeting was to take place. As I reached the second-floor landing, I heard what sounded like a chair smashing into a wall. The janitor hadn't stored everything away. I stopped to investigate. As I did, Julie and half a dozen others scattered. Two or three counselors and teachers charged into the two rooms to halt the destruction. Reading materials, cuisenaire rods, puzzles lay strewn beneath overturned chairs and desks. As I surveyed the damage, most of which was repairable, Julie and his mob were being rounded up and headed to the director's office. I followed.

On the way up the stairs to the office, Vincent pulled me aside and begged me to swear that he had returned the stolen money. Since the issues between me and Julie's mob remained to be settled and I was not at all sure if Vincent had participated in the second-floor vandalism, I made no commitment. I was trying to discover whether events on the second floor were connected with those on the fourth, where we had been playing the City Game. Later it occurred to me that Vincent had probably not taken part in the second-floor melee; his mind was on his bank-robbery troubles. Still, many of the boys who had been rounded up on the second floor were part of Julie's mob.

I was not present during the meeting between the boys and the director. He asked everyone but the boys to vacate the premises. I only had time enough to tell him the barest essentials about the bank robbery. There was confusion. The next day I learned that everyone in Julie's mob had been expelled except Vincent; he had been suspended for his part in the hold-up.

The next day a messenger called me to the director's office. Vincent Ortiz's mother had been called in as part of her son's parole procedure. Vincent sat docilely in a corner. Mrs. Ortiz, a heavy-set woman with five children to raise, sat on a chair. She didn't speak English, so Judy Perez, who had been drinking coffee in an adjoining room, came in to translate.

"Have you told your mother why you're here?"

Vincent shook his head. "I ain't had time."

"Miss Perez, please tell Mrs. Ortiz that her son was suspended because he robbed the bank."

Judy translated.

Vincent's mother blanched. She turned on him angrily. "Robaste un banco! A tu edad, robando bancos! Cretura!" She clenched her fists and rose from her chair.

"Mama! . . ." Vincent cried. He spoke an unrepeatably fast Spanish while scurrying behind a chair.

Judy Perez was nearly hysterical with laughter. "She thinks he robbed a bank! A *real* bank!"

"Oh, my God!" said Tom.

Judy Perez hurriedly explained.

To my astonishment, two days later the entire mob returned from exile. At one of the administrative levels of the program, someone had argued that Julie was the very kind of boy for whom the program was intended. Whoever made the argument had prevailed. The day before the mob returned to Broad Jump was the last day the boys were responsive to administrative discipline. Everyone got the message: it took murder to get you thrown out of Broad Jump. A steady stream of disciplinary infractions followed. Kindness had been read as weakness.

At about the same time, side effects other than those attributable to Julie's brotherhood began to show. Many of these could be related to the differences in mental and social age between the ten-year-olds and the fourteen-year-olds. Older students were using a variety of devices to extract funds from younger children in the program.

FCB (First Class Bank)

The techniques used to separate a man from his money varied from extortion to pickpocketing. By encouraging all students to secure their money in savings accounts, we were able to cut down the outright theft. At least students learned that.

But by far the most dramatic defense against the hustle was initiated by fourth-graders themselves. They talked Bob Forest, a counselor, into helping them recoup their losses. With his guidance and their perseverance, they formed the First Class Bank (FCB). The First Class Bank was the first corporation to evolve in a Micro-Economy setting.

Each fourth-grader agreed to contribute all his income and any savings he had to the FCB. In return, the corporation issued to each contributor shares proportional to the amount of the investment. With the ownership problem settled, the group divided into teams of two or three students. Each team chose a leader, and each leader directed his team in one of the four sections of the City Game. Bob Forest met with each team separately and helped it to plan strategy and to recognize its best opportunities. Using the profits made in one game to fund development in the next, FCBers got the most action out of their otherwise idle capital. Within a week, the ten-year-olds became a significant force in each one of the four games. Within two weeks they were dominant, owning as much as 30 percent of the property. While each team bought and sold property, the other FCB teams readied houses for new acquisition. They placed their improvements on the property immediately after a purchase, and thus maximized the income from their investments. The turnabout in the fortunes of these youngsters came into clear relief during a marketplace period.

Julie, Vincent, Gregany, and Julie's brother Victor sat close together in a corner of the room. They were surrounded by FCBers.

"You owe us twelve hundred dollars, Julie."

"Get off me, you little punks."

"We want our money."

"I know, I know. You'll get your money. I always pay my IOUs."

"And you," said ten-year-old Alfons to Victor, "you owe us five hundred. Better pay now or it's gonna get doubled."

"Shi . . . Will you get off me? Here, take the money. Just get outa my hair." Victor counted out five hundred dollars.

Another kid came running up to Julie. "You owe me a hundred and fifty."

"What you mean?"

"You landed on my property."

"You ain't got no house on it."

"Yes, I do. It's up there." He pointed to a cardboard structure on top of the closet.

"Man, these little punks are cleaning me out." Before my watchful eyes Julie counted out his money. "Victor, you collect our rent?"

"Yeah."

"How much we get?"

"We pulled in about fifteen hundred."

"That's all of us?"

Victor nodded. "Julie, we paid out three grand. We gotta do sumpin' about those little punks before we go broke."

But it was too late to do *sumpin'*. Our six weeks together had expired.

On the day before the auction, FCBers met with Bob Forest to divide up the corporation's income. Each student received an envelope that contained his cash.

"We rich!" said one joyously.

They were. In the last week, they had raked in between $5,000 and $10,000 a week. With that pot they would be heard from at the auction.

The finale came at the auction. Everyone looked forward to it. There were several hundred items: basketballs, educational toys, games, tee-shirts, candy, cake, soda, notebooks and other school supplies, a couple of watermelons, and hundreds of paperback books donated by a children's-book publisher for the occasion. Every item would be put up for sale and be sold to the highest bidder.

The auditorium filled with students and with their excitement. We did our best to keep order. As each item was sold, there were groans from the disappointed; the successful let out shrill whistles and screams of delight. I noticed that groups had formed. Brothers were pooling money with brothers. Kids from the same block were going in together to buy something really good that they could share. Bob Forest donated a camera to the sale. It was snatched for $7000 ME. As the auction progressed, excitement became so intense that neither sharing auction duties nor using a microphone saved our voices. No one went home empty-handed. We went home hoarse.

As I left Trinity that day, I ran into two students who were sometimes lugging, sometimes rolling a huge watermelon down the sidewalk toward the subway. They got to a hill and it started to roll. They started after it, tackling it just before it reached the street. They picked it up exuberantly. Another boy passed me with a basketball. Every third or fourth bounce, he'd stop dribbling to spin *his* basketball on his forefinger.

Near the end of the summer Tom Edwards asked me if I wanted to continue my experiment in the fall. Part of the money he had raised had been budgeted for the continuation of the City Game in the New York City school system. By coincidence, Gino Capoletti, one of the teachers in the Broad Jump program, had approached me with just such a request. Within a few days, arrangements were set. I would be spending a day or two every three weeks at P.S. 126, a school located in the Two Bridges area of Manhattan, helping Capoletti implement the Micro-Economy system in a fourth-grade classroom.

5. P.S. 126

Public School 126 lives in a brick building on Catherine Street. The street runs down to the river from that old alcoholics' retreat, the Bowery. Red brick housing developments that New Yorkers call "projects" tower for half the street's length on either side. Despite superhuman efforts to make them indestructible, many of the new buildings seem to be falling into disrepair. Most people regard the "projects" as a step up from tenement living. For one thing, inhabitants of the newer structures earn more money than tenement dwellers. For another, the housing authority employs policemen to protect residents against the unsavory element that loiters in the adjacent playgrounds. A common thread weaves through the lives of the people on this street: a search for security, a thirst for safety. The richer you are, the more you spend quenching that thirst. You send your children to Catholic school or to yeshiva. You don't go out at night. And when you walk during daylight, you make sure you have company. If you asked those who sense the danger to point to a place that worried them particularly, more likely than not they would point to a playground near a school. The playgrounds are the neighborhood in microcosm. They belong to the toughs and the footloose: to teenagers, to dropouts, to drug addicts, and sometimes to schoolchildren working their way into the ranks of the dispossessed. A fringe people in a fringe world, they make this concrete ground their own. A public place becomes their private one. Anyone foolish enough to walk through it with a lesser force than the one the natives command may be called on to pay for the privilege.

Compared to the sophisticated economic and political monoliths on the borders, Wall Street and City Hall, the schools and the Lower East Side community have only the most primitive political and economic institutions. The massive funds that spill through Wall Street and City Hall barely trickle into the communities adjacent to them.

Thirty to forty years ago Jews, Italians, Irish, Ukrainians, and Poles swarmed into the Catherine Street neighborhood. They and their sons and daughters have disappeared. The last twenty years have seen two new migrations—one Puerto Rican, the other Chinese—and 90 percent of the children attending P.S. 126 come from these two groups. Something like 4 percent of the school is white. Another 4 to 6 percent of the school is black. Puerto Ricans fill nearly 40 percent of the seats in school. The remainder, 50 percent and growing, are children of Chinese ancestry.

In P.S. 126 and in other schools bordering on Catherine Street, ethnic patterns appearing on the outside remain in force in school. In part, this occurs because children experience the same uncertainties in school that wed their parents to ethnic groupings in the neighborhood. Idealists looking in on the Lower East Side romanticize the diversity by calling it a melting pot. A closer look reveals something less homogeneous: a fragmented community. Overwhelmed by everyday details, by the energy it takes to cope with children who know little or no English, by loneliness and fright, and by new innovations on old discipline problems, schools offer little more than lip service to the idea of ethnic and racial integration. Indeed, the tracking systems which operate in P.S. 126 and in schools like it, separating apparently bright from apparently stupid children, subvert any possibility of melting.

As a rule, children are not tracked into grades or into classrooms by conscious ethnic or racial considerations; grade assignments depend on age, and classroom assignments on achievement scores on annual reading tests. Nevertheless, a high correlation exists between reading achievement and social class, and between social class and race. These correlations appear to be strong enough to replicate in school the segregation patterns that hold for the neighborhood. Also, most middle-income white families on Catherine Street send their children to Catholic or to other private schools, leaving public-school seats to those who can't afford to be elsewhere. Thus, on a broader level, disparities in family income produce socio-economic fragmentation.

In P.S. 126, stratification occurs because the stereotype characteristics of Chinese children cause them to be perceived as the middle-class counterpart of white students, with the same values and behavioral characteristics. The gap between the groups might be measured best on a scale calibrated to the tolerance for violence. For Puerto Rican, black, and even white students in the school, peer status depends on one's success with one's fists; everyone beneath you in the hierarchy is someone you can beat up and everyone above is someone you can't. Chinese children, by and large, refuse to participate in the hierarchy of muscle. They avoid violence. Sometimes they get exploited because of this, but, for some curious reason, they usually succeed in isolating themselves from confrontation.

If Chinese children shun physical combat, Puerto Rican and black children at P.S. 126 thrive on it. Chinese children come from families where filial piety continues to be a cornerstone of family relationship. One Chinese student, for instance, dirtied his shirt in school one day and refused to go home, claiming that he had dishonored his family. Puerto Rican children, with much weaker family ties, have an entirely different concept of honor. Honor is linked intimately to ritual or actual combat. It means you throw out your chest, a sign of fearlessness, of willingness to engage in combat if provoked. Sometimes a push or a curse will drive a potential enemy away. At other times one must go further: take something that belongs to an enemy, ritually insult an enemy's mother or sister, or threaten a beating after school.

The Professionals

With the exception of a handful of teachers on the staff who had moved into the Two Bridges neighborhood to be close to their jobs, the professional staff of the school commuted to the Lower East Side from white sections of Brooklyn, Queens, and Manhattan. In all, the staff numbered approximately forty. Thirty-three of the forty teachers were women. A large majority of the total staff were still in their twenties. The oldest teachers were in their late forties. P.S. 126 was a young school. It was also a Special Service School, which means that federal funds had been earmarked to support "compensatory" programs in the school.

To the majority of the teachers in the school, teaching was employment. Few had approached the profession with a sense of mission. For most it was the best job they could find. For many women, it was one of the best jobs that could be found anywhere. For some men, the classroom provided a safe haven from the draft. The increase in wages was owed primarily to the growing power and militancy of the United Federation of Teachers. Among other things, it had produced an increased willingness to put up with the disappointments of the job; also, it had won a daily fifty-minute preparation period that served as a period of rest and recreation from the ongoing classroom war. Still, many looked forward to the day when the union would rescue its members from discipline problems altogether. Indeed, the new contract took a step in that direction for the schools throughout the city by assigning 450 guards to the schools.

John Bern, acting principal of P.S. 126, sat in a small office on the first floor of the building, veteran of more than twenty years in the system. As is the case with many administrative posts, each step up the ladder brought an increase in pay, an increase in contacts with teachers, and a decrease in contacts with children. The job he'd been hired to do couldn't, he said, be done with the power he'd *not* been given to do it. He had the office and the pay, but neither the resources nor the power to do what everyone thought he ought to be doing.

In theory, a school administrator can influence the quality and direction of school activities by applying pressure to his organization at five points: (1) through budget and expenditure decisions, (2) through hiring and firing, (3) through the selection of curriculum materials and their distribution in his school, (4) through the training or retraining of his staff, and (5) through invitations to individuals outside his organization to come to his aid with additional services or with directions for his staff. Because the system does not allow for it, John Bern could not apply pressure at any of these points. He had control of 1 or 2 percent of the school's operating budget. Teachers were assigned to his school through the central district offices. For all intents and purposes, he could not fire a teacher once assigned. On paper he had some control over curriculum purchases, but a large part of his curriculum budget went to replacing worn or lost readers, math texts, and work books. Similarly, principals in New York City may not oblige members of their teaching staffs to undergo additional or new training, and have no resources to attract individuals from other organizations to aid them.

The growth in the power of the United Federation of Teachers, city-wide, was mirrored in this local school. The union's recognized network and leadership competed favorably with the principal and his network of control. A principal seemed, more and more, to become an adversary in an employee-employer relationship. The chapter chairman, in contrast, seemed to teachers more a colleague than a boss, protecting the teacher's position and prerogatives against dilution or added administrative burdens.

Maintenance of proper behavior required the full-time energies of all administrators. Whenever a teacher expelled a student from class for misconduct, the APs (assistant principals) accepted the expellee. Expellees had to go somewhere. One disruptive student could tie down an assistant principal for an entire morning. To avoid this, the assistant principal usually dressed the student down and quickly returned him to class. In more extreme cases, APs took the banished children with them on their rounds. Continual appearances in the assistant principal's office usually led to parent notification and to a request for a parent appearance. If the parents responded to the request, which they often did not, the assistant principal conducted the interview. Occasionally, a mother threatened her child with a beating. More often than not, the interview backfired and the mother took her son's or daughter's part. Doing so guaranteed that she probably would never be called upon by the AP again.

In return for peace and support, the principal had several things to offer parents. He had a certain amount of patronage in the form of paraprofessional employment. Also, the children of the more vocal parents sometimes received preferred admission to classes where reading, rather than discipline, occupied children for most of the day. Parents were given a voice in the disposition of Title I funds. Indeed, were it not for parent pressure, an administration might devote every cent it received to the suppression of discipline problems. As it was, approximately half the federal funds allocated to the school were absorbed by the operations of a pre-kindergarten class originally sought by the parent group.

In the same year the school lost four staff positions. The average pupil/teacher ratio rose from 22:1 to 29:1. Spending on support materials diminished dramatically. Budget limitations put severe constraints on the willingness and ability of teachers to improve the quality of instruction.

The Value of Work

I arrived at P.S. 126 a week after school had opened. It was clean and well lit. The glossy brick walls of the corridors had a childproof quality I remembered from other schools. Everything standardized. Brick. Concrete. Steel. Formica. Indestructible fixtures and furniture. In one room students sat in neat rows copying exercises from the blackboard. In another the whole class seemed involved in a caper. One set of combatants lobbed paper balls at each other. Four girls played jacks in a corner, ignoring their screaming teacher.

Gino Capoletti, who had taught in Broad Jump and invited me to try the Micro-Economy game in his fourth-grade class, looked at me through the glass of Room 321. He smiled and unlocked his door.

"Sorry about the door. Have to keep it locked. Keeps out intruders."

Mildly interested faces looked up from what they were doing. Three quarters of the children in Gino's class were Chinese. The other quarter seemed to be an even split between whites, Puerto Ricans, and blacks.

"I have the best class in the school!" Gino smiled at the children in front of him. "We start this afternoon. I've told them all about the game. Did you bring the materials?"

"I have the money here. Didn't have time to design a new currency. Hope you don't mind using Broad Jump dollars."

"Too bad there's not something Chinese on them. Oh, they won't mind. We'll call it Micro-Economy money."

I held up a bundle of currency. "It comes in fives, twenties, hundreds, and five hundreds. And if I get a chance, I'll print some seventeen, thirty-fours, and eighty-nines so you can get some extra arithmetic practice. Mr. Capoletti, can they start earning these greenbacks today?"

"Whad-you-mean?" said a boy in the first set of tables. "He owes us money already! You gonna welch, Mr. Capoletti?"

"You know me. I'm no welcher. Don't worry, you'll get what's coming to you."

"So you've started. Good!"

"To put it mildly," said Gino with a wry face, "my kids would sell a brother or a sister for a Micro-Economy dollar. Kai Lee, the boy who asked me if I was going to welch, keeps track of what I owe everybody. He's going to be the class banker or my special accounting secretary. Keeping track of my bills is a full-time job, so I figured why not give the responsibility to someone who needs the arithmetic practice? He'll be the best math student in the class in a month."

Gino's limitless energy had established him as one of the more promising teachers in the school. A frustrated actor, Gino had turned his classroom into his stage. From there he had launched a string of successful productions. Most experienced school people will tell you that a flair for the dramatic is just the sort of touch one needs to make it in a classroom. Gino himself said: "When all is said and done, what you're doing is performing. It's a production. You're an actor in your own play. Just better have what it takes to keep the audience with you. Otherwise, forget it."

At lunch, Capoletti asked me, "What do you want me to do this afternoon?"

"Before we get to that, you better tell me what you're paying your students."

"I pay them for tests and homework. They get half a dollar a point up to fifty dollars if they get a hundred on a test. I pay a flat wage for completing homework and a bonus for doing some extra project. You know what I like about this? I've stopped *making* them do homework. Now if you do it, you earn a living. If you don't, you don't get paid. No more hassles."

"Do you find them being more productive, working harder?"

"Some. Not all of them. Most of them work in spurts. A few work all the time. One thing sure: they do more for money than they did for grades. Robert Green came to me and asked for an extra test. He wanted it all by himself. All I have to do is make each kid his very own special test."

"They're not all that innovative, are they?"

"Thank God. But this class is good, very good."

"About this afternoon, I have a suggestion. How would you feel about adopting a more flexible wage pattern than the one you're using?"

"What do you have in mind?"

"Right now schools have one path to success: academics."

"Right."

"One way to succeed makes a few winners, but also makes a lot of losers. Create some other ways to win. You don't have to worry much about people who learn for learning's sake, or about children who achieve in traditional academic terms. I mean, you have to worry about them, but not as much as you worry about someone who doesn't make it on the academic track. Some kids are good in athletics. Some work hard. Others make civic contributions. Let's make labor the common denominator. Pay kids because they do, because they work. Academics, employment, civics—treat work as something valuable."

"I'll think about it," Capoletti said.

At the 1:30 bell, Gino Capoletti headed downstairs to meet his class. He left me in his room alone. Room 321 faced a playground adjacent to the school. Below, children were playing ball. I watched what seemed to be the leader of the mob land his fist in a victim's stomach.

So it's the same, I thought to myself.

I heard Capoletti's class approach. The door swung open.

"Class, take your seats. Mr. Richmond is here, so I can pay you what I owe you!"

"Whoooweee!"

Capoletti handed Kai Lee a bundle of Micro-Economy money. "Do you have the list? Take the money. Pay them one by one. As Kai pays you, Mr. Richmond will tell you about things the money will buy."

"Mr. Capoletti said if ya got rich you could maybe buy a basketball, a transistor radio, maybe even a dodgeball. That right?"

I looked at the boy. "Tell me your name."

"John Chang."

"Well, John, I give Mr. Capoletti a hundred American dollars three times a year. That's three hundred dollars. Each time I do, you and your teacher decide what you will spend it on."

"Three hundred dollars! Wow!" said several disbelieving voices. Others applauded and whistled.

I allowed them time to calm down. "Has anyone asked why we are doing this? Doesn't anybody care? Well, Mr. Chang, what about you?"

"Like Mr. Capoletti says. That money's for prizes. It's a game and that's the prizes."

"In a way it's a game and in way it's not. Ever heard of a game that pays you for your work? Most games are based on luck. This one will try to be based on work."

The class looked puzzled. I looked at Capoletti. He was thinking about it, too.

"Stop scratching your heads. It's simple. We pay you for the same reasons that the school pays teachers. Teachers come to school. So do you. Teachers work here. So do you. Teachers get paid because taxpayers value their labor. Well, we value yours. Most people run away from work. But someday maybe you'll discover that one measure of who a man is is the work he does; it's what you do with your life. Work gives dignity. Now, some kinds of work don't dignify as much as other kinds of work. We're going to learn about that."

Capoletti's class accomplished a good deal in the first six months. In addition to going through the regular curriculum, the class managed to play Micro-Economy one or two afternoons a week. Kai Lee made a go of the bank. He offered savings and loan services. He administered the teacher's payroll. Using the Micro-Economy game as a starting point, students constructed two or three dozen model buildings out of cardboard and waste materials brought from home and from the street. Two students started a materials-supply business. A third began constructing houses for sale. By January nearly every student had joined a partnership. This pleased Capoletti, who was keen on having his students work together. Every day differed from every other. One day they discussed rent control. On another the topic changed to the design of a building or a park, or to contracts and how to enforce them. He and his students were smitten with the unending possibilities of their miniature society. It was, therefore, no surprise to learn that they were holding P.S. 126's first trial.

The Lawsuit

"I won't pay you to be good. I pay students for work, not conduct."

Julia looked at Capoletti. She couldn't quite comprehend what he was saying. She wanted a no or a yes. Instead, Teacher had given her an explanation, something that took time to grasp; she tried, but wasn't up to it. She hit her head. Sometimes a slap made it do what she wanted it to do.

"Gonna pay me or not? I need the money."

"Julia, I don't pay anyone just to be good. Don't you understand? My answer is no. I won't pay you if you're nice all morning."

The "no" registered.

Ten minutes later Capoletti heard the familiar beginnings of uproar. Yells. Thuds. Crashing chairs. Angry voices. Julia ran for cover behind Capoletti.

"He hit me! Mr. Capoletti, you stop him!" Julia twisted out of Bo's reach. "Lemme 'lone."

A look that was half exasperation, half pity, registered on Capoletti's face. He put out his arm to block access to Julia. "Bo, go back to your seat."

Bo was seething. "I'm gonna tear her hair. Better stay away from me. You'll be sorry."

Julia stuck out her tongue.

"Wait till this afternoon. You won't be in school tomorrow, piggy."

"Bo!" exclaimed Capoletti.

"If you can't stop her—man, I will. With these!" Bo, the only black child in Capoletti's class, held up his fists. "See these? They gonna make you black and blue."

"Make me black like you," Julia taunted.

"Bo, act your age. You know Julia can't help herself."

"She betta learn, the dummy!"

Bo threw Julia his most frightening stare and spun toward his seat.

"Lord," Capoletti sighed. Julia seemed to be at the source of every uproar. He could feel the strain. For the last six months he had been making a constant effort to attend to her needs, and it distracted him from the others. Although she was not conscious of it, Julia held enormous power over the class. When she was absent, you could feel the difference. When she was there, you couldn't ignore her. Capoletti knew that no one would allow a teacher to have it perfect. As the months passed, the anger Julia drew increased until it could no longer be contained.

"She stole my jacks!" cried Mai Ming.

Capoletti looked up from his desk with a frown. "Julia, give them back!"

Julia ignored this order. "I askst permission."

"No, she didn't. She asked after she took 'em," countered Mai Ming.

Before Capoletti could react, Bo tackled Julia football style. The two tumbled to the floor, Bo twisting Julia's hand until it released the jacks.

"Gimme the jacks!"

"They ain't yours!" replied Bo, handing them to Mai Ming.

After Capoletti had sent Bo to cool off in the AP's office and Julia to the principal, four students confronted him.

"What can I do for you gentlemen?"

"We want to put Julia on trial. We wanna sue Julia."

The thought of it nearly made Capoletti's own anger evaporate. "Who gave you the idea you could do that?"

"Mr. Richmond said that we should do something when we get mad—that if we don't like what someone do to us, then we should make a trial, so to tell a person."

Chen Ling seconded his friend Billy Tom. "Yeah, when someone owe money or someone punches you, then you should sue."

"What will you charge her with?"

"Crimes against us!" Billy Tom's voice implied that he found Capoletti's question incredible.

"But you don't have a court. You don't have laws. You don't have a judge. And what do you expect to do with her if you find her guilty?"

"You be judge," responded Chen Ling. "We got rules, don't we?"

Dudley Tsuroka, the third member of the party, looked at the others. "Maybe we don't have it right." The others looked at him forlornly.

Gino sensed their disappointment. They really wanted to do this. "Wait. Maybe there's something to this. Maybe we can run a court on common sense and base what we do on the rules we already have. Toss a little Perry Mason in and . . . maybe it'll do some good. Okay . . . but you have some problems to solve even if we do it."

"Yippee!" the boys yelled in chorus.

"Don't cheer yet. How do you know Julia can get a fair trial here? Aren't all of you against her?"

Chen Ling looked at Gino Capoletti. "We'll be fair." The others nodded.

"Then one of you will be her lawyer."

No one said anything. Capoletti turned to the class. "If we have a trial, will anybody volunteer to be Julia's lawyer?" Capoletti waited, but nothing happened. "How can we have a fair trial if no one will defend Julia? I guess we can't. There's your answer, boys."

Dudley Tsuroka, president of the class, said, "I'll do it. I'll be her lawyer. But there hasta be rules."

"Rules?" queried Capoletti.

"There's gonna be a jury, right? Before the jury says Julia is guilty, everybody on the jury says she's guilty, or she gets off. One person thinks she's innocent, she gets off—and everything they say against her they gotta prove, otherwise the judge has to say the evidence is no good."

Capoletti smiled. "Sounds like the prosecution is going to have its hands full."

Chen Ling took a deep breath. "Maybe we shouldna do it. Dudley very smart."

"But everybody knows she's guilty. Even him," said Billy Tom.

"Okay, okay," said Capoletti. "I have only one question. Dudley, tell us why you agreed to be Julia's lawyer."

"I'm president, right? You always say a good president does the stuff no one else wants to do. That's the way I think."

The class spent portions of the next five days establishing a court. Marilyn Harp, one of the more astute and verbal of Capoletti's students, won election as judge. Upon assuming that post, she instructed prosecution and defense lawyers to submit a list of students from the class acceptable to them as jurors. Children appearing on both lists were then interviewed by opposing lawyers. Six were chosen to fill the jury.

Marilyn granted requests by both prosecution and defense for permission to hire investigators to help in preparing the case. These lawyer-investigator duos began interviewing prospective witnesses. Interviews took place during recess periods, during lunch, and even on the street after school. To help them along, Capoletti scheduled an interview day. To diminish the climate of secrecy, he established two tables in the rear of his classroom where the interviewing could be done with a minimal amount of disruption. This innovation proved to be a boon to Dudley, who kept painstaking track of his opponent's interview schedule.

Kai Lee stood up at the prosecutor's table. "I am suing Julia for crimes against everybody in this class. She always is getting in trouble with someone and it's time we found her guilty because she is guilty." Kai sat down. He fingered two dozen sheets of paper in front of him. He nearly had them memorized, but he pretended to read them anyway.

Marilyn looked over to Dudley expectantly. "You want to say something?"

"Yes, Your Honor. Someone told me Kai is going to put up a hundred charges. He has them on a paper. I think maybe it could take a whole year to hear all of them. I asked Mr. Capoletti about it and he said we didn't have so much time. I want to motion that Your Honor tell Kai to choose one charge out of the hundred. Then he and me argue about it."

"I object!" roared Kai. He approached the bench. "I spent a whole week getting all these charges." He lifted up a dozen sheets of ruled paper. "You do what Dudley says and I worked all for nothing. It's not fair!"

Marilyn looked to Capoletti for guidance.

"Dudley has a point. We don't have the time. We have this afternoon and maybe one or two more if we need it. Marilyn, you decide what to do."

"I want to think about it." Marilyn tucked her hand under her chin and frowned. "Okay. I thought about it. Kai, choose two. We don't have time to hear the other ninety-eight. That way, at least, if you don't make the first one stick, you get a second chance."

Kai looked downcast. A week of fact-finding down the drain. The class watched as he leafed through his collection of interviews. Capoletti half expected him to break into tears. When he had separated what he could use from what he couldn't, he rolled all but two pieces of paper into a ball and tossed it into the wastebasket. "For nothing!" He looked at the jury—didn't want the blame if the prosecution turned out poorly.

Dudley leaned back in his chair in triumph. In the first five minutes of the trial he had succeeded in getting all but two charges dropped. But this quick victory didn't lull his defense. Dudley wanted the material Kai had collected, the material in the wastebasket. In a flash of intuition, he felt that Kai's work might be made to work in Julia's favor. He would have to be cautious. He wanted to surprise his opponent. He leaned over and whispered to the student who had helped him conduct his investigation.

Marilyn looked to Capoletti. "Can we begin?" Capoletti waved his permission. Marilyn looked anxious. She was a thin, spindly girl with streaky blond hair. "I pledge allegiance to the flag. . . ."

The class, caught by surprise, stumbled to attention to join the chorus. Capoletti watched backs straighten, smitten himself by her clever attempt to weave ritual into the proceedings. When the class finished the pledge, Marilyn called the court into session.

"Who goes first?" asked Kai.

"In a real trial the prosecutor goes first," said Capoletti.

"Which one of them is the prosecutor?" asked Marilyn.

"Kai!" someone called out. "You're the judge, you supposed to know that."

"Order in this court! That question was for Mr. Capoletti. He's the court's adviser. Anyone speaks out of turn and I'll contempt him. And sumpin' else. Two lawyers get called by their first name with one difference. You put Mr. in front of it. Sounds more realer that way. Mr. Kai, you can start."

Kai Lee got up from his seat. "Do I call a witness?"

"You're the prosecutor," Marilyn said, looking at him as if he was dumb.

"I call Roosevelt 'Bo' Weaver."

Everybody knew Bo hated Julia the most. Capoletti thought it might be because next to Julia he was the "baddest" in the class. "Bo," as almost everyone called him, had a temper. Capoletti half believed that if Julia had been in some other class, Bo might have been twice as bad as he was. As it was, he had to be different to keep from being lumped together with Julia, which meant he had to be good.

"Okay, Bo. What you got to say about the time Julia got after Wendy?"

"I say plenty. One day we was comin' out of school. There was a big crowd in front of the school like every day. Well, Julia came up to Wendy and grabbed her bag and started runnin'. She ran up the block. Wendy ran screamin' after her. Wendy caught up and Julia hit her. She fell. Julia made her bleed. When she saw all that blood, Julia got scared and run away."

Marilyn peered over at Dudley. "You have any questions to ask Bo?"

Dudley shook his head. "No questions, Your Honor, but give me permission to call him back later if I figure out something I want to ask him?"

"Sure. Next witness."

"Liz Somoa."

"Liz, swear to tell the truth?"

"I do."

Kai walked over to where Liz had taken a seat. "Tell your story."

"I saw it just like Bo. Wendy came out of school with me. Most times we go home together. Someone bumped Wendy on the stairs. I think maybe it was Julia. Wendy had candy in her bag. Julia saw it before we got ready to go home and Julia asked her for some. Wendy say no. After, she got bumped. Wendy dropped her bag. Julia picked it up and ran down the street. When I catched up Wendy she was crying. Julia hit her with her bag."

Kai raised his hands in satisfaction. "That's good. No more questions."

"How about you?" Marilyn turned to Dudley.

"I have questions." Dudley moved toward the witness. "Bo said Wendy was bleeding. You didn't say nothing 'bout that. You say she was crying?"

"I didn't see no blood."

Dudley smiled at the jury. "I suppose someone poured catsup on her when you weren't looking. Or maybe Wendy cries red tears."

The jury thought that was real funny, and laughed.

"I saw the blood!" yelled Bo as loud as he could.

"You the only one," Dudley shot back. " 'Nother question, Liz. You said Wendy dropped her bag on the stairs. Bo said Julia grabbed it. Which is true?"

"She dropped it."

"She grabbed it," whispered Wendy loud enough for everyone to hear.

"Wait a minute!" Dudley walked over to the jury. "Which one do we believe? Can't convict anyone for a crime when we don't know what's true. That's one of the rules in a court."

The bell sounded.

"It's three o'clock," said someone.

"Ooo-ooh an' jus' gettin' good."

"Sorry, we'll have to recess the court till tomorrow." Gino Capoletti looked at the disappointed faces in front of him. "Think of it this way: you have all night to think about it. Justice takes time."

"I recess the court, don't I?" asked Marilyn. She stood at her table, faced the flag and sang, "Oh, say, can you see . . ."

The class, already in the throes of its departure, stopped in its tracks to join in the singing of the national anthem. When they finished, a smiling Marilyn recessed the court.

Kai shook his head. He would have to prevent Dudley from doing the same thing to him the next day. He would have to make sure his witnesses told the same story. And better not call Bo again, he told himself. Bo would mess it up because he hated Julia too much to think straight.

Something else occurred to Kai. There had been a memory lapse. The first charge had taken place nearly four weeks before. Memories were short on the details. Next time he'd choose something really recent, something everybody remembered, and something Dudley couldn't twist around.

For his part, Dudley felt good. He suspected that the next day would be tougher. Kai would adjust, be more careful. It would be harder to outdo him. In any case, the class might put up with one loss, but everyone wanted a conviction. It would take something special to get Julia off. Instead of attending Chinese school, where Dudley went every afternoon, he headed home to watch Perry Mason. Maybe, just maybe, it'd make him think of something.

Julia purred to herself all the way into the street. "I got a goo' lawyer," she said over and over to anyone who would listen. She said it with even greater gusto to Kai. Outwardly, he ignored her. Inwardly, he grieved.

The next afternoon Kai Lee charged Julia with theft. Unlike the previous day, he came prepared to do battle. Witness after witness detailed the episode involving Mai Ming's jacks. This time the story held together. Nothing Dudley did could pry it apart. Even Bo told it straight. Julia was oblivious to what was happening. She was losing, and didn't know it. She seemed to be enjoying it. It puzzled Dudley. She had no idea how hard he was trying and how badly he was doing. As the trial came to a close, Dudley pulled out the last trick in his bag.

"Your Honor, I want to put up some new evidence."

Marilyn looked over at him. "New evidence?"

"Evidence Mr. Kai collected."

"Where'd you get that!" Kai exclaimed.

"You threw it away. This stuff here is important. I think we should hear it."

"Your Honor, you said only two charges. He can't bring in no other charges now. I object!"

"These aren't charges."

"Why you introducing them now?" challenged Kai.

"Because I think this whole trial ain't right. We ain't been true."

"Whadayoumean?"

"Half the people who Kai talked to say Julia acts crazy. I been watching her through this trial. She don't know what's happening. She don't even know she losing. How can someone like her be guilty? I watched Perry Mason. If you don't know what you doing, you not guilty. That's the truth. A crime is something you do wrong on purpose. Julia didn't do what she did purposely. She do it because she can't help it. She crazy."

"I ain' crazy!" shouted Julia. She couldn't control herself and tried to push Dudley.

Several children pulled Julia off Dudley. "Julia, he's trying to help you!"

"He call me *crazy!"* She broke into angry tears. "You not my lawyer!"

"Julia! Julia!" shouted Capoletti. "Don't move. We're going to finish this trial. He didn't mean any harm to you. Sit down! Go on, Dudley."

"That's all I got to say."

"What about you, Kai?"

"Me neither."

"Marilyn, do you want to say anything to the jury?"

"Yes. This court works by common sense. If you think Julia breaks the law, then she guilty. If she crazy—then you decide she is not guilty. You all know her. You decide." Marilyn pointed to the door. The six jurors got up and went out into the hall. They left an air of suspense behind them. Capoletti felt sure that Julia would be convicted. She had caused too much grief to get off scot free. But if they found her guilty, what would they do to her? Make her mother come to school? Make her do some chore? What?

It took two minutes for the jury to reach its verdict. The brevity of the deliberative period had to do with the fact that children don't rehash the evidence; they don't deliberate very much. They decide.

"Well, what's the verdict?" asked Marilyn.

"We decided Julia was guilty of doing all the bad stuff Kai says, but we also think Dudley right, sometimes she don't have no control. Our verdict: not guilty!"

When the words "not guilty" fell on the ears of the class, Capoletti expected at least a groan. Instead, he heard cheers. They jumped up and down. They congratulated Julia. Some children wept. A line of well-wishers formed. It was the most incredible thing Capoletti had ever seen.

A week later Julia went back to her old ways.

The Turn of the Screw

Jane Baron joined the P.S. 126 staff in early January of 1971. Late in February, at the principal's suggestion, she brought her class into the Society School project. At the time, her students were emotionally restless and extremely disruptive, having already dispatched two of Miss Baron's predecessors in the first four months of the school year. Jane received her allocation of scrip, established a wage scale, and began paying her students for their academic work. Everything seemed to be going well until four boys raided her closet.

The thieves succeeded in lifting a good chunk of her Micro-Economy money.

When she exploded upon discovering the theft, her students couldn't have been more amused. Chagrined at discovering that the thieves had earned the admiration of their peers, a crestfallen Miss Baron came to me. After telling me about the "Micro-Economy debacle," she asked to be relieved of her commitment to the program, saying, "I just don't see myself teaching children to be thieves. It defeats everything I'm trying to do in there."

"I have a saying," I interrupted, "every setback has an opportunity hidden somewhere."

"It's just complicating an already miserable situation," Jane insisted. "They've gone through two teachers already. Some days I'm sure I'll be the third." She looked at me. "What do I do?" she asked in a strained voice.

"Let them keep what they've stolen."

"What!"

"Hold an auction next week. Sell them things for the money."

"You're crazy! You'll make them professional thieves!"

"They're already professionals, Jane. We've got to stop pretending they're innocents. By the time they're twelve they'll know more about sin and corruption than you'll know when you're thirty. I'd guess the rest of the class thinks they're hot stuff after that caper. Especially if they got you upset."

"They just loved my reaction, you can bet."

"Turn the tables."

"How?"

"Do what I've said."

Jane looked at me. Slowly she began to realize where I was leading. "They'll get it, all right," she said with a chuckle.

Jane put the plan into effect. A week later she auctioned off $45 worth of candy, cakes, toys, records, and athletic equipment. As predicted, the four thieves couldn't resist the temptation to outbid everyone, including each other. In fact, they came dangerously close to spoiling our plan in their mad competition against each other.

Two of the four boys exhausted their stock of Micro money before the auction ended, leaving the other two to divide up most of what remained.

It wasn't until the auction was over that they noticed the trouble they were in. Angry faces seemed to be everywhere. One of the thieves offered his best friend something he'd bought, in an effort to buy off his displeasure. The friend accepted, but it didn't change anything. The room rang with complaints anyhow. One student came right out and said the whole auction was a fake. Another said he wouldn't do any work "if stealers get everything."

"Wow!" said Jane. "They're practically kowtowing, those four. I really think they know they did something wrong. They feel it. For the first time!"

Something even more dramatic happened. Not a single Micro-Economy dollar disappeared for the rest of the year. One of the thieves happened to find one on the floor one day and, instead of pocketing it, announced the find.

"Incredible," Jane said again and again.

The change might be explained in any of several ways. Perhaps Miss Baron's students stopped stealing because they disliked being victimized themselves. It is also plausible that, as a result of the auction, they began to regard the Micro-Economy program as something worthwhile, worth their cooperation. Thirdly, it is just possible that the drama of theft-payoff-cost posed a serious threat to the peer hierarchy itself, creating the possibility of property theft on a heretofore unimaginable scale. Somewhere, in the labyrinth of anger the episode produced, lurked an ethical system or an unwritten code with established rules of fair play. If those rules had been penetrated, the reduction in thefts might be explained by an informal decision to diminish the uncertainties the penetration had produced. It also seems possible that the changes came about because Miss Baron's students wished to avoid the vagaries and uncertainties of preying on each other. For at least some of the children, the anger the auction produced was something to be wary of in the future.

Each of these insights has a life of its own. But the prize for the most compelling logic probably belongs to a simpler explanation. Four boys ripped off fifteen comrades. At first blush the entire group of nineteen saw the work of the four as a celebratable teacher rip-off. Applause for that. Sometime during the auction it dawned on those present that the real victims of this larceny had not been certified to be teachers. Second blush uncovered the real victims. Instead of applause, the four thieves found themselves the objects of abuse. Villains, not heroes. Honor among thieves? Call it what you like. Either because some article in the peer code had been broken or because the thieves had to live with their victims, it no longer seemed worthwhile to steal. Indeed, the thieves seemed to be spending considerable energy undoing the wounds they'd caused.

Without a careful job of research, all of these explanations remain suspect. Whatever explanation is favored, one thing seems certain: interesting possibilities for investigation had opened up. If community pressure, the reduction of anonymity, and the institutionalization of peer pressure contribute to a reduction in criminal behavior, it's worth finding out how much and under what conditions. Realistically, very few teachers are equipped to explore these possibilities or to build a model for school-based justice. This is especially true because the possibilities of building the model are complicated by levels of moral perception that, according to Kohlberg's research, are linked to cognitive development. If this connection holds, it means that engineering a legal system must be accompanied by a drive to extend the cognitive capacity of students to understand abstract legal issues. Taking an optimistic view, this extension may occur more effectively if real, instead of hypothetical, moral dilemmas provide the impetus for moral reasoning.

6. Different Teachers, Different Games

"So what's new?" I looked at Gino Capoletti expectantly.

"Teachers are coming in here all the time. That never used to happen." Gino eyed me carefully. *"They* want to know what's new! I tell them Micro-Economy. They wanna share."

"You mean they want to play? You think we should expand?"

"Why not? Spread what's good around."

"I don't know," I said reluctantly. "What's to spread? Currency. Merchandise for an auction. A real-estate game. An idea. Pretty flimsy. Can't spread you, Capoletti. You're an inventor. How many other teachers improvise the way you do?"

Capoletti smiled. "There are other good people. I'm not the only one."

"Who?" I pressed.

"My friends. Those curiosity seekers. Tobias, Goverman."

By June of 1971, the end of the school year, seven members of the P.S. 126 staff, in addition to Gino, had become affiliated with the program. Each joined for a different reason. Some were friends of Gino. Some liked what was happening in his classroom. A couple joined because they thought the currency might help them motivate their children. A few others entered the fold at the suggestion of the principal, who, impressed by the talk around the school, decided to get me to work on three of the "problem classes." But most joined because they understood they were not being asked to give up instantly everything they believed or everything they were doing. They had been told by Capoletti that the Micro-Society approach built on the strengths of individual teachers. I don't think any felt something had been imposed from above, or that they had to do something they did not want to do.

This meant, of course, that every teacher's experience differed from every other's. All had received a call to activity, a call to do and make. Some responded powerfully, others pretty meekly, and a few negatively. Those who responded negatively did not participate in the program or at least minimized their participation in it.

Capoletti

Capoletti's students played the Micro-Economy game for six months. By the end of that period, both he and his students felt that they had exhausted its possibilities. A few students had succeeded in monopolizing most of the property. The improvements they made on the property pushed rents very high, with the result that non-owners began protesting every time someone suggested they play the game. Since protesters were in the majority, the landlords' counterprotests fell on deaf ears.

A movement by landlords to continue playing led to several notable discussions: landlord-tenant responsibilities, rent control, city planning, environmental problems, model building, housing finance, and the economics of the marketplace. When it became clear that very little support existed for continuing the Micro-Economy game, Capoletti agreed to purchase back the property from its owners at half its assessed value. At least, he reasoned, they wouldn't lose everything.

During the six months the game lasted, students initiated and completed an impressive number of construction projects. Cardboard houses, ski slopes, farms, factories, schools, sports stadiums, and the like rose on shelf space around the entire perimeter of the class. The construction materials used were varied. Some students stuck pieces of cardboard together. Others invented houses using milk containers, ice-cream sticks, plastic, and construction paper. One or two students had located enough wood to embellish their houses.

In addition to construction and Micro-Economy game activity, Capoletti continued to invent and improvise new ways to integrate Society School activities with the traditional program. He pushed Children's Theatre productions into an economic dimension. Actors, set designers, prop men, and costume makers received wages for contributions to the productions. He also attempted to develop a mathematics unit on measurement, relating it to the building program of the Micro-Economy game.

In the early spring Capoletti decided to turn the usual elections of class officers into an elaborate political experience. Each candidate had to raise money for his campaign. Each solicited volunteers to help persuade voters to elect him to office. An expensive and elaborate advertising campaign generated a host of colorful materials that ultimately spread onto hallway bulletin boards and into the bathrooms. Capoletti also allowed his students to launch the first trial, described in detail in Chapter 5.

Mrs. Tobias

According to Gino, Mrs. Tobias had a reputation as the best teacher in the school, a dedicated professional, someone who, year after year, chose to work with the difficult children, and who, when the school fell short on its promises to provide her with the materials she wanted, paid for them with her own funds.

So, with an introduction from Gino and an invitation from Mrs. Tobias, I began to work with her sixth-graders. After two or three sessions, problems began to arise. She had not distributed Micro-Economy money to her students, and without the establishment and distribution of the currency, students would have nothing to exchange for property available through the real-estate game.

But it became clear that personal anxieties were dominating her attention. A close relative was seriously ill, and she was required to care for him. She missed school frequently, and then came in exhausted. The resulting discontinuities between what we had set out to do and what we were doing convinced me that it would be wise to suspend our arrangement for the time being. Mrs. Tobias agreed.

Tina Goverman

Tina Goverman's nine-year-olds, although the same age as Capoletti's students, were about a year behind Capoletti's students, as measured by reading-test scores. Judging by their behavior in class, an equal gap existed in emotional maturation. Goverman's children seemed more awkward about new experiences. They seemed more willing to depend on their teacher to solve problems. A larger number of her children seemed to tune out when explanations of Micro-Economy were being given. We responded to what appeared as a lower level of cognitive maturity by moving at a slower rate and by intensifying our efforts to make abstractions concrete.

These students preferred saving money to spending it. Students passed what seemed to be weeks counting their earnings. The counting lure finally blossomed into a refusal to part with their savings on any count. Finally Tina and I conspired to move her children to the next threshold by holding an auction. It worked. With their currency holdings being visibly translated into goods, more and more children began forming new opinions about the functions of money. Although this significantly diminished the counting mania, it also posed new problems. An enthusiasm for collecting Micro-Economy money replaced the drive to count it.

When I introduced the real-estate game to her class, I discovered very few children with any interest in investing their funds in real estate. At least money was concrete—you could spend it at the next auction. What was real estate? It took several sessions of playing to get over the hump. Finally, one or two children ventured into the real-estate market. A session later, the first angry tenant paid the first beaming landlord. The cognitive dike broke. An immediate rush to buy and then to build followed. Everyone wanted to taste the pleasure of collecting rent from angry classmates.

Goverman, a sensitive and creative teacher, took advantage of the openings Micro-Economy provided into other parts of the curriculum. She responded to the counting craze by using Micro-Economy money as a concrete math material. She discovered that students understood her explanations of arithmetic problems a great deal more quickly when she expressed the problems in dollars and cents. She even began to explore the possibilities of using currency to express fractions. This also seemed to work well.

Capoletti's children worked whether there were inducements or not. Goverman's students seemed to have far less of this natural achievement urge. She decided to try spurring her students to greater efforts by offering them Micro-Economy money as an inducement. The resulting experience was a divided one. Probably the majority of her students reacted positively and strongly to the incentives. For a time they produced more paperwork than she wanted to handle. Another segment of her class responded periodically. The closer an auction date came, the harder they worked. Some children in this category seemed to respond more strongly when the inducement was linked to a competition or a contest—i.e., girls against boys, team against team.

A third group appeared to be experiencing cognitive difficulties. A few insisted to the bitter end that the money we were using was fake. The fact that it purchased things seemed to make no difference. United States currency was the only currency worth working for. One or two children refused to respond to the incentive at all. Goverman's best efforts failed to uncover the reasons. These children just didn't communicate what the obstacles were.

Phil Ware

Phil Ware, one of the few black teachers on the P.S. 126 staff, brought his class into the program late in February; like everyone else who joined after the midyear, Phil's experience was comparatively short. His class had the best reading scores on the sixth grade. Like Capoletti's children, they eagerly welcomed the opportunity to explore new experience. In addition to following what was becoming a well-worn path—introducing currency, developing a price system, and establishing and operating the real-estate game—Phil Ware went further than any teacher before him in turning full responsibility for operating the program over to his students.

He trained students to operate the bank, to run the real-estate game, and to administer his payroll. His students took the initiative in developing a flexible pay structure: computed weekly by a wage commission, based on the value of the work to the class, the ability and efficiency of the worker, and the time spent doing the job. His students also succeeded in establishing and operating a successful savings-and-loan association with borrowers paying and lenders collecting interest.

Philosophical and contemplative by nature, Ware pressed the Society School experience into that mold. When conflicts arose, he used them to explore philosophical and ethical issues. He asked students to think about what rich people owe poor people and vice versa. He asked them to consider the ethics of inheritance and of inheritance taxes. His class considered how much work was worth. They studied why managers get paid more than blue-collar workers. On the less contemplative side, Ware's students developed the first newspaper. Another group in his class developed an employment agency that advertised available jobs in their classroom newspaper and conducted interviews for prospective employers. Ware took the occasion to help students learn to write résumés and to interview for jobs.

Dunne, Fay, and Baron

Early in March of 1971, John Bern called me into his office. When I came in, he was puffing away on a thin cigar.

"I have some problems I want you to work on. I would like three teachers upstairs to try your program. Three of my problem classes. Look, you're working my easy classes—I thought you'd like the challenge."

I smiled. He was baiting me. I saw the hook. "I don't have much time to spare, but I'll see what I think can be done. Don't expect miracles."

"Who said anything about miracles?"

Jane Baron

Jane Baron, who earlier "turned the screw," came to P.S. 126 from a parochial school in another state. If she imagined that her experience in that school would prepare her for rough-and-tumble public-school life, she became quickly disabused of that notion. Nothing prepares one to live in New York, let alone teach there. In the first two months after her arrival, her Lower East Side apartment was burglarized twice. The second time she was robbed by a junkie at knife point.

After looking around for a job in a private school, she decided to apply for work in the public-school system. Such jobs were still easy to get and they paid a lot more than private schools were willing to pay. Also, she knew the things she had to give would enrich children needing enrichment, while they would help her grow and to understand urban life. Within the first week, Jane Baron was more frightened by her class than by the burglars. The violence she saw in her ten-year-old students made her desolate.

"I need all the help I can get," Jane Baron told me. "I'm the third teacher they've had this year. I think they think I'm going to reject them, too. They're angry about a lot of things." Out of the corner of her eye she caught Charlie Frazer wringing someone's neck. "Charlie!"

My eyes followed the action. Charlie was playing deaf. He wouldn't let go. He even turned his back to her. She moved. It almost seemed as if her movement compressed the air. Her movement, not her voice, warned him of impending danger. In an instant, Charlie dove out of Miss Baron's reach. It was only after he'd reached the safety of the back of the room that he turned his shining, victorious eyes on his pursuer.

At lunchtime that day, Jane and I walked over to a diner near the Bowery.

"You look weary."

Jane smiled. "Then I look the way I feel. God, how I love the lunch break. Except for the last ten minutes. I use those to tool up for a brutal afternoon. We don't have much time. Let's use what we have to best advantage. Bern said you might help me. So far, you've said you might not be able to do much."

"You find yourself in the middle of a classroom war. Your opponents don't even behave like an army. Sometimes they don't even behave like an enemy. They're guerrillas. Sometimes they're angels. If you defend yourself on one side, they attack you on the other. They attack and attack until they wear you down. Every day you come to school, you wonder if they'll succeed in driving you out before they drive you crazy. Does that sound right?"

Jane Baron nodded. "Minus some detail."

"I think you have two choices. This is going to sound like a cliché. You come at these kids with love. Most of them probably think you're a weak sister. For a lot of them love's not enough. The day you stop loving, get out of teaching. But for the ones who don't respond I prescribe three things: buy them, expel them, or turn them on."

"Buy them?" Jane looked at me incredulously.

"Look at it this way. Children have different needs. Some want affection. Some want praise. Well, affection and praise work for some, but not for everyone. And some won't think the affection is real unless there is a tangible reward. Some children will do anything for a baseball glove. Some children want to be bought and loved. Others won't be bought *or* loved. They cut themselves off from every kind of human transaction. Those children need something you can't give. All I'm saying is: recognize your limitations. Don't set impossible goals."

"Are you telling me to bribe them?" Jane countered.

"I'm saying pay them for their labor. I'm saying give them permission to work for material goods. I'm asking you to put a very middle-class attitude about learning into proper perspective. These are children of an under class. They want material things—but then so do the middle and upper classes. Why withdraw permission to want them? Very few teachers work for no pay and some of them can afford to."

"Okay. Tell me something concrete. I don't need any more philosophy."

I pulled a bundle of Micro-Economy money out of my pocket and set it on the table. "I'll back your currency with about a hundred dollars. You begin by buying those who can be bought. You continue loving those who are prepared to receive. And then you do everything you can to excite the rest. And you expel anyone left over."

"I just want you to know that I didn't come into teaching for this." She held up the bundle of money. "I came to reach children who want to learn."

"You make me feel like the Grand Inquisitor."

She laughed. "Aren't you? Bread vs. freedom. . . . I'm sorry."

"Don't apologize."

"I just believe that if you care enough . . ."

"You can rescue anyone."

"I suppose."

"The missionary. They have to rescue themselves or they won't get rescued. You probably create greater dependency than I do."

"Where do I begin?"

"What's the interest span of your students?"

"Two, maybe three minutes."

It was going to be very difficult.

Jane and I developed several simple procedures. Every time a student did something constructive, Jane reinforced this behavior with Micro-Economy money. She wanted to ask children to do things they could succeed at, and to reward children who took an initiative. Thus, if a student came up with his own suggestion for an activity and implemented it, she paid him more than someone who took one of her suggestions. In addition to this strategy, Jane established a basic wage for all her students. She linked this basic and uniform system to the curriculum materials her class was using. For instance, students were paid a dollar for each page they completed in their reading workbooks, and another dollar for every two pages they completed in a basic reader. One student had taken almost four months to complete her first workbook. She took only four days to finish a second of somewhat greater difficulty and length. Not every student responded as dramatically. However, nearly all did respond. Two boys who didn't found themselves shuffling between Jane's room and Mr. Good, the assistant principal.

Jane tried rewarding students for extending their attention span, but found it too complicated to administer in a consistent manner and so discarded the attempt after a brief trial. Instead, she focused her efforts on implementing Skinner's suggestion that positive responses to stimuli be followed by immediate and positive reinforcement. She posted an economic chart that compared the average aggregate income of the boys and the girls in her class. Predictably, it kindled peer pressure mechanisms and, in turn, helped her students pour even greater commitments of energy into productive enterprise.

She carried with her a supply of Micro-Economy currency, readily dispensing it to students as they completed assignments. She also added her praise to the inducements and continued to supply strokes of affection to children who wanted them. To the never ending chant "How much will you pay if I do . . ." she learned to respond with, "Well, how much do you think it's worth?" She also reached an important insight about that question. At first glance, she regarded the question as expressing simply a desire on the student's part to make money. Later she began to believe that something else lay at the crux of it: She began interpreting it as need for affection, as desire to do something to enhance self-esteem, and as a clear signal of a student's desire to win. As time passed, the Micro-

Economy money began to seem to Jane less a simple inducement to work and more a useful psychological tool, less the tool of a corrupt society and more an expression of affection.

In May I visited her classroom. During my entire half-hour visit her students worked doggedly on panels from a Science Research Associates reading laboratory.

"How did you do it? Your children once upon a time had an interest span of two or three minutes. Do you remember?"

Jane smiled. "You know, it's funny. It happened so gradually, I hardly felt the difference. I still don't feel like I've accomplished anything. So they've settled down, so what? It's still not the kind of teaching I want to do."

I stared at her in disbelief. "You go from chaos to this and you still think you're a failure?"

"I suppose I'm very middle-class. I probably should be back in a Catholic school. There's no intellectual excitement here. You helped me establish routines they need. But those same routines seem deadly to me."

Miss Fay

In what might have been taken as an omen, Miss Fay's door opened to our knock with a roar. A young woman stared out at us from the chaos behind her.

"Pleased to meet you," said Fay. "Children! The principal and Mr. Richmond are here. Better shut up!"

She turned to me. "You're the one with the money game. I heard about you." She gestured at her students. "I'd use anything on these monsters."

Half a dozen children were in earshot. She seemed to believe they could not hear what she said.

A girl in the first row threw her a hateful look. In my own anger, I gave in to an irrational desire to help her students, something I was in no position to do.

"I'll be here tomorrow, Miss Fay. Can we talk during your preparation period?"

"Let me think. Friday. Fridays I am free third period." She whirled. She had detected Robert taking something from her closet. "Get back to your seat, monster! They don't listen to anyone. Little thieves. Animals. I would never believe kids could be this bad. I tell them they'll never amount to anything. You think they listen?"

I looked at her students. Never minding her ear-splitting shrieks, they ignored her. It took discipline to play deaf.

I saw Fay as scheduled. But I was beaten before I even began.

When I went to her room for my first session with her class, I didn't know it would be my last. Her students took their seats at my request. Order appeared where there had been chaos. I reached for their attention. What I reached for they gave willingly. I was careful to do all I could to hold it. During a quarter-hour my presentation was interrupted at least ten times—by the teacher. She had taken a seat in the back. From there she watched her students like a hawk. At the slightest sign of inattention a scream cut through my words. Every cell in my body suppressed a desire to scream back.

By the tenth interruption I'd lost the attention of the class and probably its respect, so I excused myself, saying that I might come back on a more suitable occasion. Some of the students groaned their disappointment. A few taunted me for giving up. The rest turned angrily or indifferently into chaos.

"See how bad you are! See what you've done! Now Mr. Richmond has to go. *You* ruined it!" she told her class. "Mr. Richmond, please come back another time."

Three weeks later Fay saw me walking in the hall during the lunch hour. Hearing my name called, I poked my head into her room. A half-dozen of her Chinese children were seated in a circle, preparing to eat a meal brought them by two of their number.

"We sent out to this restaurant down the street. Good food. Doesn't it smell good?" While saying this, Fay examined the bill one of the boys handed her, and the change. She counted it. "The idiot!" she chuckled. "Let's have an arithmetic lesson." She moved to the blackboard and began chalking figures on the board. Her calculations confirmed her hypothesis. "A dollar mistake! In our favor!" She looked at me and then at her children triumphantly. "The stupid man who gave you the change better go back and learn his arithmetic."

A slender Chinese girl, not more than ten, raised her hand. "Shouldn't we give the man back the money? Maybe he pay it back if he makes mistake. My mother told me. She work in restaurant."

"Do you think I'm stupid too? Come on! He pays for his mistakes. Learn your arithmetic so *you* don't make them."

I stared at Fay in disbelief. She had given them a lesson but not in arithmetic.

Dunne and Point

Faith Dunne and Eve Point joined the project in April. Both took the program into their classrooms and implemented the currency and wage steps without any problems. In what remained of the school year, Dunne established the currency, created a wage-and-price system, developed a reinforcement strategy for each student, and began playing the Micro-Economy game.

Point's fifth-grade class, the most advanced of its grade in reading ability, took easily to the program and integrated the mapping curriculum they were doing with the Micro-Economy game. The result was a plan for a new city. Collaboratively, her students were even able to erect seven or eight buildings of their "ideal city" before the closing bells in June.

George Richmond

The first year at P.S. 126 proved at least one of my hunches correct. It had been apparent to almost everyone in P.S. 126 that the traditional incentive system was not working. Children just did not react strongly to the old system of grades and petty favors. Most of the children who did respond came from highly socialized families that reinforced the school's reward system at home. That reinforcement usually took the form of praise, but it often took the form of material goods or assurances of success in life. In contrast, the majority of students of low socio-economic status, while scarcely immune to praise and other intangible rewards, preferred tangible reinforcers to intangible ones. In other words, the kinds of reinforcement wanted by students with pressing physical needs tended to be the kinds of reinforcer that met those needs.

I concluded that the existing reinforcement program, consisting mainly of intangible reinforcers, needed to be broadened to include tangibles if the Micro-Society approach was to meet the real spectrum of student needs. This in no way meant that spiritual payoffs should be diminished. If anything, the opposite would be the case. It did mean, however, that students who had been promised, offered or urged to strive for spiritual payoffs—of which there was no great surplus—would now be offered tangible and intangible payoffs in combination. I had discovered that children and adults were similar when it came to their wants. Only a handful of adults behave purely from principle or for purely spiritual ends. Similarly, only a minority respond solely to the stimulus of material advantage. The vast majority of people respond to a combination of stimuli, some tangible and some intangible. It follows, therefore, that schools should be offering students the full spectrum of stimuli so that children can arrange them in combinations that are suitable for themselves.

Money is useful as an instrument of motivation, not only because most people recognize it as an incentive, but also because it serves as an emblem of achievement along a wide range of the continuum of intangible to tangible payoffs.

Currency, furthermore, permits trade to occur. Under the old system, one simply accumulated grades and service points and hoped to cash them in at college-recommendation time. The Micro-Society approach, if it allows trade, also allows saving, immediate consumption, or investment. The greatest source of the Micro-Economy money power comes, not from its utility as an incentive, but from its combined economic functions; it gives students and teachers access to a more precise tool for establishing priorities, for planning, and for distributing student and faculty energies in the most sensible way. In other words, money permits the budgetary and allocation mechanism to operate so that students and teachers can be active and effective: plan their business, or change their society and their school. Together, these attributes produced an incentive far more powerful than grades, far more powerful than gold stars, or, for that matter, green-stamp payoffs. As an incentive, money is by no stretch of the imagination perfect. There are and there will always be children (or adults) who decide to behave on principle despite monetary inducements to behave differently. True in the world, it is also true in school, and thank goodness.

School currency can facilitate changes in teacher-student relationships. Teachers who find it difficult to reach certain children may do better dealing with them in terms of concrete rewards. Also, teachers are in a position to offer students the full spectrum of incentives and thereby supply different individuals with suitable combinations of extrinsic and intrinsic rewards. In combination, these two changes point to the substitution of an employee-to-employer relationship for that which now approximates a relationship between serf and overlord. Critics will argue that very little distinguishes the two, or, worse, that the substitution replicates one of the worst features of modern society in a classroom. I would disagree, and I think the whole history of the labor movement supports my position. That history suggests that the development of a self-consciousness as a laboring class precedes the drive to improve general working conditions, membership welfare, and access to the kind of experience that leads to self-determination.

Other shifts in student-teacher relationships occur as well. Unlike the old currency of grades and demerits, the new currency can be saved and invested. Accumulations of capital and the liberty to dispose of them carry with them corresponding opportunities to make public policy, and to budget resources for enacting policy decisions into practice. Potentially, a true investigation of these opportunities could lead the school community into investigations of the social and political organization of school society, and to the implementation of measures designed to organize and structure student experience in society building. In far more modest terms, students eventually accumulate resources by performing work for their teachers. A time comes when these resources swell to the point where student entrepreneurs compete with teachers for the disposition of student labor. A time comes when students develop and operate their own networks and organizations. And a time comes when these networks and organizations organize to gain their own political and social objectives. From our experience, it appears that these organizations produce new authority systems managed by students and, as a consequence, diminish existing authority systems controlled by adults in proportion to that growth.

A school-based currency system can also encourage shifts in student peer relationships. The inducements traditional schools offer for cooperation have little or no impact on political and social relationships among students of low socio-economic status. To the large majority of these children, grades, commendations, praise, demerits, and other devices teachers use in governing a classroom vibrate on a different wave length than the compliance measures based on brute force which are administered through the peer community. To underline the old aphorism: "Sticks and stones will break my bones, but words will never harm me," it seems far wiser, where compliance depends on force, to risk displeasing a teacher than to risk getting punched in the gut by a peer.

Compared with peer-group compliance mechanisms, school compliance measures appear necessarily abstract. A school-based currency system offers something more concrete. Second, a currency system permits an enormous shift to occur in the peer group. That shift can amount to the generation of a new class based on wealth that competes with the present muscle-based order. This new class eventually organizes itself to protect its interest, person, and property. Eventually, its drive to secure itself against the muscled crowd should make it a valuable ally in the attempt to link informal and formal compliance networks. Indeed, Raoul's and Ramon's experiences described in Chapter 2 of this book suggest that the outlaws of today may well become the policemen of tomorrow.

In addition to influencing political relationships among students and between teachers and students, the new currency works as a planning medium: it allows the school community to collaborate in a budgetary process that reflects agreed-upon priorities and allocates resources to achieve them. For instance, if teachers and students agree to emphasize reading, then they allocate a disproportionate amount of the total budget toward achieving that goal. If the school community wishes to stress a work program of, say, community service, then budget resources flow in that direction. At the very least, it makes allocations of student and teacher energies a conscious and planned process.

Most teachers will distribute resources they receive to several categories of activity. These will include academic work, various kinds of student employment, civic and cultural activity, and athletic and leadership activity. Many teachers will see some advantage in posting their priorities publicly and in discussing on a weekly or biweekly basis the path most appropriate to attaining agreed-upon student-teacher goals. Such postings may be deemed especially helpful if a group requires constant reminders to shift its energies from low-priority to high-priority budget items. The tables on the following two pages suggest four possible distributions of a weekly classroom budget based on an allocation of $3,000 a week in Micro-Economy money to a teacher with thirty students.

These shifts in the reward structure point to a principle. In traditional reward structures, students make it on the academic track or they don't make it at all. In contrast, the scrip system, coupled with sensible additions in the range of available opportunities, is flexible enough to recognize accomplishments in non-academic areas with the same currency. This is central to the Society School model. It insists that we multiply the paths to success, and that educators tolerate paths they may secretly deem less worthy than others. In turn, this principle points out two overriding objectives of the model:

SALARY MATRIX 1: Suggested budget aimed at increasing student activity and effort (based on a weekly allocation of $3,000 ME for 30 students)

	Assigned tasks	Extra labor	Creative or social contribution
Reading		400	
Math		400	100
Writing		400	300
Total academic	1,600		
Employment	100	400	300
Total employment	800		
Social service		100	100
Arts		100	100
Total civic and social	400		
Athletic		200	
Total athletic and leadership	200		
Total	3,000		

SALARY MATRIX 2: Suggested budget aimed at dealing with disciplinary problems, rewarding completion of assigned tasks, and encouraging athletic achievement (based on a weekly allocation of $3,000 ME for 30 students)

	Assigned tasks	Extra labor	Creative or social contribution
Reading	600	200	
Math	300	200	
Writing	150	200	
Total academic	1,650		
Employment	600	100	
Total employment	700		
Social service	200		
Arts	100		
Total civic and social	300		
Athletic		350	
Total athletic and leadership	350		
Total	3,000		

Salary Matrix 3: Suggested budget aimed at fostering the development of reading, writing, and arithmetic skills (based on a weekly allocation of $3,000 ME for 30 students)

	Assigned tasks	Extra labor	Creative or social contribution
Reading	400	450	
Math	200	200	150
Writing	200	200	200
Total academic	2,000		
Employment	200	200	100
Total employment	500		
Social service	50	50	50
Arts	50	50	50
Total civic and social	300		
Athletic		100	100
Total athletic and leadership	200		
Total	3,000		

Salary Matrix 4: Suggested budget aimed at encouraging creativity (based on a weekly allocation of 3,000 ME for 30 students)

	Assigned tasks	Extra labor	Creative or social contribution
Reading		300	
Math		300	300
Writing		300	400
Total academic	1,600		
Employment		300	300
Total employment	600		
Social service		150	100
Arts		150	300
Total civic and social	700		
Athletic			100
Total athletic and leadership	100		
Total	3,000		

(1) to engage students in society building as a means for sustaining individual and community growth, and (2) to connect children early with a variety of careers and with meaningful kinds of work.

I came to several other conclusions as well. The first year at P.S. 126 helped me isolate three important features of the model: (1) that the transition between the traditional school and the model occurs gradually and through a well-defined incremental process, (2) that the model adapts readily to most, but not all, situations in urban classrooms, and (3) that the personality of any one implementation of the Society School will be determined by the inputs made from the collective experience and from the adventuresomeness of all its participants. In other words, the model comes closer to being a process than to being a collection of elements poured into a mold. Outcomes and outputs of that process will differ dramatically from site to site, and from classroom to classroom.

To say it more pointedly, the Society School model permits a variety of outcomes. As it is an incremental process, each new step is reinforced and, in turn, reinforces all the preceding steps. Practitioners who wish to explore the process need not subscribe to the theory behind the Society School in its entirety. Practitioners have only to commit themselves to each step and to walking. For some, these paces amount to going through a proof en route to building a practice. The practitioner's experience either confirms the theory or defeats it. If it is confirmed, the practitioner tries the next step, if need be on faith, but preferably because it makes sense in the given situation. If it is defeated, the implementor begins making his or her contribution to the theory of practice by experimenting with other approaches.

The following formulations flow from the P.S. 126 experience. In classroom situations in which both teacher and students behave responsibly and predictably, transitions from traditional school processes to Society School processes occur easily and quickly. Progress at a slower rate likewise seems possible in situations where either party, students or teachers, behaves predictably and responsibly toward the other. In this second situation, one contacts and works through whichever party seems to have greatest control over itself in the environment. The slower pace of development can be attributed to distractions that crop up in connection with emotional or interior interests and problems of the participating individuals. In situations where both teacher and children seem emotionally incapacitated, the movement from traditional to Society School process cannot take place until the school develops some procedure to deal with students and teachers who are experiencing emotional breakdowns. To educators and humanists who would have the school become everything to everybody, I can only say that they have a better opinion of the schools than I do.

As for flexibility, I would argue that the Society School model makes better use of teachers with skills outside those normally used by teachers. Teachers with interests in law, architecture, city planning, medicine, health, and so on can easily make these part of the school experience. The sum of those contributions will determine the particular shape of any implementation of the theory.

To a rather large extent, the universe of these experiences and skills can be expanded either with materials or with contributions from professionals and graduate students in fields heretofore excluded from school. Thus, books, films, reading laboratories, philosophers, architects, bankers, judges, and the like must be called upon to make a fitting contribution to connecting children with the process of civilizing the immediate environment.

At a more concrete level, many teachers have checking accounts and most students don't know what a checking account is. The Society School process provides the impetus for making such accounts a part of school life. Similarly, most teachers engage in some form of financial planning. Most low-income students and their families don't. A school can teach this also. Few teachers have more than a vague idea about how the justice system operates. Both they and their students attend to this ignorance by building a legal process of their own. Most children in theater companies get a rather clear understanding of staging and acting in a production. Very few even consider the financial arrangements that make theater possible or impossible. School should attend to this. And so on. More and more, the Society School model attempts to connect children with the web of social, political, and economic experience that surrounds virtually everything we do.

From this exegesis, it should be evident that Society School implementations require a far broader experience in the world on the teachers' part than does the traditional school. The more vital the life of the teachers, the broader the experience of the adult contributors, the richer the implementation of the model will be. Today you will find very few teachers in elementary school, or in any school, who are familiar with the workings of law, government, agri-business, social-service agencies, medicine, architecture, economics, or any field other than pure teaching. The narrowness of the teachers' experience cripples possibilities for broadening student experience and understandings. Even well-intentioned efforts to inform children about the world around them tend to be shallow.

One solution is to improve experience. During the early stages of the school's transformation to the model, it may be necessary to import experienced people from the professions and service industries into the school to share with both teachers and students the life skills they have mastered. This will probably be a useful, if expensive, stopgap measure. Eventually, however, teachers will have to be trained and selected for employment because they bring these skills and understandings to the job. Teachers already employed by school systems will have to agree to a period of retooling that probably will involve them in organizations other than schools. Teachers will have to be enriched if they are to improve the experience of the children they teach.

In combination, the incremental process, adaptability, and flexibility make the chances of implementing the Society School exceedingly favorable. The process's incremental feature works to allay the fears that school personnel have about entering a period of rapid and disorderly change. Every change takes its own time and proves itself before a new step is introduced. The model's adaptability to most classrooms gives it broad rather than narrow appeal. Children who work to acquire material goods have as much permission to do so as other children who do things because they are ends in themselves or because they are linked to the satisfying ideology of society building. Finally, the model's flexibility allows the school community to make the best of what it has while spelling out the kind of community it wants, and seeking the people it needs to sophisticate teaching practice.

Early in June, during what was to be the final meeting of the faculty, the teachers who had participated in the project and some others who wanted to expressed the desire to continue the Society School for another year. It was not my intention to work in New York a second year. I was living in Cambridge and studying at the Harvard School of Education, and didn't much like commuting to New York. But the enthusiasm of the staff and the developments during the first year overwhelmed personal considerations. By the end of the meeting I'd agreed to seek funding for a second year and to plan for September on that basis.

7. The Micro-Capitalist Society

"Sarah Dubin and I do not expect to hear how our fund-raising effort turns out until late October. If it turns out badly, we will have to close down." I looked at Sarah. She was watching the teachers at the meeting, wondering whether they had understood what we were saying.

Sarah, a friend who had worked with me in New Haven when I directed the Transitional Year Program, had joined me in the P.S. 126 venture in early summer. Vivacious, energetic, and committed, she had all the energy of a twenty-five-year-old, although she was almost fifteen years and four children beyond that. At the prospect of working without being paid, she had waved my warnings aside, saying, "I'll gamble. Pay me retroactively if we raise the money." Something in her look made the risks I was taking less threatening. With her presence, I could almost feel a doubling of the energy going into the project.

"What George is trying to say is that he is going to finance the project until the foundation money comes through," said Sarah.

"If it doesn't come, I suppose I go broke."

The teaching staff listened numbly. A few eyebrows raised. "Does that mean that we can have the auctions?"

"I'll commit myself to a Christmas auction. If we don't get funded, we close up, or I close up, during the Christmas break. Some of you may decide to go on after that on your own. Any questions?"

"I hope you're rich," said a voice.

"I'm not," I said matter-of-factly. "Life's full of risks. We've all talked about what we plan to do individually. I hoped this meeting would give us all a feeling for the project in its totality."

Sarah began passing out sheets of memos.

"The top part of the first sheet approximates the time frame we'll work in. It's rough. It may take longer to set up the legislature and courts than it says. We may find we're trying to do too much. If we do, the plan changes. A number of us have minor disagreements; some of you have quite different commitments to what we are doing. We'll have to work out these differences as best we can."

A lengthy discussion ensued about the organization of the project and the delegations of responsibilities. After almost everyone had expressed a view, an interest in one area of the program, a disinterest in another, I suggested we organize the discussion and duties into four areas: Micro-Economic, Micro-Political, Micro-Social, and Academic. In a concession to anxieties some teachers felt about working with other teachers they did not like, I asked each of the participants to commit himself or herself to one of the four areas. To no one's surprise, friends ended up working with friends. Each group then chose a nominal leader. I took responsibility for the economic side of things. Gino Capoletti took responsibility for the political area. Riva Thel agreed to oversee legal development, and Sarah Dubin agreed to coordinate the Children's University.

Other exchanges continued through the lunch hour. Most of the main issues had been settled the year before. There were no hesitations about using Micro-Economy money in the classroom. There was very little discussion on the level of educational philosophy. Teachers understood that their beliefs would translate and shape whatever happened.

The Orange Business

Manuel watched the other children impatiently. "Why don't they hurry up and eat?" His eyes scanned the breakfast trays in front of him. They were filled with oranges, milk, cold cereal, and other ingredients of the school's free-breakfast program. Sometimes his eyes stopped on the faces of the children noisily gobbling down the provisions. One saw him measuring, calculating.

Mannie was ten years old. For slightly more than a year he had been assigned to a Sanctuary class, which meant he had caused enough trouble to warrant special attention. Sanctuary classes provide troubled students with special services. Mostly, children with temper problems found their way there. But, as with other special classes, the children in them were labeled losers by most kids and teachers. The "bad kids" who don't pay attention and who get into fights end up there.

Mannie wasn't bad. Teachers just found it hard to cope with him. He was a troubled person. And whatever he covered it with could be broken down by a false word or a wrong look. Like many such children, he put up a tough front, but the anger sometimes rose into his throat and the effort he made to stop it before it got out wrung tears from him. So it was not unusual to see Mannie fighting and crying at the same time, like watching a windmill in the rain.

But now he had channeled his energy into the orange business. Someone might have forbidden it, because it was different from what usually goes on in school, but no one did. No one helped him either. Mannie just figured out what to do and did it. And instead of stopping him, everyone was glad to see him being constructive and excited.

"Hey, Mannie, what you doin'?" his friend Greg inquired.

"My business!"

"Come on," insisted Greg. "Ain't we friends?"

"Okay. But you swear you won't tell and you won't mess me up?"

"What's the big secret?"

"Swear or git!"

"Okay, man, I swear."

"See these bags?" Mannie opened two large shopping bags. At the bottom of each Greg saw a half-dozen oranges, four or five cartons of milk, and two boxes of cold cereal.

"You collecting garbage?"

"Garbage? You stupid!" Mannie spat on the floor. "The stuff in these bags is grade A double A. And I gonna be rich."

"Ain't no A double A. That garbage comes off them trays."

Mannie screwed up his face. "You retarded. Know nothin' 'bout nothin'."

"Tell me, then."

"You really wanna know? Okay, then. You gotta do it to learn it."

Greg shrugged. "What you want me to do?"

"Keep your eyes open and take one of these bags. Collect food that ain't touched. Get oranges, they the best. Then milk. Then cereal. Put 'em in this bag. You stand here. I'll stand t'other side."

The two boys hovered like birds of prey on either side of the lunchroom. As soon as a child got up from breakfast, one or the other of the boys scurried over to his table space, looked over the tray, and squirreled any untouched foodstuffs into one of Mannie's brown paper bags.

Mannie had his eye on one of the parent aides who looked disapprovingly in their direction.

"Cool it, Greg. Old lady over there, she gonna start messin' with us." The two nimbly escaped to the other side of the cafeteria. Fortunately for them, Mrs. Mouhley didn't run after them. Miss Dunne, the Sanctuary teacher, had also been watching them and came over.

"Collecting food?"

"Yeah," answered Mannie as though he knew he had done something wrong.

"What will you do with it?"

"Sell it!" Mannie looked at Greg with a smile. "I'm paying Greg to work for me. We going into the food business."

Miss Dunne looked amused. "You mean you're going to sell this for Micro-Economy money?"

"That's right!" Mannie slapped his hands together. This teacher obviously liked what he was doing, so he became expansive. "We gonna make a sign! Mannie and Greg Company. Hang right in our room. And maybe a pushcart too. So we can sell stuff after school."

Miss Dunne peered into their bag. "That milk will go sour by 3 o'clock. No one will buy it."

"Guess we gonna have to throw it out."

"Come with me." Faith Dunne walked into the cafeteria kitchen with the boys at her heels. "Mrs. Chambers, these are two of my students. They're going into the food business."

"They are?" laughed Mrs. Chambers. "Cooking or distribution?"

"Distribution. They're collecting all the food children throw away and—" Faith Dunne turned to the boys—"where do you sell it?"

"At lunchtime in the schoolyard and after school in front," volunteered Mannie.

Mrs. Chambers frowned. "I suppose it's better than having it go to waste. What you do with the money you earn?"

"Spend it in the auction," Mannie said, looking as if he'd been asked something incredible.

"We have an auction in our class about every two months," explained Faith Dunne. "My students buy things with the money they earn. I'd consider it a special favor to me if you'd let these boys use a little section of your refrigerator to keep the food they've collected from going bad. That way not only would the food be going into stomachs it belongs in, we'd be sure of its condition when it arrived. Would it be okay?"

"Okay by me. Do better than that. Some days there's leftovers. Doesn't happen every day—just some days. Those days I'll help you boys out. Put your things in here!" She opened a refrigerator.

Greg and Mannie smiled. "Wow! Man! We got a refrigerator."

It was not long before their business grew and the two started gathering leftover food during the lunch period. To their surprise, the boys discovered they could market breakfast foods at lunch and lunch foods at breakfast.

Faith Dunne, who told this story to me, felt it didn't matter that they were profiting from their enterprise. For Faith it was paramount that Greg and Mannie should taste what it was like to be winners. "That's satisfaction," she said, "seeing losers become winners. That's why I'm here."

Greeting Cards

In December, Faith Dunne's class decided to make greeting cards and sell them to children in Micro-Economy classes. To encourage their business venture, I agreed to increase the dollar allocation to her classroom economy by one American dollar for every $500 ME the class earned. Using funds budgeted for economic development, Faith purchased linoleum blocks, tools, paper, ink, and ink rollers for the production effort.

"Who we gonna sell them to?" asked a dubious Roberta. "No one buys from us."

"Mr. Richmond will buy some. I know a lot of teachers who'd buy our cards," Faith countered. "You just watch."

"They Jewish. What they want Christmas cards for?"

"Jewish people send Christmas cards to friends who aren't Jewish and Hanukkah cards to people of their religion."

"Whatsa Hanukkah card?" demanded Gail.

"It's just like a Christmas card, only it has a Star of David—and sometimes nine candles instead of Santa Claus or the Virgin and Child.

"We should make both. We can sell to everybody."

It was agreed. Several children began carving the linoleum blocks. As they finished, other children in the class began the printing sequence. Some rolled ink onto the surface of the block. Others set the inked blocks on a piece of paper and tapped them with a hammer until they left an impression.

The cards they turned out were hung on a clothesline to dry. Others were spread on tables around the room. After initial tries with red ink, some children began experimenting with green and blue. In a little more than two days Faith's children produced more than 500 Christmas cards and 100 Hanukkah cards.

Word of these productions, fueled by "gift" samples to teachers in the fourth, fifth, and sixth grades, spread quickly. The sample cards, beautiful in a primitive way, produced a flood of orders from students and teachers. Many teachers offered to buy the cards with U.S. currency, reasoning that their purchase of Sanctuary cards replaced purchases they were planning to make at local stores. Students bought literally hundreds of cards with Micro-Economy money. Sales to teachers netted nearly $24. Sales to students earned $6,000 ME. In all, something like 600 cards were sold, yielding the class about $36. Faith Dunne's students voted to spend their earnings in a local Chinese restaurant.

The greeting-card story didn't end there. As when a pebble is thrown into a pond, the impact rippled beyond the origin point. Sam Chin and a student in the fifth grade purchased a few sample cards and took them home. At a gathering of friends, he happened to display them. His uncle offered to buy a dozen if Sammy could get some more.

Sammy got to thinking. If his uncle liked them, then other people would like them, and if other people liked them, then they too might buy them. He decided to visit Miss Dunne's class first thing.

"Miss Dunne, my name is Sam Chin. I'm in 5–430. I saw the cards your class made. Can I buy some?"

"Certainly. Class, you have a customer."

Two girls ran up to Sam, each with a handful of cards. "Buy mine! Buy mine!"

"How much?" Sam asked.

"Ten Micro-Economy dollars each!" both children shouted.

"Only good ones," Sam said resolutely.

"They all good. How many you want?"

"Two hundred."

"Two hundred!" gasped the girls. "You got a lot of friends?"

"My uncle wants some. Also friends."

The girls began to count the cards and put them into a box in bundles of ten. When they counted out his twenty bundles Sammy paid them $2,000 ME and left.

A week later Miss Dunne ran into Sammy in the hall. "Did you use all the cards you bought?"

"I sure did," said Sammy with a smile. "Wanna know a secret?"

"Sure."

"Promise you won't tell."

"I promise."

"I sold all them cards for ten cents apiece."

"To whom?"

"My uncle, the lady next door, a priest, two friends, and everybody in my building."

"You must be a rich man."

Sammy Chin looked over his shoulder and then took out his wallet. In one of the compartments Sammy showed her two U.S. tens.

"Better put them in a safe place."

"At lunchtime," Sam said, "I'm goin' to the bank."

The Newspapers: Regular and Underground

Early in the fall Riva Thel's fifth-grade class, the same class that had contributed so much to the program the year before, launched the Society School's first newspaper. They called it the *Junior News* and published it at irregular intervals of about three weeks. The paper consisted of original student articles, comic strips, stories, gossip, letters to the editor, news, word games, and editorials.

To ensure a distribution of journalism experience Riva asked her students to elect three people to be newspaper editors. Each editor was then allowed to select volunteers from the class for the various positions on the newspaper: assistant editor, copy editor, business manager, circulation manager, and layout. Each publishing team was then assigned a publishing date.

When all the copy for the paper had been collected and copy-edited, the editor in charge produced a plan for the layout. I brought the copy with me to Boston, where I typed it into columns. Following the layout plan as best I could, I prepared the dummy for delivery to the printer.

There were articles of every possible description. Moy Ha Long wrote the following article about a fight and a trial.

> On Tuesday Tony had a fight with Eddie. It started when Eddie pushed Tony. Then they started pushing each other. And at lunch time Tony said he would get Eddie outside. Which did not happen, because Eddie left before Tony got him.
>
> After the lunch period Eddie told Mr. Z—— that Tony had said he'd get Eddie. Mr. Z—— said that we would have a trial. At his trial, Eddie was found guilty. His punishment was to sit on the bench during gym. After Eddie's punishment, Eddie told Tony that he'd get his brother to beat him up. But Tony said if you get your brother I'll get my brother. And then Eddie's brother said you better not touch him.

There were also poems, crossword puzzles, word games, spelling riddles, gossip columns—one called "Dear Diary"—and advertisements:

> ADVERTISEMENTS: $5 micro-economy money for students per line. $.25 U.S. a line for parents and businessmen who don't have micro-economy money.

and advice to merchants:

> ADVICE by Cindy
>
> If your class is in the micro-economy program and uses credit cards, I advise you not to use too much on credit because when it is time to pay up you may not be able to afford it. You may not be able to pay back the money you owe people. And then people will sue you. And you will be put on trial. You would get yourself into lots of trouble by using a lot of credit. If you can't pay, you will find yourself in a mess!

A problem arose in the distribution of the paper. Unlike the greeting-card venture, most classes were content to buy half a dozen copies of the paper and share them. Six times fifteen classes adds up to a demand for about ninety copies, barely enough to warrant the expense of printing. It therefore became necessary to secure the commitment of all the teachers in the program to use the paper as part of their regular reading program. Most teachers agreed to this, but a few did not—for reasons known best to them.

In spite of the encouragement I gave the venture, it was unable to grow into anything more than a classroom effort. I had envisioned a school-wide newspaper with contributions from participating classrooms. It didn't come off. In retrospect, bringing off such a venture at the elementary-school level requires some very keen organizing skills. A school-wide paper might have happened if we had been able to allocate enough teacher time to the effort or if we had been able to draw students from the entire school. Existing staff allocations weren't sufficient. So instead of developing one school-wide newspaper, we ended up having two classroom-generated newspapers and a third from what its editors called "the underground press."

Two other newspapers developed during the year. The *Daredevil News* grew out of fierce rivalry between children in Mrs. Thel's class and children in Lena Andrews' class. In actuality, both newspapers appeared to be very similar in make-up and in organization. Where the *Junior News* came to be the expression of the world inside Thel's classroom, the *Daredevil News* expressed the personality of Andrews' fourth-grade children.

Still, the *Daredevil News* surpassed its competitor in at least one area: it had the best cartoonist in the school. For a while the *Daredevil* adopted a marketing strategy superior to the one being followed in Mrs. Thel's class. Instead of trying to hawk newspapers one by one, the *Daredevil*'s business manager decided to sell thirty copies to each teacher at a special discount. Until the competition imitated it, the *Daredevil* had the widest circulation in the school.

As with some of our other ventures, we found ourselves seriously strapped for manpower. We could for instance have developed markets for the newspaper among parents, at local newspaper stands, and in nearby schools. Advertising revenue might have been generated by soliciting local businesses serving the school population. Along the same lines, it might have been possible for some enterprising student to develop a business brokering advertising space in various school publications. Like many other routes, this one remains to be traveled and examined for possibilities. One day a student somewhere will start an advertising company that not only solicits ads, but also designs them.

Mrs. Tobias' class had been blocked by their teacher from participating in all but the legislative functions of the Society School. The blockade was not one I was asked to enforce. It was imposed by their teacher on her students and justified on the grounds that they had to spend the time on activities judged by their teacher to be preparation for junior high school. In general, these activities followed more traditional lines involving ever increasing doses of reading, writing, and arithmetic.

Mrs. Tobias' children, however, felt short-changed. Enough interaction existed between children in the school for them to have a pretty good idea what they were missing. When they received copies of the *Junior News* and the *Daredevil News,* many of Mrs. Tobias' children also wanted the chance to produce a newspaper. Mrs. Tobias refused to allow them this responsibility. She had, in her own mind, cut herself off from the project. "Like a paramecium," she said, "it spreads and multiplies. And I don't want any part of it."

I had made up my mind to respect Mrs. Tobias' wishes and viewpoint, although I had my regrets. She held the reins on the brightest sixth-grade class in the school. Tapping the energies of those children might have had an immeasurable impact on the school.

I felt slightly uncomfortable when I was approached by four boys from her class who said they wanted to start an "underground newspaper" called *D.E.L.T.* because it combined the first initial in each of its four editors' last names.

I looked at the boys. "Has Mrs. Tobias okayed this?"

One of the boys nodded. "She said as long as we do all our work we can have a newspaper."

Past experience dictated proceeding carefully. "All right. I will do for you what I do for the other classes publishing newspapers. You bring me the raw copy. I'll type it and have it printed. I bring it here every week. You distribute it. Now tell me this—what's underground about it?"

Jimmy Dewey, the leader of the group, smiled. "I don't think my teacher likes the idea." And then he added mercifully, "But she said yes."

Three weeks later I encountered Mrs. Tobias in the hall. "Mr. Richmond, I want to speak to you."

For just a second I felt like a boy caught with a hand in the apple pie. But I turned with a smile. "How can I be of help?"

"It's about the newspaper. I find my children spending too much time on it. One of my mothers has complained. She says her boy spends all night on the phone talking to other editors. He's neglecting his homework."

"Haven't you taken this up with them?"

"Of course I have. I just want you to know there will be no more *D.E.L.T.*"

And no new issue of *D.E.L.T.* appeared. When Sarah inquired about it she discovered that the editors had, at least officially, agreed that there wasn't enough time.

Banks: Savings and Commercial

Nearly every class with Micro-Economy money developed a savings bank. The least sophisticated of these institutions merely provided children with a safe depository for their funds. These depositories became a necessary part of classroom economic life as children discovered that the money they were earning had value, and that if it was left carelessly around or displayed openly, chances were good that it would change hands.

Nearly all the teachers also used the bank to get their students to do applied arithmetic. Upon opening an account at the bank, each student received a bankbook. Students inscribed in this book their deposits and withdrawals. The savings-bank manager, in most cases selected for being a capable arithmetician, maintained records of each student's account in a special bank notebook. Every transaction entered in that notebook had to be initialed twice, once by the bank manager or manager's assistant, and the second time by the depositor. Teachers reported it as commonplace to see children adding and re-adding their bankbooks. Children imbued numbers with enough meaning to require teachers to expend some effort distracting them from comparing sums and turning their attention to other activities.

Sarah Dubin devoted a considerable amount of her time to developing and operating a commercial bank in the school. The bank she started relieved some of the pressure on classroom savings banks. Several teachers felt that helping students keep their accounts straight took too much time. Bank errors happened frequently enough to call for teacher intervention in order to untangle them. To appease teachers who resented the extra duties, we decided to provide a central banking facility.

Sarah began pilot work on the central bank in February. Several months later, experimentation seemed to have produced a sequence that was both simple and effective. Even then Sarah continued to streamline bank operations.

The materials Sarah developed included a sheet advertising the bank's four major services to customers: (1) safety for deposits, (2) interest on deposits, (3) checking accounts for students, and (4) checking accounts for teachers. Another form listed the steps by which students and teachers could take advantage of the services being offered. A third form outlined step-by-step instructions for filling out checks and establishing two banking days for each class.

To open an account a student filled out a form with his name, class, Micro-Economy number, the amount of the opening deposit, and a record of the depositor's signature. Each new depositor then received an envelope to use for deposits and withdrawals along with instructions for its use:

a. Put your name, class, and ME number on this envelope, with a deposit slip or withdrawal slip (provided in each envelope).
b. If you are depositing money, put your checks and cash in the envelope with the deposit slip.

c. Give the envelope and its contents to your class treasurer. He will give it to the banker assigned to your room.

A fourth form announced that students could start checking accounts by purchasing a book of twenty checks for five Micro-Economy dollars, and announced the interest rates that would be paid on deposits (1 percent interest on amounts left in bank for six weeks).

In offering its services to teachers, the bank followed a slightly different procedure. Teachers received a special form that authorized the direct deposit of teacher currency allocations to their Society School bank accounts. The student bank managers also provided to teachers a quantity of checks so they could draw on these deposits. This privilege allowed teachers to delegate check-writing functions to student accountants in their rooms. In addition to this service, the bank gave teachers a regular weekly statement of their expenditures and balance, a service very much needed since several teachers habitually overdrew their accounts.

The bankers, for their part, learned to keep accurate records, use an adding machine, and, when a miscue occurred, answer customer complaints. In one desk drawer the bankers kept notebooks for each class, and in another, checks and other kinds of records to verify their transactions.

Although Sarah succeeded in developing the mechanics of banking in school, it would be misleading to say she solved the problem. Poor children know next to nothing about banks, for the simple reason that their parents don't use them. The simplest transactions seem mysterious in an almost unfathomable way. For example, it takes a great deal of energy to convince a child that his money will be safer in a bank, where he is guaranteed against loss, than in his pocket or his house. For the poor child, safety and proximity correspond. The closer one is to one's belongings, the surer one is that they are safe. Likewise, many students simply refused to believe they had the power to write checks. Checks came from bosses or from welfare. One cashes checks, one doesn't write them.

One of the bankers, for instance, went with Sarah to a wool store to purchase supplies for the Children's University. Sarah paid by check. The banker, himself a check casher, couldn't believe that a man would give Sarah $10 worth of wool for a piece of paper. It seemed almost magical.

I had seen the problem before. In one of the Broad Jump summers a student took home a check only to have it appropriated by his mother. The next day, together with her son, she visited a bank, attempting to exchange her son's Micro-Economy check for real money. After a few short moments of confusion and a few others of consternation, the teller was reported to have looked at the parent and said, "Sorry, we don't carry soul dollars." To the mother's embarrassment, he began giggling. The poor woman, sensing that something was amiss, examined the check more closely. Humiliated, she dragged her son by his ear into the street. For the boy, his Broad Jump check seemed little different from the checks his mother received from her income source, even though he had been told they were negotiable only in school.

Cognitive problems of this kind arose at every step of the banking process. Some students, after depositing money, insisted on seeing whether the bank still had their cash the next day. Shown figures in the bank's books reflecting their deposits, these individuals might reject the figures and demand to see the bank's currency. Early in the bank's development some children refused to be paid by check, because they didn't regard checks as money. Similarly, Sarah never discovered why the bankers refused to put their own money in their banks, and finally attributed it to quirks that would eventually be ironed out.

Becoming depositors gave some children a rather extraordinary sense of importance. Many demanded personal attention and found frequent occasion to visit the bankers on some small matter related to their accounts. The four bankers, one a potential discipline problem according to his teacher, rose so high in their own estimation that it was sometimes hard to bring them back to earth.

To compound the cognitive problem, many teachers neglected to take advantage of the arithmetic opportunities the bank provided, some because they did not feel comfortable dealing with banking, some because they didn't see the opportunities, others because they didn't know how to make use of them. However, several teachers helped their students study interest, word problems, fractions, algebra, using transactions related to classroom business.

Accountants, Bookkeepers, and Secretaries

As the number of organizations in a classroom and in the school proliferated, the amount of paperwork increased correspondingly. Since most teachers had enough paperwork to do as it was, most of them quickly became disposed to turning over these burgeoning responsibilities to capable students. Although the pattern differed from room to room, student help generally took the form of secretarial, bookkeeping, and accounting assistance.

At my insistence, teachers prepared two students to undertake secretarial and bookkeeping chores right at the outset. It thus became possible to shortcut a financial sequence that entailed counting money, arranging for the student to deposit it in his account, and bookkeeping as well, by bookkeeping most transactions from the beginning. Most teachers were therefore able to debit the student's account and credit their own with a simple verbal command. The bookkeeper immediately noted the entries in the appropriate accounts as directed. At the end of the day, a second student, designated accountant, tallied all the entries for errors and prepared a simple financial statement that summarized the debit entries and balanced them against the credit entries.

In the P.S. 126 project, only a few of the teachers had had enough experience in accounting to develop a system of double-entry bookkeeping like the one described above. Most relied instead on a single-entry system that consisted of debits to student accounts. At week's end, when all the student accounts were summed together, the account secretary informed the teacher how much had been spent and how much remained to be disbursed. Teachers then balanced this sum against their scrip allocation of $100 per student per week.

Most teachers stayed within the recommended limits. However, one teacher quickly discovered that the pricing structure he had adopted was exceeding his weekly allocation. In other words, he was paying out more than he was taking in. After an appeal to me failed to augment his supply of Micro-Economy money, the teacher decided to issue bonds. In other words, instead of getting money from me, he decided to borrow it from his own students. No sooner had he explained this proposition to his students—together, of course, with an elaborate description of how interest was computed—than he discovered that his students had learned the lesson too well. Students were willing to lend him money, but not at a price he really liked. "I'll have to declare bankruptcy," he said. "That'll teach 'em," but of course he didn't.

The Post Office

Early that spring a teacher's meeting unearthed a suggestion for linking writing in school closer to its actual communication function. A week later two girls from Dick Sewall's class began working on the development of a postal service that would allow children to communicate with children in other classes. The steps taken to establish the postal service consisted, first, of convincing me to subsidize the office's operations for a trial period, then of designing and decorating two mail envelopes for each classroom—one for incoming and the other for outgoing mail—and finally of distributing and installing them in all the classrooms willing to participate.

In the beginning, the novelty of being allowed to send letters to friends in other rooms produced a correspondence boom. Gradually, however, the postal service lost its luster. A month after its celebrated and well-advertised beginning, the idea was abandoned. The reasons for the failure of this organization to reach its potential were many. First, the mail drops and pick-ups took place only once a day. The children wanted to do it more often, but Sewall objected to the frequency with which the girls were out of the classroom. Secondly, the school economy just hadn't grown large enough to sustain a postal service. Third, administrators and teachers preferred generally to use their own network of monitors to distribute school circulars and so bypassed the mail service the children established.

These reasons contributed to the postal service's demise. But probably central to it was a reluctance on the part of the staff, with many other pressing things to do, to give the thing the push it needed. In part this attitude may have had roots in worries over the abuse of the mails. Students, in the very first week, managed to send enough obscenity through the mails to cause a small commotion. Even when the novelty of sending anonymous graffiti to someone across the hall had passed and genuine letters were being exchanged, teachers continued to be wary.

Whether the postal-service idea works as planned or not, the idea strikes me as a useful way to foster communication. Possibly as important, the service provides a student enterprise with access to the entire student body of a school, a privilege now reserved to adults in education organizations. As for the obstacles and issues raised in the Sewall effort, none appears to be insurmountable. To avoid classroom interruptions, for instance, a central postal system might be established in the hallways outside the rooms. To keep pace with demands for more frequent service, deliveries and pick-ups could be made once every hour. It also seems likely that the number of letters and other forms of mail would increase with economic growth, and if Society School activities were allowed to take place during after-school hours, the correspondence generated, say, in the course of business operations from three o'clock to five might make the service worth the effort. Other improvements might include a mailbox placed outside the school for evening and weekend drops, greater controls on the use of special monitors to distribute school circulars, utilization of mail service instead of loudspeakers, and providing penalties for abusing the mails.

Comic-Book Makers

Early in the fall, students in Miss Andrews' class launched an operation for making comic books, in response to my offer to purchase their work. My original intention was to reproduce those that clearly deserved to be. However, I ran into production problems. Most of the children used color in their illustrations, which made it too expensive to reproduce them. Second, Andrews' class produced so many excellent hand-made comic books that to select one example and not others might have been interpreted negatively by those whose work was not chosen. So I decided to try the much less expensive Xerox process. Here again I was frustrated: the copies just weren't good. With the failure to find a cheap and effective method of reproduction, the effort collapsed.

The Comic-Book Lending Company

A friend of mine at Harvard pointed out that school-age children *voluntarily* buy 250,000,000 comic books a year, making comic books the most popular children's reading medium in the United States. It seemed sensible, therefore, to use them in school, where persuading children to read consumed a good part of a teacher's energies. I looked around to see if a comic-book reading series existed. None did, so I was thrown back to using those commercially available.

Purchasing more than a hundred of these, I decided to give some thought and energy to developing a distribution system that maximized the number of readers each comic would have. As an experiment, I employed four students to handle distribution. Each was asked to develop a list of subscribers willing to pay $25 ME a week for the privilege of receiving a comic book each day. Each of the distributors was permitted to develop ten subscribers and each was given ten comics to circulate among these customers.

This system worked smoothly until spring vacation arrived a month later. When the distributors returned, most reported that their stock of comic books had nearly disappeared in the interval between the closing and reopening of school. Some reported that customers had lost rented copies. Others attributed the attrition to brothers and sisters. To keep the operation going, I resupplied the distributors, but the operation never reached its previous exuberance. A number of student subscribers complained that they had not received their money's worth, and refused to subscribe again. Records of transactions were lost or badly kept. The comic-book lending business, thus, never became more than a shadow of its former self.

Other Businesses

A variety of smaller enterprises developed in individual classrooms. Several of Mrs. Hand's children produced candles and sold them to other children for Micro-Economy money. In Miss Andrews' class, a group of children developed a popcorn business. The ingredients were popcorn, butter, a popcorn maker, a hot plate supplied by the teacher, and paper bags. In different classes a number of children with "swift tongues" offered their talents for sale to children in need of legal assistance. A good deal of construction activity took place in classrooms using the Micro-Economy game. In Riva Thel's class, students developed an entire street of commercial stores along the shelves that stretched almost the length of two classroom walls. One child wrote about how these stores worked.

ALL ABOUT STORES *by Elaine B.*

> In the beginning of the year, class 5–427 started Micro-Economy for the second time.
>
> We started to build stores to make more money. Some of the stores were made out of white paper or cardboard. If you want to, you can paint the store. They are all sizes and shapes. Some are big, small, fat or wide. Most of the stores are stationery stores. They sell jokebooks, games, toys, doll clothes, books.
>
> In order for us to put our stores somewhere we have to buy land for $15 a month. Some stores make money, others don't.

Two other students advertised their wares in the *Junior News:*

> SALE!
>
> I would like to introduce you to a great store called Stationary and Things. The owners are Amelia J—— and Michele F——. In the store we would like to advertise telescopes, dolls, doll clothes, combs, good books, rings and glass cases. NOT EXPENSIVE! You can have refunds if you aren't fully pleased. In Class 5–427. Ask your teacher for permission to come when we have Store.

In the April term of the Children's University, Marlin Sangre, who had failed in his campaign for president (a campaign described in Chapter 8) came to our office wanting to know "if there was gonna be uniforms for the volleyball teams."

"You want uniforms?"

"How you expect us to be a team without uniforms?"

I looked at Sarah. "You know, the boy has a point. Then, turning back to Marlin, I said "You ever tie-dyed anything?"

"In the settlement house we make all kinds of things, like bands for your head, skirts, all kinda stuff."

"How about making shirts for the teams?"

"I ain't making shirts for everybody. Maybe for my team. But not everybody."

"I thought you were smarter than that. You could make a fortune. Maybe even get rich."

"Yeah?"

"Yeah. You could sell a tie-dye shirt to every kid on a team. Hundred Micro-Economy bucks each."

"You know, that ain't a bad idea. Teach, you real smart."

"Never mind. You figure out where you're going to get the shirts. I'll get you the dye. You also have to find some place to do it."

"That's easy, I can do it at the after-school center. But where I get shirts? . . . Lotta kids got white tee shirts. I get them, color them."

"How you going to get them?"

Marlin grinned minus one tooth. "I'll take them off them."

"You'll do no such thing," Sarah laughed.

Marlin shrugged. "Okay, I'll ask, but if they don't wanna give . . ." He didn't finish.

"Talk to the captains. Get them to collect the shirts and the money to pay you."

"Sounds good. When we going to buy the dye?"

"Find me at three o'clock."

"You can get it down the street. They got a lotta colors."

Marlin met me that afternoon and we went shopping. Several days later he walked into our office with a bundle under his arm.

"I been collectin' shirts. Almost my whole team brought in their tee-shirts. We gonna have beautiful shirts, man, beautiful. I'm making the arms yellow and the body red. Beautiful."

No sooner had the first dozen shirts been produced than Marlin received orders from all the other captains in the tournament. I didn't hear from him for some time after that except for requests for new dyes. When he had finally outfitted nearly eighty of his fellow students, he came by.

"Hello."

"Hi, Marlin. Where you been?"

"Been? I been gettin' rich."

"Hope you are doing it legal."

"Yeah, I am. I got seven thousand forty dollars. That a lot?"

"Most in the school probably, except for the bankers."

"You like my shirts?"

"Beautiful."

"Want to know a secret?"

I looked at him. "What's the secret?"

"The last twenty shirts—I didn't do them. I just sold captains the dye for the same as if I did the work. Now ain't that something?"

"Sure is. You found a secret way to get rich by being a middle man who does nothing. Now think about it."

8. Micro-Politics

While in retrospect all this activity seems impressive, at the time I had the feeling that our real possibilities had only begun to be tapped. Dramatic differences in commitment to development existed among the staff. In my most private thoughts I dreamed of a time when every individual might function near capacity. When that time came, I believed, our collective energies would transform the school. At the same time, I was forced to look at things pragmatically. For whatever reasons, we had ignited some and not others, and it was these others, whether teachers or students, over whom I constantly puzzled.

At the teachers' meeting in September, Gino Capoletti agreed to undertake the organization of a school-wide political system. As an aficionado of children's theater, he saw the task in a special way. Micro-political organization was a year-long production with hundreds of actors participating in a cinéma vérité. The role of director in this production suited him well in his new position. He had become a cluster teacher for the fourth, fifth and sixth grades, which meant he had no class of his own and instead provided classes with a drama or music program once or twice a week (and thus provided teachers of those classes with their preparation periods).

Gino began organizing the political system in these classes. Students heard his plans with interest. His characteristic zest and enthusiasm ignited theirs. After several weeks of planting political seeds, of training a small cadre of student organizers, he decided to issue the call for a constitutional convention. The ground had been thoroughly prepared. Not only had Gino reached students, he had also reached every teacher on those three grades. Within days of his request, every class elected two representatives and one alternate to the convention. Largely out of respect for Gino, even teachers who stood in the way of student participation in the other programs of the Society School sent representatives.

The convention held its first session on the second Thursday in October during the regular time of the Children's University. As its first act, it constituted itself. By a voice vote, it agreed to hold its sessions in secret, as its second. No one I asked could explain the secrecy. It seemed to add some sort of special drama to what they were doing. It made the participants feel important. It gave them a feeling of power.

Students spent the next four months wrestling with the concept of government. None of the participants had ever before taken part in a student government, let alone undertaken the awesome task of establishing the kind of government that might one day regulate economic activity, tax citizens, foster social programs inside and outside school, and construct a court system and related legal frameworks.

After completing administrative preliminaries, listing members of their classes, and choosing a chairman, the group fell to discussing its responsibilities to its constituents.

"Do we tell them what happens here? Or do we bring here what they want us to take up? Do we write the constitution and then ask them to vote on it? Or do we let anybody who wants to submit a law? What's a constitution? If we make a law, who makes sure nobody breaks it? And if someone breaks it, then what happens?"

"I never had so many questions," Gino said with pleasure. "It must mean they're thinking."

Debate began on who should be allowed to be in the convention. A group of fourth-graders proposed a resolution inviting third-grade classes to send representatives. Sixth-graders led by Dewey Yang, feared that the third-graders would dilute their influence and make it impossible to operate. They opposed it, and a vigorous, almost riotous debate ensued.

"We shouldn't let them in. They won't understand," argued Dewey.

"You in sixth grade. You won't be here next year. Then we'll have to break them in. Get them started now," retorted a fourth-grader pushing for the measure. "Anyway, I was in third grade jus' four months ago, and I know what's happening."

"Ask the second grade too. Ask kindergarten!" said a boy named Benie. "We do what you say and we have a mess."

After a continuous hour of exhausting debate, Capoletti urged a vote.

"Wait! Wait! We should vote to have a vote. If not everybody wants to vote, or someone wants to add a new idea, then maybe we should wait," said Dewey Yang.

"He wants to stall!" said a fourth-grader accusingly.

"No, he's right," said Capoletti. "I know it sounds complicated, but legislatures vote on the resolution to vote before they vote on the resolution itself. Okay, how many vote to vote on the resolution?"

"Point of order!" shouted Dewey.

"What is it now?"

"I think we should have a ten-minute recess before this vote. We should talk among ourselves before we vote."

Capoletti smiled "If you think that, you should say you want to amend the resolution. Then we vote on your amendment."

"I want to amend the resolution."

"Tell us your amendment."

"My amendment is that we talk for ten minutes before voting on whether to vote. Just ten minutes," Dewey whined.

"Okay, vote," said Capoletti. "Get it over with."

"All in favor of the amendment raise hands."

Dewey's allies raised their hands. A count gave him two votes more than he needed to win. During the ten minutes the vote purchased, Dewey attempted to line up the votes to defeat the resolution. His count uncovered a clear victory for the other side, so he used the remainder of the time to persuade some of the shakier people to back a compromise.

When the recess expired and the vote took place, it went against Dewey, the fourth-graders stood and cheered. Minutes later the drama of legislative process began infecting everyone. Students leaned forward in their chairs to follow the debate. The room filled with all the tension of an athletic event. Of all those there, however, only Dewey made a head count, made mental notes on whom to avoid and whom to befriend. He wanted the leadership of the convention.

Just as the chairman was preparing to read the resolution that would admit the third grade to full membership in the convention, a boy sitting next to Dewey took the floor. "I think it's a good idea if we take another ten minutes to talk about this among ourselves. Then we vote."

"Second the motion," said Dewey, trying not to show how much he wanted the time.

"All those in favor?" said the chairman. The vote was unanimous. Children spilled out of their seats, forming and reforming in knots around the room. By the end of the recess Dewey had fifteen votes to defeat the resolution, two votes short of a majority. He hadn't reached everyone, so he couldn't be sure of the outcome. He decided not to chance losing. When the bill had been read, Dewey rose and said, "I want to amend the resolution. When we got talking, I changed my mind about the third grade. We should let them in. I also think that they're too young. So I want to make a suggestion. We let them in as watchers. They get to vote next year. That's my amendment."

"That's called a compromise," said Capoletti. "Sometimes when two people or two groups have different opinions about an idea, they make a deal. A little of this, a little of that." Capoletti's hands mimicked his voice.

"All in favor of Dewey Yang's amendment raise hands," called the chairman of the convention.

Nearly all the hands went up. Seconds later, the convention adopted the resolution as amended.

Democracy or Police State?

The next time the convention met, Capoletti posed a question that took nearly a month to answer. "What should it be? A communist government, a democracy, or a police state?"

Capoletti's question presented considerable difficulties. Most children in the legislature didn't understand the question, or if they understood it, they had only the faintest notion of what the choices meant.

"What's a communist government?" Capoletti looked around the room.

A fifth-grader stood up and said, "Whatever it is, it's bad. Is communist the same as commies? If it is, my father says it all the time when he swears."

Capoletti called on someone else.

"Communism means they tell you what to do. The opposite of free."

After several more stabs at it, Capoletti spoke. "A lot of you have a little bit of an idea of what it is. First of all, it's a planned society. So you plan everything that you want to happen. Then, nobody can have private property. For example, if you had a bike, everybody would own it. Everybody could ride it."

The thought of this made some children squirrel up their faces as if they had just whiffed a bad smell. "Look at your faces!" Gino laughed. "It also means you get to ride someone else's bike. Communism means the government can tell you what job you can have, where to live, how much money you make, and how to raise your children."

"My grandfather, he come from China. He says the commies kill people just because you don't do what they say."

"Doesn't sound very good, does it?"

The discussion continued for the rest of the afternoon. When it was almost time to go home, Capoletti decided to take a poll. "How many of you would want a communistic form of government?"

No one raised a hand.

"If they voted yes, it would have been the same," said Dewey as they filed out of the room. "The school wouldn't allow it."

The convention spent its next meeting debating the pros and cons of having a democracy or a police state. Unlike the discussion of communism, this debate divided the convention.

"Look at the halls! It's not safe in the playgrounds! Some bad things happen in the bathrooms!" said a voice. "Drugs right outside school!" said one of the sixth-graders. "Maybe they come inside if we don't do something. Mr. Bosch says so," said the stern voice of an eleven-year-old. "We should have more safety squad. They our police. Anyway, sometimes there's a fight and the squad members just stand there and look on. Some just plays around. We need a government like the safety squad. Let it stop fights when they start."

"Yeah, yeah," said Dewey Yang. "But strong kids don't make the economy work, or the courts. We need smart people running things."

"You say that because you in the best class!" shouted someone in the opposition. "You want to run things!"

"I don't want to run anything. I'm saying it's complicated and hard and you can't solve all problems with a punch in the mouth."

After an hour of similar harangues, you could have cut the tension with a knife. Someone wanted relief. "Let's quit talking and vote."

"Yeah!" others agreed.

"Wait a minute," said Dewey's sidekick. "This is too important to just vote. We should take this back to our class. Let them discuss. Let them vote. And then *we* vote. I want to know what the people who I represent want."

"Second the motion!" said Dewey.

The motion carried unanimously. As soon as the measure passed, you could feel the relief.

"Hey, this is hard," said one student to another. "Now I know what a Senator feels. Man, you can't fall asleep. Someone gonna put something over on you."

"Yeah, I know what you mean. All we been doin' is sitting and I feel like I runned a race."

From all accounts, most of the representatives to the convention succeeded in consulting students in the homerooms by the next meeting. If any expected the results of these classroom polls to simplify the decision they were making, they were sadly mistaken. The deadlock in the convention reflected the opinion of the school as a whole. Or, if one prefers, those who reported the convention's wrangling to their classmates influenced the votes toward whichever direction they favored. If this occurred in some classes, the reverse happened in others. Dewey, for instance, said everything he could think of to get his constituents to vote for a democracy. In a resounding rejection of his entreaties, his class voted 26 to 7 for a police state "modeled on the safety squad."

The true politician is an artist. The truer he is, the greater his abilities to turn defeat into victory, to make a minority a majority, and to turn a vote against him into a vote for his advantage. Dewey Yang, if not a master politician, at very least had the makings of one. When he returned to the convention with the stated preferences of his constituents in hand, he masked what he considered a personal defeat and began looking for a way to turn that defeat around.

"I have a problem," Dewey announced to the convention. "Or should I say I have a question? What I want to know is, is there a rule that says we have to vote what our classes say? Or do we vote our conscience?" To the untrained hearer, his question might have seemed a simple matter of philosophical inquiry.

"If you want to stay in office, you obviously vote the way your constituents say," said Capoletti.

"But what if you believe something that they don't? What then? What if you care about something enough so you don't care they vote you out?"

"I don't know," answered Capoletti thoughtfully. "Ask the convention."

A debate ensued. Some children took a simple stand: "We are the representatives and we should vote the way the people who elected us want us to." Others insisted that representatives to the convention were picked because of their ideas, principles, or qualifications. If a class didn't like what the person representing it voted for, it could vote him out of office the next time. While in office, however, three voices insisted that representatives could vote the dictates of their conscience. Dewey, however, found little reassurance on either side of the argument. He decided, therefore, to vote for a police state if it looked like a sure thing. If the vote got close, well, then he'd have to think again.

"We have a motion on the floor." The chairman of the convention held up a piece of paper with some scribbling on it. "We want to decide what it's gonna be—a police state or a democracy. Whoever gets the most votes wins."

"I move that we make it a secret ballot," said Dewey, still looking for a way out of his dilemma.

"Anybody second the motion?" asked the chairman. There were no seconders.

"Then the motion is defeated. Did I hear someone ask for a vote on the resolution?" asked the chairman with a sly grin.

"I make the motion," said a girl.

"I second it," said someone next to her.

"Roll call!" shouted the head of the group leading the faction that wanted a police state.

It is impossible to say just what Dewey thought. If we accept Gino Capoletti's insight, he faced a measure which, while it meant other things, fundamentally affected his political future in the school. If the convention established a police state, Dewey—taller and stronger than most, but by no stretch of the imagination a boy who lived by his fists—would have little to do with the Society School's governance. The toughs would own the school. On the other hand, if the convention voted for a democracy, Dewey probably had the best chance of winning an election. If you believe Dewey Yang, it was simply a matter of conscience. "I want to live in a democracy." He said it over and over again until it sounded as if those words had become his personal property.

To be sure, Dewey found himself inside a paradox. If he ignored his constituents and voted for a democracy, he would be adopting a very undemocratic means to achieve democratic ends. On the other hand, if he followed the dictates of his constituents for democratic reasons and voted for a police state, he was on equally tough ground. "Maybe I should tell them that when they voted for a police state, they gave me the right to represent them—so vote the way I want to." Saying this, however, did not relieve the doubt he felt.

The roll call began.

"Police state."

"Democracy."

"Democracy."

"Police state."

"Police state."

Dewey watched the votes being recorded. He tried his best to keep track of them. It was going to be close. He began edging toward the far side of the room in an attempt to have his vote recorded last. When his turn came to vote, he looked toward the chairman. "What's the score?"

"Vote! Vote!"

"Maybe my vote won't matter. I'd like to abstain."

Capoletti, who was looking over the shoulder of the tally keeper, smiled at Dewey Yang. "It's tied."

Dewey twisted in agony. "Democracy."

A cheer rose, followed by stomping, clapping, and then by laughter.

If one stage of the political sequence had come to completion, others were just beginning. The convention spent the next two months drafting a constitution for its democracy. When the draft was completed, Capoletti scheduled a constitutional assembly in which all the children of the fourth, fifth, and sixth grades could adopt or reject the work of their representatives.

Despite a best effort, many of the children attending the assembly probably understood very little of what they were being asked to vote for or against. The constitution was read. Four speakers, two for adoption and two against, were given the chance to speak. When they finished, the chairman rapped his gavel on the wooden table.

"All in favor of making this our constitution, raise your hands."

Three hundred of perhaps four hundred children raised their hands. Clapping began, inducing some of the less sure to add their arms to the majority.

"All against."

Fifty hands rose and fell.

"Then the constitution wins!"

The announcement brought cheers, whistles, and applause. Teachers reacted to the bedlam with stern faces. Commands rang out through the hall. The threat of mayhem subsided.

Political Campaign

The adoption of the constitution moved political developments to their next stage. Capoletti issued two calls, one to elect two representatives from every class to the legislature, and a second for the election of four officers to the executive branch. Several classes honored the first call by returning their constitutional-convention representatives to the legislature. Four or five classes elected new representatives. One or two devoted considerable time to the electoral process itself, allowing candidates to campaign, advertise, and compete against other children interested in the posts.

At about the same time students interested in executive posts began circulating nominating petitions. The constitution required candidates for the offices of president, vice-president, secretary, and treasurer to collect fifty signatures to get on the ballot. For a week, students who decided to be candidates were allowed to visit classrooms between two and three o'clock to enlist support. By week's end, two candidates for president, three for vice-president, and two for the other offices succeeded in winning places on the ballot. Dewey Yang, from Mrs. Tobias' class, and Marlin Sangre, from Mrs. Sallin's class, each collected enough signatures for president.

Marlin, charismatic, Puerto Rican, and member of the bottom class on the sixth grade, vs. Dewey Yang, reputedly the smartest kid in the school, Chinese, and from the top class on the sixth grade: the match-up smelled of an old-time ethnic political duel and excited everyone. Students began taking sides in the contest, and they were not the only ones. Every teacher in the school admired Dewey Yang. He had everything: looks, intelligence, maturity; Dewey at the age of twelve clearly seemed scripted to be a winner. Marlin, on the other hand, had everything going against him. He could barely read. He preferred playing to studying. He got into frequent fights. But there was a genuineness about him, a natural quality, a softness about his toughness, a warmth that endeared him to other children immediately. Everyone knew his "rep" for justice and fair play. They knew he got into trouble a lot. Mostly his trouble had to do with a strenuous effort on his part to defend the honor of family and friends. His penchant for fighting got him into some teachers' books. Others adored him for it. The election pushed some of their adoration to the fore. There was something about his pint-sized underdogness, something so powerful about the kid who all his academic life had been a loser, that some of the teachers who admired Dewey Yang most prayed secretly for a Sangre victory. Heads said better Yang than Sangre. Emotions ran the other way. You could see it, plain as day, when Sangre's forces marshaled a soapbox parade in front of the school during the lunch hour.

"We want Sangre! We want Sangre! We want Sangre!" Fifty youngsters with signs, banners, and ribbons inscribed with Sangre's name and the Puerto Rican colors. "Sangre's ragamuffins," one teacher called them. All the secretaries in the principal's office looked out the window expectantly. No one had ever seen anything like it. They half expected to hear the sound of broken glass, but if they heard anything at all it was the sound of political rhetoric.

"We stick together, we gonna win!" shouted Sangre. "And we gonna make this a better school. We gonna have teams and everything!"

"SAN-gre! SAN-gre! SAN-gre!" chanted his audience.

"Hey, Sangre, want us to take care of Dewey Yang?"

"Get Yang! Get Yang! Get Yang!"

Sangre raised his hands to quiet the multitude. "That ain't how I do things. That ain't the way I want to win. We win fair and square, you hear me?"

"Get Yang!" shouted someone in the crowd who rather liked the idea.

"Anybody touch Dewey Yang, they gotta deal with me. I ain't running for nothin' if he gets touched. You vote. You line up votes for Sangre and *we* will win. If we win, we get everybody's respec'; if he win, *he* get everybody's respec'."

Capoletti had scheduled the nominating convention for the next day. The children's-theater aficionado added the little touches: the lights, the staging, the microphones, the banners, and the rest. Capoletti used his magic to turn a play into a major production.

When the classes on the fourth, fifth, and sixth grades paraded into the auditorium the next day, everyone felt the drama and excitement. Every class had its own banner. The most partisan students carried homemade banners. Candidates, their campaign managers, children employed by Capoletti at the entrances and exits, and safety-squad members milled around the edges of the crowd. Even teachers seemed enthralled.

The lesser candidates and their backers spoke first. From the first row you could see beads of sweat on the foreheads of the nominees. Hands trembled as each of the speakers in turn addressed the crowd. After each speaker, Capoletti played band music over the loudspeakers. Finally, after the last of the vice-presidential candidates had made his speech, Mark Lee took the podium to introduce Dewey Yang.

"Good morning. Dear members of the student government, my name is Mark Lee. I am most grateful and honored to be here today. I am here to introduce a favorable candidate for president of the student government of P.S. 126. Before I introduce him, I would like to say something that I hope you won't mind. I hope you vote for the best candidates for the student government like Dewey Yang.

He has the ability to do his best now that the government is running. Thank you."

When Dewey walked onto the stage, the audience, clearly divided in its loyalties, responded with an even mixture of cheers and boos. Dewey, a picture of poise, raised his hands to quiet the crowd.

"My name is Dewey Yang. I'm running for president of the government of P.S. 126 Manhattan. But what is P.S. 126 Manhattan? Is this school just a building with a number, with people walking in and out of its doors? I want to make this school known as the best! We play sports, right? Is there anything against having school teams, uniforms and all? We can even challenge other schools! We're a school together, not separated. We have to prove that we're a strong student body! Do you know what that means? That means Student Power! That's what we need here! Students should have a voice!"

His remarks brought cheers from the audience. Student Power had become one of the key phrases of the campaign. No one knew exactly what it meant, but then very few political slogans are designed to have an exact meaning. When the cheers quieted down, Dewey continued.

"I'd like to thank our convention and Mr. Capoletti for creating the superb constitution that you have adopted. But many things have been left out of your constitution. And it will be up to this first government to complete that constitution and to add the rights of the students. You need someone with experience, someone that will do things for you. I am that someone. Vote for me and this school will be made the best. Today is a very important day of our school history; today is election day. Vote for me and improve this school. I have been to many classes to campaign. If I did not get to your class, please vote for me anyway. I need your vote to help me to help the school. It's your vote. Use it correctly. Vote for me."

The next student to take the platform was David Lord.

"Hi, my name is David. I am Marlin's representative. How did you like Marlin's parade yesterday? Good, right? If you vote for Marlin for president, I know he will be a good president. I think if you gave Marlin a chance, he could be a good president. I don't have much to say. But vote for Marlin for president. Now, here is Marlin SANGRE!"

A cheer went up from the crowd. Marlin went to the podium and tested the microphone. "I just wanna make sure you hear me. Thanks, David. I don't have much to say. I am Marlin Sangre. If I am elected president I will obey the laws and you obey them also. If you want me to be president, I expect you to obey the laws of our government. If anyone sees a fight, just don't stand there and say, 'Go on, hit him good'—stop it.

"I don't want this school to become one of enemies. I want all of us to be friend. Also, please listen to your teacher. When there are fights, a lot of you safety-squad members just stand there and look on. Do something. Just don't stand there. I could name five of the safety squad who do a good job—Palito, Yin-Yang, Kai and Dennis and Sam. Lots of others play and dance all the time. Also, many of you think it's fun to play with the firebell. If you keep playing with the firebell, one of these days you gonna be dead. Yesterday I heard firebells. Someone is not obeying the law. Please think before you pull the firebell. Like they say with the matches, think before you strike. Yesterday the kids in the parade hit Dewey. I stop it. We went to exit three. The kids said to say a speech. I said it is like a game, but I play fair. When I play a game, I want to win. And this game, I want to win it fair and square. This game not over yet. But this game I am going to win without no fighting. Peace, brothers!"

It was not what he said that moved them. And then again, it was. When Sangre finished, the audience rose and gave its thunder to him. Mrs. Parsen and Mrs. Salling were dabbing their eyes with Kleenex. "Did you ever hear anything like it? Oh, my God, I'm crying."

A day before the election the *Junior News* published an interview.

AN INTERVIEW WITH DEWEY YANG

Dewey Yang 6–415 is a candidate for President.

Q. What do you promise?

A. I cannot promise anything if I do not know our school

budget. But if I knew, I would have the curtains repaired and get better school supplies.

Q. Why should you win?

A. I would like to repair this torn apart school. If I win, this school will be repaired. I want to win that's why.

The Monday following the election, a special edition of the *Junior News* announced the results.

DEWEY WINS PRESIDENCY BY 3 VOTE MARGIN 177–174
10 STUDENTS ABSTAIN FROM VOTING

The legislature, directed by Dewey Yang, spent the remainder of the school year trying to perfect the constitution. Particular attention was paid to making the court system function. At its last meeting in June, the legislature passed the following resolution:

Resolved, that we set up a court system. Each class will have its own court. Anybody who wants to sue someone in another class uses the grade court. Anybody who wants to appeal a decision by the court in a class, appeals to the grade court. The legislature is the court that you appeal to last if you don't like the decision of the grade courts.

9. The Judicial System

After Miss Markowitz had decided to return to school to complete her graduate work in psychology, Riva Thel took her place. The moment she walked into the room, she realized she had never seen a class like this one. Children had special jobs at special pay scales. Other children had stores, and regular times when they opened. She felt like a tourist in a foreign city. Riva, who went to law school at night, was delighted but stunned to discover students settling their differences in a court of law. "My husband won't believe this. Never!" As the class most experienced with the Society School program, as well as the most experienced with courts and law, Thel's class, not surprisingly, called the year's first trial.

The burgeoning commerce in Thel's class led her students to create credit cards to facilitate transactions during the daily fifteen-minute period in which the class "opened store." They behaved naïvely at first, giving credit to everyone who asked. It was only a matter of time before someone bought more goods than she could pay for. Given Julia's difficulties and her interest in owning new things, it should have been equally obvious to us that she would be the one to do it.

Julia ran out of money the fourth week. The amount she spent exceeded the total amount she took in selling goods in her own store and from other sources. Her creditors, caught unawares, reacted as merchants would anywhere. They screamed. They ran to the teacher for justice. They tried to repossess articles they had sold. Finally, they demanded that the contents of her store be auctioned off and that the proceeds from the sale be distributed among them.

Riva responded to their demands with an indulgent smile. "Wait! This is something a court should settle. The court should decide what's fair for Julia to pay."

"A trial!"

The merchants to whom Julia owed money gathered together and chose from among themselves someone to argue their case in court. Because Julia had few assets, the court appointed a lawyer to defend her and asked Riva Thel to foot the legal bill. Riva agreed.

"Hear ye! Hear ye! The court is now in session. Case of Julia vs. June, Lee, Parks, and Bo."

Marilyn Harp looked for the court assistant. "Read the charge."

"Yes, Your Honor. Julia is charged with buying things from stores with her credit card and could not pay. The people who sold her stuff want their money."

"How does Julia plead?"

Bruce Long got to his feet. "We plead guilty. Julia didn't know what she did."

Marilyn Harp looked at the defendant, who was watching her intently. "In that case the court has to figure some way to make Julia pay. She have any money, Bruce?"

"Three dollars maybe."

"How much does she owe?"

"She owes me thirty dollars ME."

"And me ten dollars . . ."

"And *me* ten . . ."

"How much all together, Sha Nang?"

"All together?" Sha Nang took out a pad and conferred with each of the children he represented. He wrote down what each said and then added up the amounts. "All together a hundred fifty dollars."

"Julia, will you pay off what you owe?"

Julia crossed her arms in front of her and put on a sullen face. "Ain't got no money."

"Then will you give back what you bought?"

"Lost it," she growled.

"Your Honor, some of the stuff was food. She probably ate it."

Marilyn frowned. Then she turned to Mrs. Thel. "What do we do?"

"I can tell you what big people do. When someone goes broke, the people owed money ask a court to declare bankruptcy. If the court does, it usually orders the sale of any property the bankrupt party owns. They set up an auction. The money from the sale gets divided up among the people she owes. Sometimes a court will garnish wages. That means a certain amount of the salary a bankrupt person earns the rest of the year goes to his creditors—to the people Julia owes money. A third thing sometimes happens. The court sometimes orders the bankrupt person to give back the property purchased."

"Okay. Everybody heard. Now Bruce and Sha Nang come up to the bench. I want to hear what you think would be the best way to do it," said Marilyn.

Bruce and Sha Nang approached the front of the room. Sha Nang looked back at the merchants he represented and scratched his head.

"Well, Bruce, say what's on your mind."

"Your Honor, Julia is the poorest kid in the class. Now, I admit she did wrong. And it would be wrong for her to get away free. But it wouldn't be so good either if she got made to pay—or maybe got fined. She'd get poorer. Wouldn't be nice to her feelings. She always lose—and it don't help nobody for her to lose more."

"What about you, Sha Nang?" Marilyn glanced at him.

"Bruce says right. But we still don't like it. She should pay something. Otherwise everybody will become bankrupt."

Marilyn ponded her gavel on the table. "This is the court's decision. Julia owes a hundred fifty dollars. She pay seventy-five dollars future money. What do you call it?" she asked Mrs. Thel.

"Garnish."

"Garnish Julia seventy-five dollars. The other seventy-five the whole class pays one dollar each. That's thirty-one dollars. That leaves forty-four dollars. That means that Sha Nang, June, Lee, and Charlie Parks, you lose $11 each. I decided this way because it's not fair you be the only ones Julia don't pay. But I also think you should remember not to let people who have no money charge it. I also think Julia has a little money. It's not good that one person be so poor."

Torts

In addition to adjudicating breaches of credit contracts, many classroom courts paid considerable attention to torts—cases in which some injury was done by one student to another. In one sixth-grade classroom, a student absent from school for three days returned to find that someone had raided the belongings in his desk. After several inquiries, Marlin learned that Rita, one of his favorite enemies, had been seen with paper belonging to him.

During the lunch hour, Marlin Sangre looked for Rita in the lunchroom, found her, and accused her of stealing from his desk. Rita denied the charge and showered Marlin with curses. But for the intervening arm of a parent aid, the two might have clawed each other to pieces. Taking a cue from goings on in other classrooms, Marlin approached his teacher with a request.

"Mrs. Sallin, I want to sue Rita. She stole from my desk and she cursed my mother. I almost beat her ass. Miss Dubin said sue her—so I'm gonna do that instead."

Mrs. Sallin looked at Marlin with not a little displeasure. She wasn't sure about the court system. She decided to give in, because she recognized that not to do so meant sanctioning the alternative—namely, Marlin taking his rage out on Rita's behind.

"Who's going to be your lawyer?" asked Mrs. Sallin somewhat disdainfully.

"Me. *I'll* be my lawyer."

"You can't be your lawyer. You're doing the suing. You have to find someone to argue the case."

"All right. I'll get someone from Mrs. Thel's class, one of them smart Chinamen."

Mrs. Sallin sat back in her chair. She could see how worked up Marlin had become. "Might as well go along with it," she said. "Get two of their judges, one boy, one girl. That way it'll be fair."

"You give me a note," Marlin demanded. "Otherwise, that teacher won't let them out."

Sallin scribbled something on a piece of paper and then looked. "I've written here that the trial starts day after tomorrow. That gives you tomorrow to prepare your case." Marlin began to move away. "I also wrote for two lawyers—one for Rita!" shouted Sallin after him.

"So?" said Marlin, leaving the room.

"I just wanted you to know."

Preparations for the trial began at once. A jury was selected by the simple device of asking for volunteers who thought they would be fair. Marlin and Rita were given the right to challenge any of the jurors. Neither of them did.

Two days later, a three-day courtroom drama, pitting Bruce against Sha Nang, began. Sha Nang opened for Marlin's side with what soon became a standard question, "What did you see?"

Witness after witness answered. But no one had actually seen Rita remove paper from Marlin's desk. One witness said she saw Rita "acting like she done something wrong." Another said she thought she saw something in Rita's desk that belonged to Marlin.

Then began the cross-examination. "Could someone put Marlin's papers in Rita's desk without her knowin' it? How 'bout you? Were you in school that day? You good friends with Marlin?" Bruce pulled apart the sometimes contradictory answers throughout the afternoon.

The next day Sha Nang called Rita to the stand.

Bruce objected. "You can't make her testify against herself."

"Get outa here!" shouted Marlin. "Let her tell the truth!"

"I object, Your Honor!"

Almost before the words tumbled out of Bruce's mouth, Rita had moved to the witness stand.

"I ain't afraid to talk. I'll tell you what happened."

Bruce folded his arms and sat down. He was angry. Who was running the trial, anyway?

When Rita finished telling her story, Sha Nang began the cross-examination. Rita had contradicted herself and Sha Nang found the weak links in her story. As for Bruce, he listened to her in utter amazement. The story Rita told the court had only the faintest resemblance to the one she had told him. The discrepancies infuriated Bruce almost as much as the thought of not being able to run the defense. He had never lost a trial, and he was proud of it. His client had tricked him. He felt ridiculous. When Rita finished giving her side of the story, Bruce rose with a look of foreboding.

"Your Honors, I want to get off this case. How can you be someone's lawyer when they don't tell you the truth?" He shook his head, put his papers in his briefcase, and walked out. A thunderous cheer rose from Marlin's supporters.

The next day the jury brought in a guilty verdict. After much debate and after an assertion by Mrs. Sallin that the "court couldn't make a sentence stick anyhow, so it's all for nothing," the court suspended Rita's cafeteria privileges for a week, forcing her to go home for lunch.

"Don't worry, Mrs. Sallin," Marlin said with a victorious smile. "I guarantee she do her time."

Teacher on Trial

Shortly before one of the most unusual cases went to trial the *Junior News* published a set of legal guidelines to help courts develop procedures that were fair.

MICRO-SOCIETY TRIALS

In the Micro-Society you can be brought to a trial if you do something that harms someone else or if you do something that destroys property.

> Anyone who gets hurt can "bring charges against" the person who hurts him.
>
> If you think you want to sue someone, talk to your teacher about it.
>
> If charges are brought against you by someone else, this is what happens:
>
> (1) The person who is bringing the charges will give you a summons to appear in court. The summons must be signed by the teacher or a judge.
>
> (2) It is very important that you get yourself a good lawyer who can defend you. You can get a lawyer from another room if you want to. If you cannot afford a lawyer, you can ask your teacher, or Mr. Bosch, or Mr. Richmond, or Mrs. Dubin to help you get one.

It almost seemed intentional. No sooner had these guidelines been established than they were put into practice, only this time a student sued, of all people, a teacher—namely, me. The same newspaper published the circumstances that had led to the trial.

> MR. RICHMOND'S STORY
>
> Mr. Richmond was taking a class down the stairs and E—— was running down the stairs. Mr. Richmond put his hand out to stop him. Mr. Richmond accidentally caught his chain with his hand.

Another article in the *Daredevil News* described the first day of the proceedings.

> TRIAL CONTINUES by Liza
>
> The trial was held Feb. 24, 1972. E—— is suing Mr. Richmond. There were six people in the jury. This is how they were chosen. They were asked to go up and were asked questions by the lawyers. E——— was asked to go up and sit down. He was asked a question by the prosecutor and the defense lawyers. The chain was broke. He wants $1.00 in US money.

Channel 5 came to cover the event. The publicity could have stymied the participants, but it didn't. Under the glare of lights, witnesses were called, heard, and recorded. The proceedings became quite heated since such different interpretations were put on events.

When the judge, Phil Ware, finally instructed the jury on what it could find, tension ran high. The jurors deliberated for about ten minutes, then returned to a hushed room. The Channel 5 camera crew, straining to pick up the drama, panned to faces, to nervous hands, and to my nervous vibrating feet. The foreman rose.

"We find Mr. Richmond and E—— both at fault."

A lot of people wanted to know what that meant.

"It means," said Ware, "that I throw them both out of court. Case dismissed!"

These courtroom sagas, and the dozen others like them, represent tentative steps toward a new approach to school conflict and its resolution. Peer courts by themselves accomplish fairly limited objectives. They can provide some measure of catharsis to the wronged parties. They stimulate community attention that can serve to deter a certain amount of wrongdoing. Some will argue that the penalties courts impose on wrongdoers deter criminal acts as well. But evidence in both society and school seems to give less than strong support to this statement.

Other, more educative benefits can be derived from court and legal systems located in the schoolhouse. In traditional schools, disciplinary issues and civil matters rarely receive the focus they should. They are handled as nuisances rather than as educational opportunities. Rational debate, group study, and even reading and writing on issues of momentous importance to the student culture receive hardly a nod from those who decide what the classroom curriculum will be. Notwithstanding, the P.S. 126 experience suggests that the minor conflicts that crop up in school often awaken keen and abiding interest in students, and that this interest can be used to fuel development of the academic and social processes.

Similarly, disciplinary issues are often settled, traditionally, through punitive means in the interest of quickness. Not only does this leave the offender with little opportunity to defend himself or explain himself, it gives the offended party no opportunity to vent and legitimize his anger. He discovers he has offended only authority, not his own community, which, in turn, implies one social contract with those in command and another with his peer community. As a result, students can be, at once, the bane of authorities and the idols of their peers.

Thus we see distrust and alienation from our legal processes beginning in school. Schools like P.S. 126 spend a disproportionate amount of energy obtaining student compliance to adult commands, playing out sagas of crime and punishment, and maintaining existing patterns of authority. This energy expenditure, if it nets some successes, also produces failures. Students learn many unintended lessons in school. They probably learn more from the structure of the school than from the curriculum. If that structure promotes and is hospitable to arbitrary and authoritarian behavior, then that structure eventually promotes either blind acceptance of authority or serious estrangement from it. Neither, it seems to me, serves the long-range objectives of a sound education process.

In such schools even the academic curriculum becomes a tool of social control. Instead of injecting excitement into school activity with materials, novel experiences, and trips, teachers tend to standardize and routinize classroom life. They do so because experience has taught them that it is easier to chill hot spots when you know exactly what every child is supposed to be doing. But this drive to be in control, even if it has short-term satisfactions, can create problems in the long run. Children who are bored by school are more likely to liven it up by playing games of Uproar, Chip On My Shoulder, Clown, Stupid, Cops And Robbers, and Make Me, than those who are not.

Even granting the short-run value of the custodial approach (if you kick someone out of school, he gives someone else the headaches), school crime statistics seem to indicate clearly that police power does not work. Last year in New York City the school crime problem and the teachers' union led to the hiring of hundreds of security guards to protect teachers and students from harm. In P.S. 126 the school's three administrators, equivalent to three security guards, spent about 90 percent of their time on discipline and discipline-related functions. And that doesn't even tell the whole story. About half the teachers in P.S. 126 receive classroom assignments that call for an inordinate number of custodial responses from the teacher. Despite all this police power, the number of disturbances in P.S. 126, and in schools like it, has grown steadily. The number of windows being broken, the number of assaults, the number of teacher beatings, the number of fires, fire alarms, etc., in schools across the country have not diminished. At best, police power is a holding action. At worst, it communicates the willingness of educators to do more of what we do so well: give wrong answers to the right questions and right answers to the wrong questions.

The spiraling school disturbance statistics may point to something more profound than a refusal by students to accommodate themselves to legally constituted authority. They could suggest a rapid decay of the formal legal conventions operating in school. It might have been possible, once upon a time, for teachers to assume all the authority roles in their classrooms. Offenses against the code of conduct were few and far between. Under these circumstances, teachers could be legislator (lawgiver), judge (law applier), policeman (law enforcer), paddler (punishment giver), and sometimes plaintiff and witness, all rolled into one. In recent years, the convention that said these roles could be assumed by one person has been made increasingly unrealistic by the sheer volume of disciplinary infractions.

From a different perspective, the decay of formal legal conventions may be seen as the growth of a dual system of authority: one formal, the other informal. In the face of competing demands from peers and from adults for compliance, students inclined to pledge fealty to the network that promises them the best assurance of survival find themselves in a muddle. On one side stand teachers, armed with demerits, detentions, suspensions, and expulsions, calling for one kind of behavior. On the other side, the student culture, threatening its own forms of isolation or straightforward body blows, commands compliance with its wishes. In their attempts to control students, statutes in states like New York limit teachers to psychological measures of control. You can shame a student before 300 children in an auditorium, but you can't, legally, slap his face, though in some communities physical punishment is permitted by law. In the peer group, no laws of prohibition apply. For where a hierarchy of muscle exists, a high incidence of physical force accompanies it.

Against this hierarchy of muscle, the school posits its authority and offers its sanctuary. In doing so, school officials make implicit promises and explicit payoffs: "Study long and hard and you will prosper." Unfortunately, the payoff for this promise takes a long time to materialize. Kids know it and discount it accordingly. If it takes twenty years of schooling to get a bicycle, most will take their chances stealing one. And whether our hypothetical student decides to take the bike or not, teachers hand out grades, service badges, and recommendations as a down payment on the future. If the press of relative poverty becomes particularly severe one year, it should surprise no one to see students devalue promises, down payments, and, ultimately, the wishes of school officials. Instead of enlisting in the army of those graduating into the promised land, they enlist in the faction of their peer group that offers the best chances in the here and now.

Instant solutions to the decay of legal conventions exist. If the state empowered school officials to expel students permanently for misconduct, as in some cases they can and do, the triumph of traditional authority over decay and peer-compliance mechanisms might submerge the opposition for quite a while. The "if you don't like my rules, get out" approach, however, creates its own headaches. Expellees have to be expelled to somewhere. Put them out on the street and more than likely some will soon become wards of the police department. When we set up custodial schools and incarcerate the expellees, graduates of such institutions will more often than not use the experience to improve on techniques that terrorize the rest of us.

A few teachers succeed in finding temporary solutions. They assert their prerogatives by exercising their personal charisma, along with the traditional sanctions available to them. Some even win a modicum of calm by skillfully manipulating the peer-compliance mechanisms that threaten them. Others succeed in convincing students that their best interests are being served by school. Notwithstanding, even the best of these teachers, at one time or another, finds her castle besieged. If persuasion, screams, and personal charisma fail, even the best-prepared lord may be tempted to use the whip instead of reason.

Suspension and expulsion offer slightly different forms of temporary relief. In New York, principals have the right to expel a student from school for a week twice in a given school year. After that, the only way to remove a troublesome student from the school is to initiate a court action. Obstacles to such actions are so overwhelming and time-consuming that few are even attempted. It is rumored that judges like to throw school discipline cases out of court for insufficient evidence or on some technicality. Similarly, rumor among teachers has it that when judges receive reams with detailed acts of student misconduct, they dismiss the case as an obvious conspiracy against the child. And if you don't get beaten with too little or too much information, rumor says the case will languish in court until the problem graduates. School officials who accept this court lore are naturally loath to seek relief in the courts.

However, the inability of school authorities to obtain relief from the courts and from children they regard as troublesome has its roots in the more fundamental character of the school's relation to the children it serves. State compulsory-education statutes make it obligatory for children to attend school whether or not they want to be there. The same statutes oblige school systems to accept children. And although both measures can be defended on progressive grounds, the negative consequences of compulsory education are apparent. Chief among these is that obligatory schooling nurtures a society of captives, in which children "do their time," and in which adults become infected with fatal authoritarianism.

The limited options available, the obstacles to extending them as solutions, and the statute that compels school attendance produce a relation between students and teachers that approaches indenture. Paralleling custodial systems found elsewhere, overt or disguised attempts by the under class to take its captors captive become characteristic of the transactions between students and teachers. In response, the overlords of the custodian regime play out the parts of masters intent on obtaining respect for themselves in the role they play.

We can no longer view disciplinary infractions as isolated incidents of terrorism. Teacher feudalism has broken down. A street ethic, more primitive and in some ways more brutal, daily challenges the right of teachers to reign, and the power and efficacy of punitive forms of control. To date school systems have dealt with the phenomenon of school crime by prescribing larger and larger doses of police power. Those prescriptions do not make schools better places or even safer places to be, at least not in the long run. They simply raise the likelihood of alienation and prove the bankruptcy of power imposed from above. If we are to stem the decay of legal convention, schools must play an educative role and construct rather than suppress. Schooling must come to mean society building and that, in turn, means that schools must encourage students to enter explicit social contracts with people and with institutions.

To say it differently, schools must address the issues of alienation at every level that produces neurotic forms of human behavior: alienation of self, estrangement from other selves, closed behavior and distrust among people in organizations and between people and organizations, and social deviance in the even larger sense. At each one of these levels, students should have the experience of working out a reasonable model for the resolution of difficulties they encounter. The model should include a way of analysis, a model of what is, a model of what could be, and a practical sense of how to get from one to the other. Most of my own proposals for dealing with alienation at the four levels mentioned above with respect to schools still require the benefit of practice and research. Thusfar, they have only taken shape in a loose sense at the level of theory, and have therefore been relegated to sections II and III of this volume, "The Model," and "The Theory."

10. The Academic Society

P.S. 126, like other public schools at least in theory, offers an academic program that emphasizes the basic skills. The Micro-Society approach did all it could to enhance this focus. The newspapers we published were full of student-created word games, arithmetic and crossword puzzles, editing and spelling games, riddles, and reading material. Individual classrooms undertook writing projects that included the writing of comic books, short stories, legal briefs, scripts for puppet theater, and letters to students in other classrooms. One teacher paid his students a dollar for every word they formed with a given set of letters. Another paid students for adding suffixes to prefixes or prefixes to suffixes as a part of word-making enterprise.

Plans were developed to program books in the school library so that students who read on their own or who used the library would be able to obtain an independent income from that source. The plan called for each student to write one question that showed he had understood what the book was about, and to answer all questions prior readers had written. The librarian was to pay the reader $5 for developing a useful question and $5 for each correct answer to the questions posed earlier.

Late in the second year, at the principal's behest, I involved five classes on the fourth, fifth, and sixth grades in the Great Reading Race. To create the race, we posted five charts in the school lobby.

On each chart we posted the name of every student in a given class on a bar graph that pictured the weekly gain in income for each student. Together with the reading specialist, we developed a sheet of price recommendations for teachers. Students using SRA materials, for example, were paid one dollar for completing each one of the first ten panels with an accuracy level of 80 percent, $2 for the next ten, $3 for the next ten, and so on. Similarly, students received a dollar for each page they completed in the basal reader workbook series used in the school. Similar steps were taken with other materials.

At the end of each week I collected Reading Race tally sheets from the five participating teachers and posted the changes on the bar graphs. At the end of the fourth week of the race, the ten individual leaders were awarded prizes and the class with the best over-all performance was given a party. One of the interesting side effects of the race was the parent interest it aroused. Mothers who saw the charts began encouraging their students to take work home. It was a kind of feedback monitoring of in-school performance that had always eluded them. For some students, it brought school and home into phase; both emphasized development of basic skills. For others the double pressure must have been a pain in the neck.

I can't fairly describe the excitement the Great Reading Race generated. Children love a competition. Although some visitors to the school scoffed at the idea of competition, not a single person on the staff did. Classroom veterans rarely scoff at anything that works, and the Great Reading Race stimulated a great deal more reading than other strategies had.

Tutorial Program

Mr. Kowalski, a disciplined and energetic teacher, decided to explore the possibility of using the school currency to develop a tutorial program. He began by putting an advertisement in the *Junior News.*

TUTORIAL PROGRAM

> There are some boys and girls who need lots of help in reading and they find it difficult to work by themselves. Five girls from my class that is 5–443 volunteer to help other people. The volunteers are Judith, Genia, Mey La, Dedra, and Me Ling. The volunteers enjoy helping others. They try to help others to do better. The people that are being helped enjoy it too.

The success of this initial effort persuaded Kowalski, who was very much interested in the problems of the non-English-speaking and of poor readers, to broaden the tutorial effort.

Under the auspices of the Children's University and with the cooperation of other teachers, he selected thirty of the poorest readers in the school for extra reading help. Half the selectees were recent arrivals from Hong Kong who were just beginning to cope with the English language. The other half had a variety of reading difficulties.

Kowalski began organizing the tutorial program around the core group already working with him. They became his team leaders. With several periods of instruction in the teaching of reading and several weeks of supervised tutorial work behind them, Kowalski's tutors ventured to the best reading classes to recruit students for reading tutorial jobs. Of the fifty or so applications reviewed, thirty children were chosen after extensive student-conducted interviews.

At the first meeting of the tutorial class, Kowalski described how the tutorial program would work. "I'm going to give every one of the children receiving tutoring a scholarship of one hundred Micro-Economy dollars a week. With this money you can hire the ones giving the help. In other words, the children who get the tutoring can choose whom they'd like to hire. I will give you the money to hire whomever you like. If someone doesn't do a good job, that's it—fire them. Does everyone understand?"

A tutor raised her hand. "You mean we work for them? Not for you?"

"That's right. You help them with their reading and they help you earn your living."

During the months that followed, Gene Kowalski continued to improve on the organization of the tutorials. He divided the sixty students into ten sections, leaders in charge of each section, and distributed the sections throughout two rooms. With the help of a second teacher, he supervised the tutors in this effort to provide slow readers and Chinese-speaking children with help.

Everyone regarded the program as one of the solid centers of activity in the Society School. Particularly impressive were the relationships that grew between tutors and tutored as a result of their cooperative experience. Some attributed its success to Kowalski's innovation: allowing the have-not readers to hire the reading-haves and pay them. However, a large part of the credit must go to Kowalski for having taken the trouble to build an organization and for having invented one whose fabric suited his purpose exactly.

Math Business

Economic activity contributed significantly to the school's arithmetic program, as will have been already apparent. Nearly every class had a bank, and every student a bankbook. Many students had checking accounts and every student received wages in check form. Students counted their money frequently. Many kept account books. Two dozen or more students worked, at one time or another, in the management of a bank. Others became account secretaries for teachers. Arithmetic skills, aside from computation, found application in various roles. Students constructed houses and learned to draw diagrams and measure area. Bonds, interest rates, teachers using money to illustrate mathematical concepts—fractions, decimals, division, etc.—all seemed to be ways to apply mathematics.

During the course of the year I developed some arithmetic games to reinforce basic computation skills. Through the following advertisement in the *Junior News* I located two groups of children to pilot it.

> WANTED: Students to make math materials for distribution.
> I supply the raw materials, you supply the labor. Negotiate

contract. Contact Mr. Richmond: 3 students who have formed a Math Company.

After several meetings in which we discussed the best way to go about organizing teams in the classroom, how to manipulate the materials, and how to score the games, I selected four captains in each class to launch a math tournament. Each of the captains received a salary of $50 a week.

It was my intention to try through this device to induce children to help each other. The four captains were the best math students in Phil Ware's class. Each was permitted to select the members of his team in a manner similar to the way children choose teams for playground games. Each captain spent three weeks training his team with the raw materials. At the end of the training period, we announced the beginning of the tournament and advertised the prizes: a voucher for each member of the winning team worth $4 U.S.

At the tournament's end the team with the highest score came to me with its point totals and said, "Now we want our prize."

I smiled at the motherly attitude Sophia, the team captain, displayed toward her victorious brood. "Okay, what do you want?"

"We want the money. You give us cash, huh?"

I scratched my head as I considered the consequences of acceding to this proposal. "No. You choose what you want and come and get me after school. I'll go with you. I need receipts, proof of purchase."

"All right. It's better," said Sophia, speaking for the whole group.

A week later Sophia, along with three of the girls on her team, approached me. "We're ready. We go to Pearl's Clothing Store. She got nice things. Billy, he wants a basketball or something. He see you separate, okay?"

"Okay."

That afternoon I followed Sophia and her cohorts to Pearl's Clothing Store, a small shop with ceiling-to-floor shelves piled high with children's clothing of every possible description.

"Why this store?" I asked Sophia.

"We like it, and Pearl, she bargain. We get a good thing for our money."

I spent the next half hour watching Sophia and her friends examine various articles of clothing, each time asking for a price and each time reacting to whatever Pearl said with a show of bitter disappointment.

"Come on, Pearl, you know me. All we got is four dollars each." Sophia eyed me surreptitiously. "Can you give us more, Mr. Richmond?"

I smiled, but shook my head.

"'Then, Pearl, it's got to be you. You gonna give us a break. We come here, didn't we? We spend our money with you, Right?"

"Ain't she something?" said the old woman. "All right. You bother me all day. These two things together worth five dollars and half. Take them. Four dollars. Get out of my hair."

And so the bargaining—and the applied arithmetic lesson—went. Whenever a member of the team needed support in her negotiations with Pearl, Sophia would step in with a "Come on Pearl," or "Give my friend a better price." And with this persistence Sophia and her friends wore down the shopkeeper's resistance.

On the way home, I found myself thinking with some surprise: They bought clothing!—almost as if I, who believe children capable of almost anything, had just rediscovered that they had common sense.

"What Do You Mean, You Missed Math This Afternoon?"

In our drive to create economic institutions in the school, it seems fair to say we made an effort to develop our own academic program. Since we possessed neither the curriculum materials to replace those in use nor the manpower to derive our own, we had no alternative but to integrate the Micro-Economy system with existing elements of the academic program. The efforts we made, however, implied a different relationship between academics and non-academics, as well as a shift in the ultimate purposes of the academic program.

Mrs. Thel, who had taken over Capoletti's old class from the departing Miss Markowitz, for instance, developed Commercial Street—a collection of stores along the back shelves of the classroom from which students sold artwork, stationery, toys, candy, soda, jewelry, and odds and ends. To facilitate transactions between storeowners and their customers, students developed a credit-card system. Every Friday the class would spend the entire afternoon totaling accounts, presenting customers with bills, collecting debts, and participating in various other activities requiring fairly rigorous computation skills. At the end of the very first Friday session, one of Riva's students, reviewing the day's plan always posted on the board, sidled up to her and whispered, "Mrs. Thel, we didn't have arithmetic this afternoon."

Riva smiled in disbelief. "Wai, you're a storeowner. How many accounts do you think you added up this afternoon?"

Wai looked puzzled.

"How many people bought things at your store last week?"

"Maybe fifteen."

"How many times did you buy something?"

"I think ten."

"That makes twenty-five math problems right there. Did you count any money?"

Wai nodded.

"And did you add up all the money people owed you and subtract what you owed, the way I told you?"

By then Wai was smiling.

"Now what do you mean, you missed math this afternoon?"

The Children's University

The Society School program produced other modifications in the academic program. For the most part, these arose in connection with the Children's University. Originally conceived as an effort to bring about the full and simultaneous participation of everyone in the fourth, fifth, and sixth grades, the Children's University linked students with teachers on a voluntary basis. Teachers advertised in a catalogue the courses they wanted to offer. Students submitted applications stating their preferences. Sarah and I matched supply and demand.

Once again the quality of the courses being offered varied considerably from room to room. Teachers, even when they designed their own courses, differed rather markedly in their ability to present material and involve students in activities. Some of the staff prepared inadequately. In general, however, courses were well received, and many of the staff enjoyed their contacts with other students in the school.

As with higher education, students distributed themselves unevenly throughout the course offerings. During the first semester, students chose their courses primarily in subject areas. However, by the third semester students seemed to be making their selections almost solely on their preference for the instructor offering the course. With respect to the UFT contract, we were obliged to recognize a ceiling on class size, so that no teacher accepted more than thirty-three students in a course. If more than thirty-three applied, we were sometimes able to produce a second section. Approximately 25 percent of the student body failed to get their first or second preference. All students received at least their third preference. On certain applications, the homeroom teacher wrote recommendations that influenced the student distribution process. For instance, if a teacher thought a student could use some extra reading help and it was his third selection, we gave special consideration to that student when we filled the roster for the reading tutorials.

During the first semester, the teachers at P.S. 126 offered the following courses: Russian Language, consisting of language study and exposure to Russian music, toys, and customs; Creative Writing and Illustrating; Anthropology, using the Education Development Center's curriculum "Man, A Course of Study"; Music, a course for which we supplied children with plastic recorders and with music sheets so they could learn rudimentary music theory; Algebra, a course dealing with basic elementary algebra for children interested in "advanced" mathematics; Yoga exercises, chants, a visit from an Indian yoga master, and some readings; Journalism, a course specially designed for those interested in working on the newspapers; Science, with simple experiments and a lot of shouting; and Law, for students interested in helping design the Micro-Society's legal system.

Many courses begun in the first term continued into the second. However, a number of teachers decided to offer something else. Russian gave way to the reading tutorial program described in the previous chapter. Mr. Gores, replacing a teacher who had declined to participate in the Children's University, offered Group Psychology. The course included group games, discourses on body language, plays, as well as discussions of what makes us do the things we do. Paul Bosch, the assistant principal, offered a course in drug education. Richard Sewall decided to launch an architecture course, in place of Political Theory. His students learned something about drafting and began constructing model houses—their favorite materials, cardboard, ice-cream sticks, and tongue depressors! Faith Dunne decided to forgo a second term of Yoga and decided, instead, to operate a school-wide Micro-Economy Real Estate simulation.

In the third term, other changes were made. With the coming of spring, both students and children felt the urge to be outdoors. So, in addition to the academic offerings, the faculty of the Children's University decided to acquiesce to student demands for an organized athletic program. Under the direction of Paul Bosch and with the collaboration of Dewey Yang, president of the legislature, two tournaments were established. The first was in punchball and the second in dodgeball.

At first we considered organizing teams along classroom lines, but after a careful discussion we decided to institute a pro-athlete-type draft. Captains were chosen for their athletic prowess and their ability to organize. On the first afternoon of the third term, all the would-be athletes gathered in a room to be chosen by captains for one of the five teams. One by one, every student in the room was assigned to one of the five teams. At the insistence of Bosch, the girls were separated out and allowed to form two teams of their own. For the next eight weeks each of the teams competed for the prizes, individual dodgeballs to be awarded every member of the winning punchball and dodgeball teams.

The Experience of Applied Intellect

Instead of writing composition exercises, children in the Society School pen letters, articles, and books for each other's benefit and consumption. Instead of limiting arithmetic study to its mechanics, students apply arithmetic concepts in pursuit of professional or business capacities; accountants, bookkeepers, taxpayers, and shopkeepers compute, while architects and city planners measure. Similarly, the reading program serves the developmental goals of school society: students read what other students write.

Despite the emphasis placed on primary experiences that contribute to the drama of building society in school, it seems only sensible to introduce secondary experiences that contribute to the same goal. Although only primitive and only a beginning, it seems conceivable that schools will eventually include subjects like architecture, medicine, law, business, government, psychology, anthropology, sociology, education, city planning, and engineering in their primary and secondary programs. In order to carry this off, however, support materials will have to be prepared and teacher training broadened with professional and service-industries experience.

Essentially, the Society School establishes a marketplace for primary and secondary experience within the school. A time may come when students will have to purchase admission to courses teachers offer in school. A time may also come when the school measures the demand for one course against the demand for another, the demand for one teacher's service against the demand for another's. And while few accountability tools now exist to evaluate a teacher's performance, it is barely conceivable that one of the indices that may one day be used will be some measure of the aggregate student demand for a teacher's services, computed over a stated period of years.

While imperfect, such a measure might at least establish who is in demand and who is not—and furnish an accountability review committee with the basic data it needs to assess teacher performance.

It is also necessary to provide students access to abstract intellectual process quite apart from the concrete social, political, and economic experience available directly through the model. A culture exists apart from school. Studying it enriches the individual and enriches his possible contribution to his immediate community. Similarly, a certain amount of time should be devoted to mastering the mechanics of reading, writing, and arithmetic, the keys to future learning. A number of educational inventors—Cureton, Gattegno, Bereiter-Engleman, to name only a few—have developed learning systems and teaching methods that allow children to unlock the meanings and sounds of words and numbers quickly and easily.

To say it differently, the Society School model moves in three directions at once. First, it attempts to remove what is least useful in the academic program in favor of direct experiences that are more useful. Second, it calls for a heightening of intellectual experience through an intense analysis of the theoretical issues that society building produces. Third, it also intensifies pure academics for those who want them. It does this by linking students to specialists in their interest areas who agree to participate in the consultant bank. As an extension of this principle, the model calls for a restructuring of the academic curriculum. Instead of tailoring the primary-school curriculum to be an oversimplified version of liberal-arts college curriculum, the Micro-Society approach links the experiences schools offer with general career categories. The implications this may have for the organization of the school program are profound. Instead of majoring in a discipline, students would put their energies into courses affiliated with their career interests. Those who did not know what their interests were would taste different experiences to see whether any seemed to their liking. Those interested in business could test this out; those interested in teaching could tutor; those who wanted to write or act could do so and find concrete reward.

So far, great emphasis in the Micro-Society school has been placed on the acquisition of knowledge through concrete experience. That is only one way to acquire knowledge, and sometimes it may be a very poor way to do so. Children from low socio-economic groups need to learn economics, politics, and social skills to survive. The Micro-Society approach provides students with insights into the political, economic, and social system. Still, if it continued to do only that, the children who became involved with the approach would continue to be deprived not of the physical necessities of survival, but of opportunities to enrich the life they led, and of awareness of what that would mean. It is, therefore, important to include at a theoretical level the arts, the humanities, the pure sciences, the social sciences in the school experience.

I would like to see elementary students cover school interiors, even exteriors, with murals, and schools develop theater companies, orchestras, puppet shows, ensembles, galleries, and the like. Similarly, I think that through the arts children can make important contributions toward improving the quality of neighborhood life by holding outdoor art exhibits and recitals, and by collecting and sharing neighborhood folklore.

In any student population there will be children inclined toward pure abstract thought, whether it take the form of science, philosophy, mathematics, or social theory. In addition to a school's general program in the liberal arts, students with special aptitudes for abstract thinking might be permitted to purchase with their scrip special tutorials from graduate or undergraduate students from nearby colleges or from interested parents.

Most important, all students, rich or poor, should have access to every level of intellectual experience. The Micro-Society will have engineers and bankers, politicians and philosophers.

PART II

The Model

11. The Model for Elementary School

The P.S. 126 implementation of the Society School closed on June 30, 1972, and did not reopen in September. The termination of the project occurred for many reasons, but the most persuasive was my estimation of the long-run prospects for building the Society School in New York. In nearly everyone's sight, we were golden. We mounted a production under difficult circumstances and the result produced virtually unanimous agreement on continuation. We received nation-wide publicity, endorsements from central administration officials, endorsements from the District 2 administrators; we even seemed likely to receive continued financial support from several foundations. Strong support existed among teachers and parents. So then, why did it end?

I recognized the P.S. 126 implementation for what it was: an improvisation that would never be more than that. True, our improvisation grew from a venture involving thirty people to one that included four or five hundred. True, the production at P.S. 126 had been the best to date. True, the per-capita cost had been far lower than any comparable program ($50 per student as compared to the $700 cost per student of the More Effective Schools program). And true, strong verbal support for the project came from every quarter.

However, to my mind, verbal support wasn't enough. I wanted

commitment. I wanted to build the Society School, not to continue a pilot program year after year. In recognition that I shared with the school system an obligation to teachers, parents, and children in the school, I offered to raise $5,000 to defray the cost of raw materials for student enterprises and school auctions. In return, I asked them to create a position in the school to administer the Micro-Society program. I would contribute my own time to the project until the new coordinator assumed full responsibility. The school system could not or would not respond. One high official in the school system said it plainly and none too proudly: "The system is committed to funding failure, not success. Everything I do to change that has failed. I haven't found a way out."

When New York failed to respond, I read that failure as an indication of the long-run prospects of the Society School in New York. Yes, it might have been possible to operate for another year or even two more years. However, the outcome would be the same. Our greatest successes would be turned into failure because the system itself had no way of incorporating success into its ongoing operations. I refused the bait and the trap, because I did not want to be caught in an untenable situation. Winning was not supervising a continual replay of our improvisations. I wanted to, and still want to, build the Society School—and research its possibilities. A sustained effort to do that and nothing else will suffice. To accept anything less would be the same as lighting a firecracker: a little light, a little heat, a big noise, and nothing after but the little memory of a bang.

An Overview of the Model

Each one of the experiences in society building helped mature and enrich the next. Taken together, Williamsburg, Astoria, Broad Jump, and P.S. 126 seem to provide the ground to sustain an effort to build a new model of primary schooling. It promises possibilities for secondary schooling as well. I have decided to call that model the

Society School or, alternatively, the Micro-Society approach. As an approach, it must be a dynamic process, one that will liberate students from a curriculum without any apparent fit to life, one that will orient students to jobs in the service industries and the professions, and one that will obtain for students a better appreciation of the world of experience. The process must have the power to penetrate the classroom and alter its way of life. In so doing, it must make the inmate-custodian culture operating in many traditional schools untenable. And although the connection with work bears emphasis, the model must also offer students opportunities to become involved in academic pursuits, in recreation, in civic projects, and other productive activity.

The rewards for such involvement can no longer be limited to "ends in themselves" payoffs. School reward structures must be broadened to include material goods as well as what I call spiritual commodities. The broadening of the payoffs must occur first, because it has always been unfair and inequitable to ask children who are have-nots to accept a currency (grades and commendations) that favors children who are haves. Second, it must occur because paying children for their work has agreeable benefits for educational institutions and children alike.

This broadening of the payoffs should not be confused by such epithets as "paying kids to learn." No such simplistic approach is intended. The payoffs for working in school fall along a broad spectrum. If a student chooses to work to produce, to work to get a material good, then we should not deny him permission to do so. Similarily, if some children favor non-material payoffs—i.e., a sense of their own competence, a certainty of their own worth, a mastery over their immediate environment, a sense of community—then these less extrinsic payoffs should also be available. It may even be that those who operate a Society School may decide to skew the payoffs toward spiritual commodities. No objection is raised here to such a procedure as long as students, obliged to manage their own material survival, have the right to select values consistent with their needs and are not to be "guilted" by middle-class people for doing so.

If this model had heroes, they might be called entrepreneurs. I do not limit this designation to the economic sphere. A model true to the Sangres, Deweys, Ramons, and Mannies of this world allows social and political entrepreneurs to emerge as well. For me, an entrepreneur is a man who makes history, someone who changes the world with his voice or ideas. I think children have the means available to make an impact on the world that lives inside what we call school. And I think understanding political, economic, and social behavior in that microcosm represents a considerable step toward mastering the world beyond the schoolhouse gate.

A process that produces economic, social, and political entrepreneurs must also convey enough information and enough feedback to students about the society, its institutions, and human interaction, for students to make intelligent assessments of themselves, of their experience, and of their capacities. The lessons learned through the model, from the medium and from the medium's message, must make accessible the knowledge and skills students need to survive. Schools must allow students who need and want to formulate and control their own destinies to do so. Those with the urge to innovate and to dream must be allowed opportunities to enact their dreams and ideas, in the face of practical considerations.

In the pages that follow, a model will be set forth on the supposition that children, who create a society of their own in school, need reach only a few steps beyond—possibly only to secondary school—and only a few inches inward to appropriate the power to transform themselves and their immediate environment. It is also set forth on the supposition that this Micro-Society approach will link students not only to the ongoing process of human history, but also to its past trends and experience. It is hoped that through this linkage students will discover the fundamental difficulties and blessings of the human condition, that they will analyze the fundamental causes of human alienation, and then affirm life in whatever form, in collective spirit or in individual imagination, it takes.

Micro-Economics

The first stage of the Society School is called Micro-Economy. During this first phase, students and teachers launch a developmental process through which they construct a society in a school. If schools now limit access to legitimate economic tools and institutions, both will become available immediately. First, the school will establish a system of currency. As an economic tool, currency functions as a medium of exchange, as a store of value, and as a unit of account. These functions make it possible for students to exchange goods and services, to establish a standard against which services and goods receive relative valuations, to represent debt (credit instruments), to store labor (savings and other forms of capital accumulation), and to plan, organize, and allocate human and other resources in response to priorities the school community may wish to establish.

As the second step in Micro-Economic development, the teacher, sometimes with the help of students, designs and implements a wage-price system. Such a system should be contoured to the economic, social, and academic goals established for each class. Thus, if a class has few children with reading and computation difficulties, it might place a premium on economic or social development. If serious behavioral problems exist, the stress will be placed on generating constructive activity. If serious reading problems exist, priority will be given to fostering growth in reading. Similarly, if teachers and parents value creativity, the incentive program will be organized to foster the arts, scientific discovery, and publishing enterprise. The model says allocate to a teacher a fixed sum of scrip based on the number of students she has in class. It leaves to the teacher and her students the task of developing a plan of expenditure.

After creating currency and defining the ways in which it can be acquired, the teacher introduces property. From the student's perspective, public schools are propertyless societies; all resources and things are owned and controlled by school authorities who operate as agents of the state; property is lent to students and retrieved after a period of time. In the Society School the evolution of property, as with currency, occurs gradually. Students can create property based on their local neighborhood, city, world, or just designate an ordinary space on a table or shelf as land. In elementary schoolrooms it is desirable to locate the map physically—i.e., shelf space around the room. Deeds are then created to permit transfers of property. In time, other kinds of property are desired as the school, now an agency for the production of goods and services, produces houses, essays, artwork, books, clothing, craft goods, curriculum materials, etc.

With a medium of exchange and wealth available, marketplaces where exchange of goods and services can take place are established. If past experience repeats itself, the first of these markets will probably be an exchange of land. To create a market, one needs a time (one hour twice a week) and a place (a large room) where buyers, sellers, or their representatives can come together to transact business. Together with currency and property, the land exchange satisfies a fundamental requirement for a simulation of a real-estate industry. All that is required to make that industry operate is a simple game mechanism that randomly "lands" students on deeded properties twice each week. As in *Monopoly*—also a simplified version of a real-estate industry—students rent to property owners. Rent is calculated as a percentage of the assessed valuation of the property. Those calculations are made by a student committee that develops its own criteria for assigning value to improvements that owners make on their property. The real-estate game is really very simple. Ten-year-old children can operate it without assistance from adults. But it can be made complex, almost as complex as "real world" real estate. The complexity depends entirely on one's willingness to sophisticate the experience.

Improvements can become, with proper encouragement and purpose, an important dimension of the economic system. A construction industry becomes possible. Typically, the classroom or school community decides what constitutes an improvement on property. The simplest kinds of improvements are: cardboard houses; compositions about the families who inhabit the property; artwork; and any other activities which all agree are constructive. More elaborate construction programs might require real-estate developers to conform to building codes, to submit building plans, and to use student architects, ecologists, cost analysts, contractors, civil engineers, structural engineers, landscapists, along with others affiliated with a construction industry.

With the growth in the diversity of occupational categories and complexity of a school economy, a market for labor will have to be organized. Simulated public employment agencies and private employment agencies form. These agencies publish help-wanted columns, recruit candidates for positions, provide employers with the vitae statements of applicants, help prospective employees write them, interview candidates, and assign them to jobs. For a start, the teacher might contract such an agency to screen applicants for classroom maintenance jobs, and help the process by teaching students how to write résumés. An employment agency might also carry out character investigations for public offices and present its findings to the hiring agency. In the traditional school, children have one role: student. In a Micro-Society, children are real-estate managers, brokers, transportation managers, auditors, accountants, model builders, draftsmen, painters and decorators, auctioneers, treasurers, teachers' assistants and bookkeepers, and so on. In the process they become students in the genuine sense—that is, they learn.

A financial market will likely be the next to form. Students will need to borrow money to capitalize their businesses. Students with excess funds will need places to invest them. Encouragement and energy will produce financial intermediaries. Experience suggests that a savings bank will form first. At a very early stage in Micro-Economy, students will want to secure some of their funds in interest-bearing savings accounts. The bank invests a fraction of these funds to make loans, to issue mortgages, and to invest in small businesses and real estate. Later a commercial bank may evolve, offering checking accounts and credit cards. As has been shown, these institutions provide incredible opportunities for doing "applied" arithmetic. Some teachers have suggested hiring accountants as bounty hunters, allowing anyone who audits an account to keep the value of any mistakes discovered. Eventually, although perhaps not until secondary school, older students may learn how to develop and operate computerized payroll systems. In time, a variety of other financial intermediaries may be expected to develop—i.e., insurance companies, savings-and-loan associations, credit unions, and investment companies.

The fourth kind of market one would expect to evolve is a commodities exchange. In the model proposed, goods and services appropriate to the interests and sophistication of the school population back the currency. Students can, therefore, exchange a part of their currency holdings for things they want and need. Monthly auctions may be held where records, clothing, books, school supplies, athletic equipment, refreshments are sold to the highest bidder. Alternatively, student government authorities may open a flea market on Friday afternoons where students can bring from home things they have found and repaired for sale. In poor communities, either arrangement has great virtue, since no formal means exists there for distributing obsolete goods among students. Although these markets fall short of compensating children for the misfortune of poor circumstances, at least it improves the access to things they want and relieves some of the necessity of acquiring them by less legitimate means.

A market may also be developed to distribute other kinds of goods. Student contractors who build houses need materials with which to build them. Someone must, therefore, gather and sell raw materials: cardboard, wood, metal, glass, plastic, paint, nails, paper, tools. Students entering the materials-supply business will allocate time to scavenging for materials, stripping wood off old furniture, collecting cardboard boxes, plastics, etc., as well as to the supplying of buyers. Some students may specialize in building the miniature houses, others in selling them. The number of small enterprises that may evolve seems to be limitless: greeting-card, newspapers, architecture, publishing, art, food, clothing, and plant and flower shops.

In addition to the market development, one may expect a major build-up thrust in the reading and computation areas. Students may concentrate on developing materials that document the experiences, skills, and events that contribute to the growth of school society. Development may also entail creating a student literature, through which the students of one generation can pass on traditions and expertise to the next, or chronicling the memories of old people and the history of the neighborhood. Each of these industries will help students learn more about themselves while they also learn to read and write.

Reading-industry businesses may attempt to program school library books for comprehension, or to create an independent reading program by programming school library books with an incentive system and thereby affording children extra income for unsupervised or leisure-time reading activity. Another thrust may develop materials that force students to raise and confront moral issues. Periodicals may develop, interested mainly in giving economic advice, or systematically exposing students to different political, social, and economic frameworks. Materials so produced may be made available to those who want them through sale or public subsidy.

Students may draw on a consultant bank, consisting of community businessmen and other professionals, to help devise technological guides for various kinds of enterprise building. It also seems likely that students and teachers engaged in this building will call on members from the community outside the school for help. In terms of the school Micro-Economy, parents, local businessmen, and retired business people will be invited to supply assistance in areas of their expertise. For example, children responsible for developing accounting systems for various groups and institutions cannot be expected to do it alone. The need for this and other kinds of technical aid foreign to the competencies of the traditional schoolteacher will necessitate the importation of people not heretofore affiliated with schools.

Some of the enterprises may draw information from the outside world. A news service, publishing enterprises geared to simplify and disseminate developments in mathematics, social science, teaching, politics, marketing, finance, ecology, etc., may contribute significantly to the deepening of the experience available in school. Students might also publish digests of important news and valuable articles appearing in professional journals in the greater society. Tutors in reading and in other subjects may develop markets for their services. As the experience has shown, the list of aids-to-reading businesses is probably endless: a post-office system, testing services, comic-book manufacturing, poetry sessions, student literature of all sorts, editorial services, curriculum development, etc.

Some critics of this model worry that children may be programmed too early for special occupational niches. Experience thus far suggests the reverse. The typical student attending a Micro-Society school who may average five to twenty income sources in a given year hardly over-specializes. Moreover, when compared to traditional schooling, the experiences available appear far more diverse. To academic activity the Society School adds a long list of work experiences. To single-lane success (or, more often, failure) in academic terms, the model adds other paths: income from employment, success in recreation activity, investment payoffs, and status and personal satisfaction for making civic contributions to school and its community.

Social Development

Social developments in the Micro-Society will probably be linked closely to various stages of economic growth. It seems fair to expect that in the early stages of the Society School, most investments in social activities (as opposed to economic activities) will be for the benefit of children attending the school. Experience says that this investment will center on the development of a comprehensive school athletic program, on the mounting of an interesting and pervasive cultural program, on making sure that arts programs provide the school with rich material, on introducing new academic courses through some device like the Children's University.

Energy will also be invested in evolving legal and other traditions. In the early stages of the Micro-Society, building efforts will center within. The social system, like the Micro-Economy, also faces a lack of expertise. Many of the social groupings will be newly formed. Many will not have traditions governing human behavior. Indeed, many of the organizations will be entirely new to children. Take the courts, for example. Few students—except those in trouble with the law—have any legal experience whatever while they are in elementary school. Few can even conceive what the social fabric of their own society is like. Since this may even hold true for teachers as well, it follows that the school will have to look beyond itself for guidance in the development of a whole spectrum of social institutions and programs, as well as their interrelationships.

As the Micro-Society matures, the school will integrate aspects of the local community—for example, ethnic traditions—with the traditions it evolves as a separate society. At more advanced stages still, students and student groups based in the school will explore ways and develop the means to contribute goods and services to communities and organizations operating in the shadow of the school. For example, it is at least conceivable that children may contribute time to the care of the elderly. It is equally conceivable that older children can participate in and operate recreation facilities after school hours. It seems even more likely that schools traditionally attuned to the task of producing literacy will focus on chronicling the history of their community and the origins of its inhabitants for publication and distribution. Such efforts may provide the basis for generating a folklore that by itself may knit people, scattered by urban society, together.

If it is foreseen that the social system of a Micro-Society will grow in these directions, problems surrounding that growth are also foreseen. Every society has its quota of conflict and its own ways of resolving it. Individuals quarrel among themselves, with others, with institutions, and even test the whole fabric of social relations we call society. At this writing the Society School model has little concrete to say about the sources, content, or anatomy of aggression. It is sufficient for the purpose here to locate conflict at four levels: self, interactions with other individuals, organizations, and society (collections of organizations and selves). Thus far, experience with the Society School and the instruments and organizations created to resolve human conflict has been very limited. And while there may be some advantage to speculating on how conflict on these levels might be handled, very little advantage would seem to derive from doing so here. Let it suffice to say that a great deal of developmental work remains to be done and that the model will not be complete until enough experience exists to complete it.

Notwithstanding, it seems useful to state some of the points that require additional work and thought. In drawing out the experience, and now in drawing out the model, an emphasis has been placed on providing individuals—in this case, children—with opportunities to manipulate their environment. In putting the stress on the exterior side of making losers into winners, little attention has been paid to personality theory or to human pathology. A complete model would require an interior perspective as well as this exterior one. Similarly, the Society School model would be improved considerably if it were linked to workable models of human interaction, of behavior of people in organizations, and of institutional behavior in society. A thorough exposition of this would require a book by itself.

Saying this makes it clear that the model needs additional work. It, like the experience, is struggling through an infancy characterized by experimentation, examinations of other practice and other theory, and many wrong turns. The directions these explorations take, however, have a singular purpose: to make what is abstract concrete, to replace what is merely theory with experience, and to bring both model and experience to a state of maturation and depth.

The caveats mentioned in the preceding pages notwithstanding, it does serve the purpose here to begin addressing the real issues raised in earlier sections of this volume related to compliance, authority, and various forms of alienating behavior. Since experience in this area has been so limited, what is said resembles more a hunch than a conviction. And since this area is such a sensitive one, the reader is urged to do what the writer, were he the reader, would do—namely, discard whatever seems to make the least sense.

If the Society School contributes to social theory in any way, it does so by positing several simple notions about schools. These notions assert that school environments can be created and manipulated in ways that support personal growth, that improve the quality of human interactions, that expose organizations and their mysteries years before they become instruments of human impotence and alienation, and that put children in a position to make social history. In applying these notions to conflict and to conflict resolution, the Micro-Society approach simply makes it possible for children to conduct their own experiments in social engineering. The Micro-Society approach, at the elementary-school level, gives children greater command of the school world. As a Micro-Society, that world has problems very similar to our own. Under present conditions, children do not address them. The model attempts to reverse this situation.

Dealing with Deviance and Other Kinds of Conflict

School organizations, parents, teachers, and other interested parties can be expected to impose certain criteria and limitations on student efforts or, for that matter, faculty-initiated efforts to cope with disorders. For instance, it would be natural to expect any model of compliance adopted by a school (1) to protect the children and teachers from serious acts of violence, (2) to defend school organizations against terrorism and disruption, (3) to reinforce constructive activity, (4) to help adults and children alike to understand their behavior, its origins, its structure, and its consequences, and (5) to conform to the special character of the school and the population it serves.

It would seem to me that a response to these criteria might follow certain principles. First, most experienced school people will agree that a clearly defined and consistent set of discipline and treatment procedures is better and more effective than an ill-defined one. Most would agree that treatment, where it is available, should precede discipline, on the simple ground that it is better to help a person to feel okay than it is to confirm his low opinion of himself and the problems such a self-estimation produce. Most educators would also agree that where alienating behavior continues and where the treatment process fails, institutions should be allowed to defend themselves against debilitation. Traditionally, that defense consists of some form of segregation.

In the same vein, most educators would prefer an active policy of compliance to a reactive one. One that is reactive singles out losers and can subvert healthy growth. Students should be made conscious of behavior, of its consequences, and of the theories propounded to explain it. Beginning in elementary school, children should start exploring the practice and theories of therapy, of behavior modification, and of traditional discipline in an effort to discover for themselves what works and what doesn't. It almost goes without saying that carrying off an exploration of these areas, let alone attempting to apply the best part of existing and proven psychological constructs, would require an ambitious effort to provide educators with the necessary materials and training for the task. Making such provision also requires social-relations theorists and practitioners to produce theory and develop practice that masses of people, rather than a select few, can understand and use. Therapy, behavior modification, and school discipline must be made understandable to parents if they are to be useful. A program that deals with personality disorders and with disorders that arise when people interact destructively has other criteria to meet in addition to those of clarity and simplicity. A program of therapeutic education must be available to children as well as to parents. Provision will, therefore, need to be made for simplifying the therapeutic vocabulary. Social theorists and practitioners will have to address their ideas, theories, and practice to lay people in a language they can understand and use.

Eric Berne and the school of therapy he founded, called Transactional Analysis, have addressed the problem of finding and developing a theory of personality and human interaction fit for mass consumption. While this theory may seem oversimplified to some, it certainly seems to have been useful to those teachers who have used it, and to students who until now haven't had the vocabulary to express their feelings or to understand them. Freud's id, libido, ego, and explanations of the psychological behavior implied aren't half as useful to the lay person as are explanations of human behavior rooted in ego states labeled "parent," "adult," and "child." These words are readily understood by children. Very little in the field of psychology competes for clarity and intelligibility with Berne's or Thomas Harris's diagrams of interactions between parent, adult, child ego states in different people. It seems at least possible that a day may come when children, adults, and therapists have equal access to the concepts and tools of behavior analysis.

Humor helps too. In *Games People Play,* Berne was able to label in some very memorable ways characteristic acts of aggression. The publication of that work removed therapy from the confessional. The book's climb up the best-seller list raised the suspicions of traditional psychoanalysts and earned it a reputation for being simple and superficial, despite the fact that Berne's other works take his readers into theory as profound and complex as any in psychoanalytics.

Despite its limitations, something on the order of Transactional Analysis that focuses on problems of self-alienation and on alienating transactions between people needs to be used in school. But this approach says little about human alienation rooted in behavior in and behavior of organizations; it says even less about alienation from economic and political conditions that arise because society is organized in one way and not another. This external realm, it seems to me, requires an approach like Micro-Society, if students are to successfully grapple with alienating conditions in the external environment.

Courts

Courts traditionally function at the broader levels of institutional and group behavior. They exist to adjudicate differences and, therefore, to treat conditions they judge to be alienating. So as far as the Micro-Society approach is concerned, greater experience has been gained in the legal sphere than in the therapeutic one. By the end of the P.S. 126 implementation of the model, I had been directly or indirectly involved in some twenty student court cases. That experience has taught me that no one legal invention will suit every classroom. However, this doesn't mean it's impossible to derive hunches and to use them to make some general statements about what is likely to work.

Schools with decaying legal fabrics face problems very different from schools without such problems. The "well" school can drift toward the creation of peer courts without the fear of being overwhelmed by criminal actions. Most of the cases that come before courts in such schools probably have more to do with civil disagreements than with criminal behavior. In these schools, courts will adjudicate contracts, disputes about fair trade, civil rights, and torts.

Schools where assaults, thefts, vandalism, and other forms of strife are commonplace may decide to utilize their courts to negotiate compliance with Micro-Society legislation. Some schools, pressed by circumstances, may even want to use courts as simple instruments of compliance. School officials may try to manipulate things so that a student court enforces their rules. Common sense advises against this. In most situations, student courts work best when they express a community's will rather than the will of individual authority. It is one thing for the legislative component of the school to pass a law that it needs and is prepared to enforce, and quite another for such a legal body to administer a law imposed by a master. Such a circumstance promises eventual doom of school courts and feeds into the desperate lot of school officials who leap for gimmicks to accomplish something gimmicks just can't do.

As with economic institutions, legal institutions must develop at their own pace. Classroom courts naturally lead to grade-wide courts. Grade-wide courts naturally lead to appeals courts. And appeals courts, partly because it makes political sense, are likely to include someone from every part of the school community. Law and law enforcement must also be allowed to progress at a comfortable rate. If the legal institutions of the Micro-Society are allowed to mature, to take on other responsibilities as they can, then there is no reason to think they will not be reasonably useful to the school community.

Over time, then, the adults connected with the Micro-Society must commit themselves to a gradual transfer of power and authority to students. Such a transfer will be required if the courts and other legal institutions established in the school are to enjoy the prospect of a long life. In specific terms, this means that courts must be permitted to recommend, with a reasonable chance of implementation, an approach, activity, or penalty for students found guilty of criminal or civil offenses.

The heart of the matter lies in an attempt to gradually build and substitute a complete set of legal institutions, many but not all operated entirely by students, in place of existing formal and peer-compliance systems and the traditional authority structure operated by adults. In placing discipline as well as rehabilitation largely in the hands of students and teachers, it becomes possible to make setbacks into opportunities or, alternatively, to exploit occasions of actual deviance to educational advantage.

So much for general directions. The early legal experiences, many of which have been chronicled in this volume, have left a legacy. One could alternatively label such a legacy a "set of guidelines." Among the first of these guidelines would rest an injunction to be cautious. Limit the growth of the court system to what it shows itself, with growing experience and tradition, competent to do. Limit the jurisdiction of classroom courts to classroom business. Limit the jurisdiction of grade courts to problems that arise between students in different classrooms. If a school has no classrooms, draw the boundaries wherever the distinct social groupings end and begin. Start small. Allow for growth. Once the legislature becomes operable, limit the jurisdiction of the grade courts to interpreting and enforcing statutes or legal precedent developed there. If an issue arises that can be settled outside the courtroom, settle it outside the courtroom. Court action should be reserved for cases that absolutely require the intervention of a legal body or the attention of an offended community.

I would propose, as a second guideline, faith in the principle of evolution. Events should be allowed to take their own time. Forcing them will very likely lead to a narrowing rather than an expansion of their possibilities. It would be well to remember that the resolution of any particular conflict should be subordinated to the larger goal of developing a social system. With that in mind, it would seem sensible to encourage the growth of a legal tradition through a combination of legislated statute and courtroom precedent. Essentially, this knits students to a historical process that tends to place in their hands tools with which to civilize and master the immediate, and sometimes threatening, environment.

The legal tradition that develops must familiarize the least member of the school society with the reasons for law at levels where students are prepared to accept them. The tradition should not only incorporate statue and precedent; it should include research into the effect and effectiveness of corrective actions taken by student legal authorities. In building this tradition, it would seem wise to take advantage of the fact that the school is a Micro-Society and rely wherever possible on the cooperative energies of the student population to make the penalties and corrective actions stick. In adopting this tack, some attempt should also be made to measure what works best: community pressure, therapy, behavior modification, or discipline.

As with economic and other social institutions, consideration should also be given to linking legal institutions in the model with courts, penal institutions, law firms, and law schools operating in the larger context. Emeritus judges, practicing lawyers, corrections officers, legislators, and other legal-system personnel might be invited to lend their assistance to the building of humane and effective legal institutions. Probably as important, the legislative body in the Society School will eventually have to decide whether school-based institutions have legal authority or jurisdiction after school hours. The Boys' Brotherhood Republic, a settlement house on the Lower East Side in Manhattan, has been operating for over forty years a peer court that resolves conflicts arising between members of the club inside or outside the facility. Unfortunately, no formative evaluation has been available to reinforce the enthusiastic claims the Republic's director makes for its effectiveness.

If it can be said with certainty that no one legal invention will suit every classroom, we can also say with about the same certainty that every classroom that embarks on a process leading to the development of an explicit legal system will face a difficult transition period. The P.S. 126 experience suggests that this period will have its awkward moments: a flurry of trials, cases brought to trial that should have been settled elsewhere, clumsy presentations of evidence, even clumsier refutations by defense lawyers, confusion about who the plaintive in the case should really be, testimony filled with contradictions that resist unscrambling partly because student powers of reasoning at times are so weak, clients who don't understand the civil rights they are entitled to, judges who don't know the law, absence of law or precedent, and interference by the legislature in the operation of the court system.

On par with these certainties, there is a high probability that teachers will, on the whole, be poorly prepared to provide leadership in a field in which they have no experience. For many teachers, the development of a peer-court legal system will mean a reorientation of values, roles, expertise, and techniques. Some of the learning that must go into these changes will come from the classroom experience itself. However, teachers will have to become as competent to operate a law-and-justice system as they have become in administering an arithmetic drill. Helping students to build their own social systems is a new frontier. Eventually, operating a court, a justice system, and a legislative body will contribute what it has to give to civilizing the urban school. When this happens the frontier will be pushed ahead.

Until then we have the job of mapping out reasonable steps to take toward the creation of a legal invention in a school that does not already have one.

1. First, a legitimate need must exist for a legal system.

2. A time should be set aside to discuss the pros and cons of each step in the development of the legal invention, beginning with the decision to create a peer court.

3. If time permits, the class should embark on a study of existing legal institutions before or while it is assembling its own. Stress should be placed on defining what courts do, and on delineating the parts individuals play in administering justice. It might also be helpful if time was spent mapping out the kinds of expertise that must be acquired so that the school community can secure the legal skills it needs to develop a legal invention that performs satisfactorily.

4. In addition, a procedure for screening students and then assigning them to legal roles should be incorporated into the legal invention. It seems sensible to avoid putting students into situations where they will not perform successfully.

5. The court must also be encouraged to perform its duties in a reasonably efficient manner. Trials should not be allowed to become drawn out. This may necessitate experimenting with different procedures, setting definite time constraints or differentiating the duties courts perform from those that might be dealt with by a third party or by an arbitration group.

6. Care should be given to delineating the rights and privileges of both witnesses and defendants.

7. The class or school must decide what punitive powers to give judges. In the early stages of peer-court evolution, these powers more than likely will be limited. As students become more experienced in administering a justice system and in developing less punitive and more constructive responses to criminal behavior, these

powers should grow. At the outset, however, judges should be able to fine, assign students to community work without pay, seize property in compensation for damages, order cold-shoulder treatment for a stated time limit, or segregate troublesome individuals for specific periods of time.

8. When a defendant is found guilty, the class accordingly must decide who will carry out and monitor the sentence.

9. If the defendant feels he has been dealt with unjustly, the class must decide the conditions for appeal and with it provide a means. If a convicted student refuses to accept the court's decision or the penalties it has imposed, then the court must have the authority to ensure compliance with its decisions.

10. Once some of these substantive issues have been taken care of, the class should devote some energy to providing a convincing setting. The drama of the legal process becomes more compelling when the set, in which roles are played, enhances the drama. A contract should be let to some group of students to prepare a theater for classroom legal productions.

11. The teacher's role at every stage in the development of the legal system should be spelled out. The expectation is that the teacher will, over time, move from the position of sole legal authority to adviser. However, it seems likely that, especially in primary school, teachers will always provide guidance.

These procedural points are offered as guideposts in a very ill-defined frontier. Few address the central theoretical issues the proposal raises or anticipate the limitations to be encountered during the genesis of a Micro-Society. One problem certain to arise will be the difficulty of obtaining objective judgments. Almost by definition, peer courts operate within near-incestuous milieu. Students with emotional bonds to one another may find it difficult to render verdicts based just on the facts. Other problems will arise simply because teachers and students have so little experience with courts, law, legal procedures, or with techniques for dealing with the disparities between theory and practice.

Other issues will arise in connection with the cognitive domain.

Children at different ages have profoundly different capacities for engaging in or understanding social processes. Legal procedure, for instance, often calls for highly involved logic that can prove onerous to teachers, let alone students. Both parties will have to simplify the issues and deal with them at whatever level they can. In dealing with cognitive incapacities, it may also prove useful to allow older children or adults to contribute to the deliberations of younger children.

Justice takes time. If problems seem likely to arise because children enlist in the process at different cognitive levels, it will probably be equally true that children, at different levels of maturation, will exhibit varying tolerances for ambiguity and for the pace of events. Experience thus far suggests that the younger children are, the greater their fondness for instant decisions. This affinity could have a suffocating effect on civil liberties. It is precisely here that the adult participant can make his or her contribution, for it is in the throes of a process with realistic consequences that the lessons of civil rights hit home.

Finally, serious objections may be raised by parents or by others to any proposal that entrusts real disciplinary powers to students. In raising these objections, most people mean to call attention to the possibility of kangaroo courts. Few of us wish to see justice become synonymous with vengeance. Again, with many similar issues, the solutions must be found through a process of community self-discovery. If children develop kangaroo courts, they can be shown ways and given reasons to undevelop them. En route to doing this, it might also be possible to engage the entire community in preparing intellectual foundations necessary to the evolution and improvement of existing models of justice.

The threat of parent protests has another possible response: parent involvement. That involvement should be invited at every stage of legal-system development. Parents of accused students should be invited to court proceedings as witnesses or observers. Those who refuse the invitation have only themselves to blame. Even better, parents might be invited to undertake the custody of sons and daughters who violate existing school laws. The terms of this custody might, if one parent wasn't working, include requiring the parent to monitor the activities of a student offender in school for a stated period of time. To oversimplify, the model tries to make the school's own social process responsive to problems that develop.

Political Development

Present political life in classroom and school is almost entirely under the control of adults. In a Society School, the sheer increase in the complexity and volume of human activity will necessitate the growth of a new political system to manage and sustain it. Teachers who recognize the benefits that accrue from economic and social growth will have to relinquish or, alternatively, delegate considerable responsibility and power to their students. To be concrete, no single teacher can even begin to cope with the twenty to a hundred institutions that comprise a Micro-Society. Students, with help from outside the school community, will therefore have to develop a workable management system. In other words, by multiplying the number of organizations and the activity they generate, we also multiply the amount of authority and structure needed to oversee development. This, in turn, multiplies the amount of power available for distribution. It is at least conceivable, for example, that a single student could manage a newspaper, be employed as a teller in a school bank, and sit in the school legislature. In at least two of the three situations, that student wields considerably more authority and responsibility than he wields in the traditional classroom.

The Micro-Economic features of the model support a similar redistribution of political power. The Society School begins with students earning wages for their labor. Their labor is defined by the teacher, who possesses all the currency that exists. Before long, however, significant amounts of currency are deposited in student hands, making students, at least potentially, competitors with teachers for the allocation of student labor. Either privately or in institutions, students can accumulate enough capital to develop autonomous and considerably powerful subgroupings within the school. These groups or individuals establish their own priorities and employ students to enact them. If one adds to this the legislature's power to tax and spend, the distribution of power becomes even more emphatic. Through its taxing and spending power, the legislature can establish social priorities and provide budgets for programs that will fulfill them. In all three cases, power is defined as the right to allocate human labor, determined by the amount of capital an institution or individual holds.

As with economic and social aspects of the model, political power evolves gradually. In P.S. 126 the political sequence included a constitutional convention in which students chose the form of government they wanted. The creation of a legislative body, an executive power, and a court system grew out of these deliberations. Subsequently, elections were held to fill posts in each of those areas. However, as would be clear from reading the experience so far, our knowledge of institutional development remains quite primitive, which means that considerable energy must continue to be invested in perfecting operations of the governmental bodies any constitution will call for.

The P.S. 126 Micro-Society never reached the point at which government could establish school-wide priorities for social and economic development, let alone institute a system of taxation so that it could raise the revenue to carry them out. Until something like this occurs, teachers will act as the de-facto government of the school, helping students to set priorities and to enact them. Once the mechanisms of government begin to function, however, it should become possible for students to address social, economic, and political experience that now lies wholly beyond reach.

It will someday be possible to decide policies that affect the distribution of income, possible to conceptualize community values and to enact proposals consistent with them, possible to debate and decide the overall education objectives and to budget resources to attain them, possible to create economic institutions to meet expressed needs of people in school and in the community, and possible to attempt a comprehensive approach to social deviance. As educators we will be able for the first time to engage students in a process approaching social engineering not for other people, but for themselves. In doing so, the time-honored debates pitting individual against general welfare, community against self, private against public ownership, punitive measures against therapeutic ones, justice against injustice, equity against inequity, conservatives against liberals, and so on, will become the substance of the educational process.

The objectives of this political process will be the formulation of state, of republic, of democracy, of dictatorship, or, if we are realistic, of something in between. That formulation will not take place in an antiseptic environment preconditioned to make sure students will arrive at an appointed goal. It will take place amid the fury of competing interests, competing ideals and principles, and competing social priorities. What develops will develop through a series of political deals and compromises, or because some part of the school organizes itself better than some other part of the school's body politic to achieve political dominance. The form of government that emerges will, more likely than not, reflect the biases of the particular community in which it grows. We may expect these biases to form from recognized needs, and from commitments to the political system that supplies those needs unless, of course, those who have received the most decide they want something even better.

A conservative suburban community will, unless its children decide to repudiate the views of their parents, form a political-economy consistent with what it recognizes as conservative principle. A blighted urban area, on the other hand, might very well organize itself and its institutions in the way that seems most consistent with its aspirations. It could be more highly planned and less interested in the satisfaction of immediate individual goals if it chose to be, or if it could not find the means to act in concert, then the school very likely would become the ground for a political struggle in which individual interest contends with community interests. Furthermore, a population that is a minority in greater society would likely spend a significant portion of its energies developing a cultural program to unite itself into a community while simultaneously acquiring the economic skills necessary for its members to claim their share of America's wealth.

In communities that have racially mixed populations or where integration occurs in school, the model may supply the means to resolve conflict. Sometimes the means will involve judicial proceedings. At other times, racial problems will have to be treated in the legislature. It is even conceivable that specialists, trained in conflict resolution, may provide the leadership necessary to surmount the difficulties and to get a frank and open discussion of existing differences. But even before events get to this crisis stage, it would seem fair to expect the complex interdependencies of participant institutions and individuals—on economic, social, and political levels—to play a healing role and to deter racial polarization.

Although the experience with the model thus far has been too limited to be conclusive, it seems likely that one form or another of the political society will produce a ruling elite, a middle class, and an under class. Partly because wealth may not be passed on, and partly because of inflationary pressures on the school currency, class divisions are not expected to be severe. At least 90 percent of most school populations should fall into whatever might be considered the Micro-Society equivalent of a middle class. If an under class emerges that is significantly larger than 10 percent, a drive by the under class for changes in the Micro-Society must be given a reasonable chance of succeeding.

12. The Model at the Secondary-School Level

No experience with the Micro-Society so far exists at the secondary-school level. Its potential for upper-grade use has yet to be tested. There are other significant approaches that attempt to link school and society, and it is important to examine such approaches to see their possibilities and limitations, and to see whether the Micro-Society school extends these approaches in useful ways that would justify a test.

The comprehensive high school and the Parkway experiment provide useful benchmarks to one of the central themes of American education: the movement to make school and society one, a movement that the Micro-Society school seeks to extend.

James B. Conant, former president of Harvard University and subsequently chairman of a committee of the National Association of Secondary School Principals, conducted a study of the comprehensive high school, published under the title *The American High School Today*. Ten years later, with the support of the Carnegie Corporation and the Educational Testing Service, he conducted a second study, *The Comprehensive High School*. In both reports Dr. Conant defined the comprehensive high school as the prototype for most American secondary schooling. He saw the comprehensive high school as a "peculiarly American phenomenon," as an attempt to grapple with diversity and pluralism of a clientele that came from a plethora of social classes and ethnic groups. In contrast to European secondary schooling that existed to perpetuate social class affiliations, the American high school existed to foster a milieu that was essentially classless or democratic. Democratic ideology forbade the use of public schools to maintain the barriers to social mobility. Indeed, the mandate of the comprehensive high school came to be the reverse: to facilitate movement out of the under class, and to prepare students to live and work in a democratic society.

The European system assigned students to a course of study that confirmed their membership in a social class; the American system allowed students, through the "election" of courses, to determine the directions they would take after graduation. In practice, the comprehensive-high-school system led to one of two options: either one entered an academic program leading to further study at a university, or one entered a vocational program leading to immediate employment after graduation.

Despite these differences, European and American schooling continued to have a great deal in common. Both served as mechanisms for quality control in their respective societies. The American secondary school, like its European counterpart, attempted to sift what it considered to be the best and the brightest into positions of leadership, leaving the rest to manage as they could. European education, on the other hand, placed a premium on birth and social position rather than merit, assigning the rich and the well-born to the highest educational tracks.

The equivalent social classes in the United States sent their children to special private schools to which children of lesser means had only limited access. By and large, the American secondary school attracted the sons and daughters of the swiftly growing middle classes and the poor. In placing side by side the children of these social classes, the comprehensive high school did all in its power to reward merit rather than the fortunes of birth. Still, the rich and well-born went elsewhere.

The comprehensive high school did, however, encourage movement over a narrow spectrum, usually from the under class to the middle class. How well it facilitated this, though, is a matter of discussion. During the heyday of the high school, the American economy grew at such a terrific rate that its graduates were virtually assured the social mobility they wanted, with or without secondary schooling. The degree became a badge of merit. As long as the high-school diploma remained scarce, most people agreed upon its significance and value. Stated or implied, you were better off with a degree than without, since employers arbitrarily limited the pool of labor to applicants with high-school credentials. As the number of high-school graduates increased, however, employers began differentiating between high schools in making their quality-control decisions, and finally required college credentials.

Whether high-school experiences routed students to advanced education or to a vocation—implying on the one hand (although not necessarily meaning) membership in the middle class, and on the other, membership in the working under class—those experiences took the shape of elective courses with prescribed time commitments. For the most part, courses that appealed to the college-bound contained highly abstract material. Vocation-bound students, by contrast, took large doses of manual training and courses heavily laden with concrete tasks. Since students "elected" courses of study and training, the quality-control function of the high school took care of itself. Students accepted or refused the opportunities offered them or the direction others urged upon them, and by these choices and these determinations their futures were arranged.

In reality, the experience offered by comprehensive high schools represented doors to further experience. Very little of the experience high school provided tied into careers or professions on the outside. Students learned discipline, read better, computed better, and followed instructions better, but this preparation provided them with the attributes to fit into the existing order, not with the knowledge to make the existing order better, richer, or more human. High school, for most of my contemporaries, was a hurdle one jumped on one's way to college, which was a hurdle one jumped on one's way to graduate school. Each year had to be hurdled to get to the next, and one always wondered where one was running and from what. The answer given was a simple one. Those who passed all the hurdles earned the right to move upward in social and economic status. Those, on the other hand, who fell by the wayside or who elected not to try flowed into vocational channels where they might learn some useful skill that would gain them admission to the working under class.

If Dr. Conant seemed to recommend the existing social order, and to voice little interest in wholesale change of the secondary-school institution, John Bremer did the reverse in the Parkway program. Bremer was asked to Philadelphia to implement a new kind of comprehensive high school that would make use of the city's resources in and around the Parkway area. The specifications for the new model of a high school had been drawn up by the then director of development for the Philadelphia public-school system, Clifford Brenner.

Brenner's original conception of the program, and the one that won the endorsement of the Philadelphia School Board, comes down to us in a memo. That memo proposed the creation of a four-year high-school organization to "serve Center City pupils drawn from all parts of the city." It located the school on Benjamin Franklin Parkway and listed the many varied resources, institutions, and physical facilities that might support the program. The memo elaborated the new kinds of instruction that would be made available by institutions in the area, suggested how the faculty might be chosen, outlined a transportation plan to guarantee students access to institutions along the Parkway, provided parameters concerning the number of students to be served, and the socio-economic and racial make-up of the student body. The memo, however, said nothing whatever about what came to be John Bremer's primary agenda: a curriculum of institutional change and individual liberation.

He coupled this agenda with the much more limited version of Parkway expressed in Clifford Brenner's memo. That coupling gave the program and its adherents something nigh religious fervor about what they were doing. Bremer called on participants in the program to engage in a process of institutional change that would lead to the self-actualization of everyone. The coupling, if it accomplished nothing else, succeeded in giving the officials running the Philadelphia public schools fits. The moment Bremer took over Parkway, the authorities to whom he supposedly reported became the enemy and target of his agency.

Beneath Bremer's call for wholesale change nested a complete set of subordinate objectives. First among these was a desire to rework basic relationships between teachers and students. In place of a model of learning that operates from the premise that it is by "the activity of the teacher that the student comes to learn," Bremer posited a communalism in which education and learning take place "as a cooperative venture, based on friendship and mutuality of interest." Reinforcing this point, Bremer writes that "education is not something done to children by teachers, it is something teachers and children do together." This doing together, according to the first director of the Parkway program, required a social organization of a kind altogether different from the one found in the comprehensive high school.

Central to both Bremer's desire to rework student-teacher relationships, and to his decision to operate independently of his supposed superiors in the school department, was a hostility to any relation between human beings that places one man at the beck and call of another. For Parkway's first director, that hostility took shape at both philosophical and practical levels. At the philosophical level, Bremer's hostility to authority could be termed a willingness to reject all attempts by human beings to appropriate Knowledge or Will. At the practical level, this philosophical stance translated into a rejection of any educational process that subscribed to the production of knowledge specialists. These specialists were seen to be individuals who had appropriated knowledge, and by doing so had obtained power over other men. Bremer saw this as an alien relation, for, in keeping with the rhetoric of radical educational reformers, he saw as one of the goals of education an opening of secrets rather than a keeping of them. To counter the specialist, Bremer proposed to make Parkway a *school without walls* that would make the manufacture of experts, as well as the reverse, the implied production of non-experts or failures, a thing of the past. The access to institutions Parkway provided seemed to Bremer to symbolize the unlocking of the secrets. If he wanted nothing else, he wanted that. For it made little difference to Bremer whether schools produced experts or failures if what ensued from the program connived at further human estrangement. In place of a learning process leading to alienation, Bremer posed a vision of a learning process without walls, and a school that distributed knowledge to anyone who wanted it.

However, for Bremer this represented only the first step. The completion of what he envisioned required, along with a rejection of appropriations of Knowledge, a repudiation of appropriations of Will. The manager, in this parallel relation, appropriates Will in very much the way the expert appropriates Knowledge. Bremer labeled the outcome of this relation in the same way he had labeled the first—namely, as alienation. Furthermore, he decided to oppose the relation in its general form: by repudiating hierarchical authority. In place of the pyramidal organization common to the school system, Bremer substituted a non-hierarchical participatory form of social and administrative organization. Participation in that organization virtually became a curricular obligation. In attempting this, Bremer intended to lead an entire school population to negate appropriations of Will. In its positive forms that repudiation emerged as an affirmation of democratic or "communal" decision making. To negate hierarchical authority, everyone had to be in the hierarchy.

In retrospect, Bremer's intentions seem, at least to this writer, somewhat more substantial than either what he was really able to carry off or what Parkway could conceivably ever become. For, in actual practice, the Parkway program, as it was implemented, and as it was modeled, seems likely to have fallen short of its objective:

to end the appropriation of Will and Knowledge. Although it may have been trying to be something else in spirit as long as Bremer was there, it would never be more than an extension of the comprehensive-high-school idea with or without ideology.

First of all, the celebrated incorporation of institutions along the Parkway into the schooling process seems, except possibly in the case of small craft industries, to have provided students, at best, with low-level experience in these institutions. Such experience can hardly qualify as more than a step toward the reappropriation of expertise that large corporations collect and possess. Few secrets of enterprise were unfolded. Moreover, as with the comprehensive high school, what little experience there was came packaged in courses. Nothing else was possible as long as Parkway and its leadership accepted the fundamental consumer orientation to the outside economy. The orientation acknowledged that worthwhile knowledge and experience resided elsewhere and that the fundamental mission of the school was to appropriate it.

Secondly, what became for Bremer a process that connected students to legitimate real-world experience was in practice more a broadening institutionalized learning: the comprehensive high school exploiting community resources without returning goods or services in kind. Instead of relying on certified teachers, the program cornered a new set of experts who, in the majority of instances, did things to students so they would learn. In other words, the kinds of experience Bremer wanted students to have in order to repudiate appropriation of Knowledge were not to be had. The well-publicized links between school and society had been forged in a single direction —consumer to producer.

Finally, a look at Parkway today would probably reveal a retrenchment of traditional authority, not because the new administration of the program willfully intended to subvert this curriculum of change, but because the town meeting had very few real things to do. Parkway produced no goods or services of economic value to anyone. Indeed, the school consumed other people's goods and services at a voracious rate. At best, its authority structure, participatory or not, amounted to teaching students a hustle that leads inevitably to the kinds of estrangement Bremer promised to avoid.

Consumers into Producers

One of the central ingredients of the Society School model is that schools which now are almost completely consumers of goods and services are made producers of goods and services as well. At th elementary-school level the Micro-Society approach focuses o building society in school. This focus translates into an effort to buil wealth-producing institutions in school together with socio-political processes that manage institution building and wealth producing so that maximum benefits accrue to the membership body of the school. At the secondary-school level that interior focus is exchanged for an exterior one. Instead of devoting all student energies to building a Micro-Society in school, increasing amounts of energy go to building society from school.

In economic terms, this means students will be encouraged to expand school-based institutions—newspapers, day-care centers, retail stores, theaters, as well as other enterprises—into the greater community beyond the schoolhouse gates. Thus, many enterprises will have dual markets for goods and services, one within the Micro-Society of the school and the other in the community. A similar expansion occurs within the economic sphere. Micro-Society social institutions that succeed in supplying services to students in school may decide to venture beyond schoolhouse boundaries to supply needed services to the local community.

The political thrust of the program of "building society from school" will come in the form of an attempt to coordinate economic and social development inside and outside school. For instance, the political body of the Society School will have to define a territory in a city as the school's sphere to influence. Once it is defined, the Micro-Society will have to decide what kinds of goods and services it will contribute or sell within that sphere. Since it is likely that the sphere defined will coincide with the sphere students come from, it is assumed that the interface between what the school proposes to do and what the community proposes to accept will be ideal.

In other words, the central principle of the society-building program is reciprocity. School-produced goods are exchanged for community-produced goods. School-produced services are exchanged for community-produced services. From this exchange of wealth, and from the actualization of a working class of students who, for all economic intents and purposes are presently idle, flow the model's possibilities.

The shape of these possibilities will vary. In addition to having school-based institutions expand into markets beyond the perimeter of the Micro-Society, school enterprises may decide to locate themselves entirely in the community. In other words, the school could lease commercial space, or purchase existing buildings as part of the school plant, for the operation of student businesses. It might also be possible to vary the kinds of ownership agreements student enterprises might have with institutions within the Micro-Society. Some enterprises might be wholly owned by an agency or individual attending the school. Other enterprises might be owned in part by the individuals operating the business and in part by a governmental agency, a bank, or an investment company located on the premises of the school. Thus, a business that ventured into the local community could turn to institutions within the Micro-Society for capital, labor, or for goods and services.

For example, a group of students might get together and form a local advertising agency. They could capitalize it by applying to a Micro-Society investment company for a loan, locate it in the local community, and sell services to enterprises in the community and the school. Another group of students might start a day-care center. The center might be subsidized by a combination of agencies—say, the Micro-Society government, a local charitable foundation, and parents of the children attending the center. Like the advertising agency, it could locate its activities in the community, draw a large supply of its labor from the school, and sell its services to parents of children with connections to the school or to the community.

In addition to hatching independent economic and social entities, other relationships with existing enterprises might be encouraged. For example, students interested in advanced work in accounting might be matched with professionals in their fields of interest. Students could spend as much as ten or fifteen hours a week apprenticed to a public accountant. In return for providing a student with in-service training, the accounting firm or the individual providing the training might be permitted to employ a student on company business for a stated portion of his training.

It seems at least conceivable that businesses operating within the school's defined sphere of interest might be bought wholly or in part for the purpose of providing students with appropriate situations for mastering occupational areas of interest to them. For example, the school might purchase 50 percent ownership in a printing facility. In agreement with the facility's operators, the school could contract for the training of ten students in the various aspects of the printing business. Firms and agencies in which the school maintained a majority ownership share might be made subject to the regulation of school-based agencies, implying both the continuous monitoring of business activity and the possibility of coordinating a local development plan from the Micro-Society.

These kinds of relationships between community and school have implications for the social sphere of the Society School. Every community has its mores, traditions, and history. However, in many places industrial society has changed, weakened, or even extinguished them. The school community could take upon itself the job of preserving and revitalizing the history, traditions, and other cultural patterns of its locale. For example, a group of student researchers might interview, chronicle, and then publish stories about the community and its people. How did you get into your business? How did you meet your wife? How did you get into politics? Describe some of the deals you made when you were in office. What good stories do you remember? What is your favorite recipe? What kind of gossip was gossiped years ago that's not gossiped today? Questions of this kind and the personal responses they engender might help rejuvenate a community recognition of itself and imbue human relations with the kinds of intimacy that seem totally missing from contemporary urban society.

The transfer of responsibilities for building community to students will not eliminate social deviance. Extortion, theft, assaults, disruptions of various kinds, drug programs—indeed, all the problems faced in mass society are likely to continue in some form in schools. This fact will require a second thrust within the social sphere. That thrust will entail developing personal, community, and institutional ways to cope with social deviance. At the personal level, this may translate into an exposure to various forms of therapeutic treatment, into therapy education, into programs of behavioral modification, or into discipline and a study of its effectiveness as a compliance methodology. At the community level, it may call for dealing with social deviance collectively or even through school-based institutions specializing in the development and implementation of corrective programs. Law, courts, correction programs, therapy, and other approaches fall within this set of possibilities.

The development of Micro-Society institutions in and out of school, along with what might be called a vital program in career education, will not obviate the need for strengthening the academic program. Students interested in secondary experience—the traditional academic disciplines—and in the theoretical and intellectual system underpinning the professions should be encouraged to pursue those interests. Thus, at the secondary-school level, where many students are interested in academic and professional programs, considerable energy will continue to be invested in academic offerings like history, English, science, mathematics, foreign languages, and so on. Offerings in those areas would be organized along professional lines; for example, a student interested in a career in medicine might take courses in physics and chemistry, but could also become involved in community health projects operated from the school, or in apprenticeship roles in local medical facilities or in research laboratories. A student interested in a university career such as the teaching of history, on the other hand, might take English courses, attend lectures at nearby colleges, enroll in classes in more traditional high schools, or contract with a historian for a course in colonial history. A student who had not yet developed a career direction could try out a number of subject areas new to him —psychology, sociology, philosophy. In other words, instead of programming students in courses to fulfill distribution requirements, students would program themselves into experiences based on their short- or long-range interests. If students were found to be narrowing their experiences rather than expanding them, the student senate or legislature would take the matter up and attempt to legislate corrective action.

Operations Specifications

A student body of the Society School at the secondary-school level might enter the program in four stages. Each stage might take a year. The first class entering might be composed of 200 graduates of the primary-school version of the model: the Society-in-School. Another 50 students would be admitted to the model by application through an admission procedure developed by the school's administrators. In each of the three years that followed, 250 students would be admitted in a similar manner until the school reached a target capacity of, say, 1,000.

For all practical purposes, students would not be organized into grades. Some reference might be expected to be made to first-, second-, third-, and fourth-year students, but this would have no bearing on the distribution or organization of the student body. However, one's tenure in the model would be expected to influence school operations. It seems fair to expect that the longer one had spent in the model, the more likely one would be to hold positions of authority.

At more advanced stages of the model's development (in and beyond the fifth year) the student population would be enlarged to include alumni of the four-year program. As students completed their four-year commitment, they could, if they chose to do so, retain an affiliation with the school organization. This affiliation could take one or more of the following forms:

• *A business connection.* A student might wish to continue working in one of the business enterprises the school had developed. If he was the original organizer of the business, and was advanced capitalization by the model or by one of its agencies, the governing body might maintain a financial interest in the enterprise. That interest might be expressed in several forms. The student would present budgets, audits, financial statements on a month-by-month basis to an appropriate agency in the school government. The entrepreneur would pay dividends to stockholders. The entrepreneur would repay money advanced him by the model's Department of Commerce, etc. The entrepreneur would participate in economic planning, carried on at the school's central headquarters, that might have consequences for his business interests. This, of course, implies the existence of two currencies, one negotiable only in the Society School, the other negotiable outside.

• *A political connection.* Alumni would retain the right to vote in student elections and the right to hold well-defined public offices. Alumni might conceivably take it upon themselves to elaborate and improve the model's political posture with the constituency of parents who lived in the sphere of the model's operations.

• *A social connection.* Alumni would be expected to provide a number of suitable settings for training students. In some cases, students would exchange their labor for training. In others, the student or the employer would compensate one or the other in return for training or for work. This compensation, as with all internal transactions, would use the school currency. Alumni would also be permitted to participate on one or more of the numerous planning committees organized to oversee community development.

• *An academic connection.* Alumni would offer courses of instruction in areas of their expertise to students who wanted them.

Physical Plant

The physical plant of the school would be designed to approximate the idea of a city within a building. In the first year of the program, it is expected that the space within a regular school building would prove sufficient for the establishment and on-going operations of the program. Among the special features of the interior would be the following:

First Floor: (1) a courtroom, (2) a legislative chamber/quasi auditorium/theater, (3) a central market area with about two dozen stores and stalls; some of these stores will have display areas for salable goods, (4) a small movie theater/experimental stage/ legislative committee room, (5) offices for model's government, (6) a miniature bank, (7) a post office and communications center, and (8) central administration offices.

Second Floor: (1) space for student offices, (2) seminar rooms for the model's university, as well as lecture halls for larger numbers of academic students, (3) a library, (4) a social-service center for the administration of the school's discipline and treatment program, (5) several rooms adjacent to the social-service center for the segregation of students remanded there by the court, (6) art rooms, (7) a snack bar, (8) university laboratories for the science program.

Third Floor: Half of the third floor would be set aside for manufacturing operations. These might include: (1) repair centers for appliances as secondhand goods, (2) a craft center, (3) architects' drafting rooms, (4) a printing plant, (5) a bindery, (6) a newspaper, (7) magazine offices, (8) publishers, etc. The other half of the third floor might house music rooms, student offices, planning offices, etc.

Adjacent to the school, and probably on the first floor, might be a gym. In addition to boiler rooms, the air-conditioning plant, and other parts of the building maintenance and operation structure, the basement might house a very large cafeteria. In addition to this central plant, the model would develop spaces outside the school and incorporate them into the plant at a speed that corresponded to student success in developing agencies in the community. Some of this space might be made available to the school and to its students at no cost. Other spaces might have to be leased from the owners.

As a rule of thumb, it is to be expected that the school would be able to obtain space at no cost from non-profit organizations that did not fully utilize the space they had during school hours—e.g., settlement houses, churches, park facilities, museums, and so on. If the academic component of the model grew beyond the space allotted it within the central building, it could make its own arrangement with such organizations for the use of their facilities. Students might make space in their homes available for small seminars. For students who apprenticed themselves to employers, the cost of facilities would not be significant. Whenever student businesses expanded their markets into the local community, it might become necessary for the school to lease space in the vicinity of the school. This space would be paid for from the receipts of the business enterprises that used it.

Curriculum: Direct Experience

The overall design of the model presumes the curriculum would contain a spectrum of experiences moving from concrete to abstract. Each "experience center" would make available to students both practical and theoretical forms of experience. For example, students might affiliate themselves with the following economic organizations as managers, employees, or researchers:

Banks, insurance companies, accounting firms, claims adjusters, advertising, employment agencies, air-conditioning equipment sales and service, radio communications, animal breeding, anti-theft experts, real estate, apartment finders, housing inspection, repairmen of appliances, architects, art galleries, artists, audio-visual consultants, automobile mechanics, baby-clothes manufacturers, diaper service, ballet classes, catering services, barbers, jewelers, beauticians, family planners, book dealers, bookkeepers, building contractors, carpenters, plumbers, janitorial services, electric contractors, movers, newspapermen, entertainers, bakers, morticians, city and town planners, clergymen, television repairmen, decorators, communication specialists, restaurant managers, etc.

Each student would be expected to design a program of direct experience for himself, and to seek help through the student employment bureau in making contacts with businessmen in the city who might provide apprenticeship roles. Each student would enter into a contract with his employer or sponsor. This agreement would be filed with the central administration of the Society School. These contracts might state the hours, working conditions, and experiences the employer expected to provide the student and the duties and concepts the employer expected the student to master. It might also state the compensation, if any, the student would receive or what a student had agreed to pay his sponsor. The agreement might oblige every employer to fill out a monthly report on the student's performance, to list the concepts he believed the student had mastered and those he still must learn. If a student left or broke his agreement with an employer, he would be required to file his written reasons with the central administration. In addition, the central administration would solicit from the employer his version of what had happened. Both accounts would be inserted in the student's employment record. That employment record would be made available to all perspective employment contacts during the course of the student's four years and, at the student's request, be furnished to employers after graduation.

Time

The school day would be extended from the present nine-to-three time block to a twelve-hour period between nine A.M. and nine P.M.

Such an extension would make it possible to gain a more optimum use of plant and to institute a scheduling pattern flexible enough to accommodate most activities that needed to be assigned fixed time periods.

Employers and sponsors would be able to schedule sessions with students with minimum interference in regular business operations. For their part, students would be free to devote larger blocs of time to projects and traineeships that required it. Parents and other members of the community who committed themselves to providing services to the model would be able to contribute them after regular business hours.

Staffing

The staff of the model would be composed of a core of professionals drawn from the regular school system, perhaps as many as a hundred individuals from various professions and service industries with commitments to the model ranging from two to six hours a week, parents of students who committed two hours a week to the project per family, and students who in addition to their other duties would be permitted to offer courses in areas of their expertise.

Since the backgrounds of the faculty of a Society School would differ markedly from the backgrounds of most regular teachers currently employed by the regular organization, it seems appropriate here to delineate the kinds of experience the project might be seeking.

- One of the teachers in the core group should have a background or be willing to train himself or herself in the broad area of law, jurisprudence, penology, law enforcement, and contracts.
- One of the core faculty should have a background in the delivery of social services to individuals, to groups, and to communities.
- Three of the core faculty should have backgrounds in business and related financial areas, including economics, banking, real

estate, insurance, political economy, marketing, systems analysis, organizational behavior, and management science.

• Four members of the core staff should have a broad background in academic disciplines: the humanities, natural sciences, and social sciences. However, they also should have been active in the theater, arts, or scholarship.

• One member of the core faculty should have a background in the health fields, including medicine, nursing, medical research, science related to medicine, and so forth.

• One of the members of the core faculty should have a background in the manual arts: crafts, carpentry, model building, architecture, engineering, city planning, etc.

• One member of the staff should have concerned himself with the operation of government, with constitutional issues, with the operation of legislatures, and with other matters related to political science.

All would become responsible for developing apprenticeships, or internship opportunities for students in areas of their specialties.

Parents and Consultants

The parent contribution to the school, although modest, is nevertheless an important one. To be successful, the model must attract on a regular basis the participation of the parent community. If a crisis arose, the issues raised would be familiar to the parent community because it directly participated in the school. Likewise, it is important for the school's future to involve a strong political base so that unfriendly forces in the community would keep a respectful distance and maintain a policy of non-interference.

The consultants, in addition to offering courses to students at the school or in agencies outside the school, would also provide a network that could guide students into advanced career training or into higher education. This network would be managed by the associate director or by an appropriate student agency. Consultants from colleges and corporations would be invited to make a labor contribution to the school. As the group of alumni grew, it is expected that they would contribute to this linkage effort.

Governance

Specifications for governance pertain essentially to arrangements for the division of authority and responsibility; law making, law enforcement; school security and school operations; task definition and distribution and provision for spiritual direction and exhilaration. As with the preceding sections of these operation specifications, the recommendations should be considered highly tentative, subject to ratification or revision in this case by all those who would participate in the evolution of the model. What follows is an attempt to establish the "specs" for a dual organization.

Central Administration. The central administration would provide supporting services for the school's operations. It would deal with matters directly pertaining to other parts of the school system, city politics, budget allocation and expenditures on plant maintenance, teacher salaries, capital investment in student-initiated enterprise, hiring and firing, scheduling of university classes, communications, public relations, community relations, and the procurement of materials from outside the closed economy. It would have little influence, or what should be called participatory influence, in matters of school discipline, the operations of the school's political, economic, and social systems. For instance, it would have no authority to set prices, to establish punishments for offenses against individuals or groups, to define the political organization of student government or its agencies, or to establish budget priorities for the Micro-Society. It could not appropriate goods or services produced by students without a court order. Neither could it regulate the press or establish directives that fell within the private spheres of individual students. It would, however, have the power to intervene in student affairs should a student break a state law. Even in these situations, it would be obliged to move with deliberate speed to turn discipline matters over to the appropriate agencies and courts established within the school for that purpose.

The central administration would be responsible to a Board of Directors. That board would consist of the Superintendent of Schools or his representative, the head of the parents' association, an alumnus of the school, the dean of a nearby school of education, a teacher, a member of the business community, a juvenile-court justice, and the director of the school (non-voting in matters pertaining directly to his own private welfare). This board would meet twice a month, and would be responsible for the financial operations of the school, for hiring and firing the director, for serving as the court of last resort for school discipline and civil suits that went to it on appeal.

The Society School. In a sense, the Society School would be a school within an organization. It would have its own institutions of governance. These institutions would have the right to tax and expend funds, to establish laws and to enforce them, to make plans for school and community economic development and expansion and carry them out, and in general to provide for the general welfare of the community. In a general sense, the central administration would provide support for the Society School, which, in turn, would support the community. The shape of the governance organization and of its priorities would be left to students to decide. This by no means implies that administrators, teachers, parents, and consultants would be excluded from participation. In later stages of development it would even be possible for adults who operate the school to be enfranchised to hold political office and to serve on committees in the Micro-Society.

Capitalizing Economic Expansion

Considerable resources would have to be generated to develop and sustain business enterprises and their operations. The resources necessary in the early stages of the model's development would likely be modest, but capital needs could be expected to increase geometrically as the model moved into later stages. Managers of this process would, therefore, need to develop sources of funding.

These sources might be found in the school system, in the local community of parents and businessmen, in the endowments of several of the large foundations, and in the federal, state, and local government.

The school system itself could capitalize businesses within the model, particularly in areas where it stood to benefit directly. For instance, monies spent on curriculum materials might be spent in school-curriculum businesses. Enterprises that created, produced, and distributed curriculum materials in the model might easily turn to this source as a market. Other school systems might qualify as markets as well. Similarly, student enterprises might develop in food and custodial services on a competitive basis with those that already existed. In addition, a premium might be paid by the school system for reductions in vandalism to school property both at the school and at elementary schools in the vicinity of the model.

Other capital resources might be found in the local parent and business communities. Both communities might be invited to purchase shares in a holding company that maintained controlling stock interest in companies developed in the school and community. Such an arrangement would also develop a natural market in the local community for goods and services produced by school enterprises.

Foundations might be convinced to provide support or capitalization through their endowment. The incentive to make this investment should be fairly considerable, since not only would it be possible to gain a return on the investment, but it would also be possible to generate a large social return.

Finally, the federal, state, and local governments all have programs designed to help small businessmen. Among the best known of these are the Small Business Administration, the Department of Labor, the Department of Commerce, and the Office of Economic Opportunity. Several agencies might support development out of interest in the model of education—for example, the Department of Health, Education and Welfare, the Office of Education, or the Department of Justice.

If the Society School at the secondary-school level succeeded in maintaining a steady rate of growth and capital formation, there seems to be little reason for such an institution to fail to increase its impact on the local community, given time. It also seems safe to assume that, over time, economic growth would be influenced by political considerations and social priorities and that these pressures might imply increasing amounts of macro-planning. Moreover, one might hope that the issues raised, political and otherwise, would take the planning out of the hidden offices of the planners, and that the plans for school-based Micro-Societies would become a matter for public discourse.

13. The Children's Income Plan

The Micro-Society approach has been advanced in an attempt to reverse an era that began by putting an end to child labor and ended by obtaining for almost everyone under the age of eighteen obligatory membership in the leisure class. During the 1920s most states passed a series of statutes known as the Uniform Child Labor Laws, which effectively eliminated children from the work force. The laws were pressed for by those who wanted to rescue children from employer abuses and by unions whose members were being forced to compete with children for work.

Compulsory education statutes, while progressive and necessary, crippled the work experience of children, for if these statutes removed children from the factories and put them in school, they also planted the seeds of what I call economic childhood. The emergence of an affluent society, with leisure time available on a scale never before imaginable, produced an atmosphere well suited to the growth of a new attitude toward work. For many, particularly the young who never had worked, the celebration of leisure made work synonymous with displeasure, and something to be avoided at all costs.

To say that these attitudes and conditions had an impact on public schooling would be an understatement. When students made the transition from the factory to the factory-like school, the amount of drudgery experienced in the schoolhouse must have seemed relatively modest when compared to the workhouse. The difference between the two probably amounted to liberation. Decades later, however, with a world increasingly shaped for leisure, the same schoolhouse with the same routines looked every bit as inhuman as the factories it had supplanted. Teachers found themselves feeding a captive population. They found themselves burdened with an obligation to keep students entertained. They found themselves the targets of the liberal press that accused them of merely keeping students occupied with useless exercises. Indeed, traditional schools found themselves being called factory schools by a generation of radical reformers who wanted to equate leisure-time activity with learning.

These radical reformers set themselves the task of redefining childhood as a period of extended and fascinating leisure, and of dignifying this "play" as intellectual development. The most popular of the "play" education movements, the Open Classroom, pushed furthest in this direction. Centering on discovering new forms of meaningful play, open-educators ignored entirely their responsibility to put children in touch with the realities of non-leisure time, and with the pleasures of meaningful work. As a result, the educative experience they advocated produced an educational dilettantism that made even the most creative play quite as ludicrous and useless as the traditional schoolhouse exercise.

Rooted in a philosophic ground that placed premiums on leisure, on doing one's own thing, on ripping off the system, on getting as rich as possible doing as little as possible, dilettantism produced no goods or services of value to anyone. Indeed, it produced the reverse: voracious consumers alienated from labor. With child-labor laws blocking access to legitimate work experience, and with compulsory-education statutes forcing students into classrooms where they spent the day performing meaningless tasks, it was almost inevitable that teachers and students would both submit to and carry on the kind of buncoism I call economic childhood. Indeed, when all is said and done, the whole movement to educate children for leisure amounts to something less than the crystallization of the philosophic experience of a spoiled brat.

Phenomenologically, economic childhood comes in many shapes and sizes. In pint-size form, it applies to a small fraction of those who are on welfare but could work if they wanted to. The really giant size applies to the rich and to children of the rich who live on the private dole.

Working people usually object to welfare (the public dole) on the grounds that people who don't work don't deserve to eat. Yet this reciprocal relationship between work and consumption never seems to apply to the goodly number of rich people who eat very well without ever doing much work. Many students in this category regard labor itself as obsolete. They sometimes justify their idleness by pointing to the machine, as if it, in its mechanical wisdom, had laid the golden egg of infinite leisure. In an extension of this absurd logic, students of the "let others work" mentality argue, among other things, that there is too little work to be done to require labor from them.

The term "economic childhood" includes other similar kinds of behavior. It covers attempts to prolong one's stay in leisure and out of work, and one's need, therefore, to find someone who will let you live off his assets. It covers attempts to legitimize idleness with even greater idleness, to rationalize extending one's education when in fact a person has little or no interest in university courses. For some, it takes the form of panhandling in the streets. A blind man begging is one thing—and even he would prefer work with dignity. A student from a middle-income family with a college degree begging is another. For others of the same category it can take the form of going on the public dole when the private dole runs out. Whatever other forms it takes, the common denominator of economic childhood is a parasitism that permits the idle to consume the produce of those who work.

The natural antidote to economic childhood is meaningful work. I don't think I'm alone in feeling that a great deal needs to be done to make society a better and more humane place. I also think I'm not alone in believing that the job can't be done by those wedded to extending leisure ad nauseam. And so I don't think I'm alone in wanting to downgrade the consumption of leisure time, and in wanting to upgrade work. The time has come, especially among the well-to-do, to treat work as a scarce and valuable spiritual commodity. Work camps established by the rich set the precedent long ago. The distribution of income has introduced, among a small minority of people, an exhaustion with leisure and the kind of life style it produces. It follows that before long parents will see the value of paying for schooling that will provide their children with meaningful labor.

The Children's Income Plan being attached to the Society School model proposes to do this on a large scale. Together, they represent an attempt to tap the enormous supply of idle student labor for what I earlier called society building. However, it would be misleading if either the plan or the Micro-Society approach was read as an attempt to solve the problem of leisure. Although the plan addresses that question by allowing the rich to purchase the opportunity to work, it also addresses the problem of putting tools and resources in the hands of the poor so that they can produce a world they can live and thrive in.

The Children's Income Plan, alternatively called the Higher-Education Voucher Proposal, is being advanced in an attempt to think out the linkages between the model and society. It is also being advanced to supply or draw out the financial context that flows necessarily or at least ideally from the Micro-Society approach. Unlike the Society School, which to me seems eminently feasible, the Children's Income Plan isn't being advanced under any illusion of its chances for enactment; it is being offered as idea, pure and simple.

One of the problems the Micro-Society approach will face at the secondary-school level is the location of sufficient resources to back the currency. According to the theory, at least some of these resources would be produced by students attending the school. Some additional resources might flow from trade between the Micro-Society and the outside world. A certain amount of resources would flow into the school from foundations and from government agencies interested in subsidizing its educational operations. Even with all these resources, it seems unlikely that a student attending the Society School would earn enough of the national currency to purchase admission to college, or to purchase advanced training elsewhere.

The Children's Income Plan is being proposed in an attempt to make the reward structure of the model so convincing that it can't be ignored by anyone. The plan consists of the following points:

1. That schools adopt something like the Micro-Society approach and provide students with income-producing employment.

2. That students attending secondary school be required to save approximately 70 percent of their earnings at an agency set up to regulate and administer the plan.

3. That students be permitted to spend 30 percent of their school earnings on consumer goods and services while they are attending school.

4. That upon graduation, students participating in the plan be permitted to draw out their savings either in cash at some fixed exchange rate for U.S. currency, or in an education voucher negotiable at an institution of higher learning and advanced training. It should also be possible to choose a combination of the two.

Financing the Plan

The Children's Income Plan would be financed from two sources: (1) from states' subsidies to state university systems, and (2) from a tax levied on those who would reap the benefits of the plan. State university costs are now paid directly by taxpayers. Under the plan those tax payments would be deposited instead at a state agency established to administer the program. Each Society School in the state would then be given drawing rights against the funds on deposit, in proportion to the number of students it had enrolled. These drawing rights would, in turn, support school currencies.

Thus, it would become possible for a student in high school to earn a part or all of his college tuition in return for work done in his Micro-Society or in his community. To balance student drawing rights, public colleges and universities would be obliged to raise tuition charges and other fees, making them competitive with private colleges. Stated simply, students would be earning the publicly subsidized education they now get for free.

Upon graduation from high school, students wishing to go on to higher education would claim the voucher (accumulated through four or more years of forced savings) and turn it in to the state or private college in payment of college fees. The state or private college would, in turn, redeem the vouchers at the state CIP agency for their cash value. On the other hand, students who decided not to begin college study would apply to the agency for whatever cash redemption equivalent of their savings. If a state wanted to encourage students to go on to higher education, it would fix the cash redemption value of the student's forced savings at a point below the voucher rate. If a state, on the other hand, wanted to discourage students from going on to higher education, it would fix the cash redemption value at a rate higher than the voucher rate and thereby encourage students to take their savings and invest it in alternative kinds of training or activity.

A progressive income tax would provide the second important source of revenue. Since much of the cost of the plan would be absorbed by rechanneled state education subsidies, revenue raised by taxation would be used to offset the rising costs of higher education, the cost of the consumer goods made available to students by the states, the cost of raw materials for student businesses, and the operations of the Children's Income Plan agency. The overall cost of the plan would, of course, be reduced in the event that fewer students elected to go on to higher education, and would rise if more attended.

Notwithstanding, it should be expected that at the start of the plan the number of students collecting vouchers would be relatively few. Costs and the amounts required to alter the cycle of subsidies to higher education would be correspondingly low. To illustrate: John Max is a senior in high school the year CIP gets implemented. He enjoys only a one-year tenure in the plan, but succeeds during that time in earning the equivalent of $3,000 in education vouchers. After graduation he elects to go on to higher education. Upon matriculating in a college of his choice, he receives one quarter of his education-voucher earnings, $750, to meet some of his expenses. Since college costs run $5,000 a year, John Max has to raise an additional $4,250 to pay his bills for one year.

Four years later Carlton Jones enters the plan. Carlton has earned five years of income under the plan, the equivalent of $15,000 in educational vouchers. His total earnings fall short by $5,000 of what he needs to meet his higher-education expenses. Carlton elects to earn $3,000 during the summers and to borrow $2,000. He will repay this loan once he joins the work force. Jill Orear, on the

Payoff Table: Cash vs. HEV Distribution

Percentage rank in graduating class, based on earnings	Just cash	Just HEV	Combination
0–10	2,000	5,000	1,000 plus 2,500
20	2,500	6,500	1,250 plus 3,250
30	3,000	8,000	1,500 plus 4,000
40	3,500	10,500	1,750 plus 5,250
50	4,000	12,000	2,000 plus 6,000
60	4,500	14,500	2,250 plus 7,250
70	5,000	17,000	2,500 plus 8,500
80	5,500	20,000	2,750 plus 10,000
90	6,000		3,000 plus 14,000 or 1,000 plus 20,000
100	7,000		3,000 plus 20,000

other hand, finishes at the top of her high-school class in earnings. When she goes to collect her higher-education voucher she finds she has earned, in addition to higher-education vouchers worth $20,000, a cash bonus of $3,000.

The application of this tentative table of suggested payoffs might be expected to result in the following: on a school-by-school basis it would require students in the 20-to-70-percent range to find additional sources of financial aid. This might involve work, borrowing, parents' contributions, or spending an extra year raising the funds. On the other end of the spectrum, nearly 30 percent of the graduating class of every participating school would matriculate in a college without having to find additional financial aid. The table also suggests the amounts of money that might be made available to students who decided not to attend college. If we assume that it would cost $30,000 to educate each student for four years, it immediately becomes clear that the state would save approximately $23,000 for every student in the highest earnings bracket who elected to take the cash instead of the voucher. Similiarly, for every student in the 60th percentile who elected to go to college, $15,500 of the cost would be assumed by the student either in loans, through work, or by agreeing to participate in a progressive tax levied on future earnings.

While it might be worthwhile to alter these figures to take account of one interest or another, the plan is being advanced in keeping with several key principles. First, it tries to draw an explicit connection between work and the rewards for work. Second, it attempts to place the burden of paying for higher education or advanced training squarely on the shoulders of those who directly benefit from it. Third, the plan tries to equalize opportunities for attending private and public colleges between rich and poor, by providing the poor with enough income or credit to wipe out the advantages the rich now have in placing their sons and daughters in leading universities. And, fourth, the plan weakens the favored status of state-subsidized universities by distributing the subsidies directly to the consumer, and through the consumer to the public and private sectors.

Effects on Students

The Children's Income Plan would provide financial underpinning for the Micro-Society approach. It would do so in the short run by providing Society Schools with the resources to support school currencies and with materials that school enterprises would need to produce wealth. It would do so less directly by removing many of the uncertainties connected with post-secondary-school training. A student who completed what he wanted to do in a Society School would have the wherewithal to contract for services anywhere he chose. In other words, the plan would strengthen links and passage from school activities to real-world activities. By the third or fourth year of secondary school a student could, with some confidence, contract himself to do something a year or two later. This elimination of uncertainty constitutes one of the important benefits the plan would provide to students.

From a psychological perspective, the plan together with the Micro-Society approach should reinforce tendencies toward self-acceptance and toward personal achievement. Not only would the Society School make available a large number of experiences in almost every line of endeavor, but through the plan it would make it possible for students to obtain consumer goods or capital to meet present and future needs as well. In combination, the plan and the Society School would leave the student in greater control of his immediate situation and with greater certainty about the future than is now possible. Such control and certainty might grant students a larger measure of independence from their families than they now enjoy. Parents would no longer shoulder the full burden of supplying their children with necessities or luxuries, and no longer assume any of the responsibility for providing their children with the money to attend college.

On the material level, the Children's Income Plan promises to be of special utility to students from low-income families. If school stores carried the necessities—food, clothing, books, school supplies, etc.—in addition to luxury goods, then students from, say, welfare families would have an alternative to being on the public dole. Similarly, children from wealthy families would be offered an alternative to being on the private dole. In either case, students would learn to rely more on themselves and the fruits of their labor and less on rich or poor legacies left them by their parents.

To these benefits we must add some costs. Any expenditure of funds for higher education, for advanced training, or for school-currency supports that exceeded current expenditures would have to be met through increased revenues from taxation. What this amount might be would depend on several variables, most notably (1) changes in state higher-education enrollment, (2) changes in the demand for non-university advanced career training, (3) the profits reaped by student-operated enterprise, (4) changes in the cost of higher education, and (5) the costs incurred in administering the plan.

If these changes and costs spiraled, the need for tax revenue to offset the costs would rise correspondingly. As presently framed, the financial underpinning for the plan would require those who benefited most directly to pay the costs. Participants in Micro-Society institutions might therefore be required to agree to pay a surtax on their income for as long as twenty years. In effect, a student without the money to capitalize his own career development would be permitted to acquire it at the point in his life when he would otherwise be least able to get it. And in an extension of that logic, it would allow that student to pay the costs of that capitalization over the course of his working life—i.e., when he was best able to do so. If one assumes, for a moment, that those who earned the greatest benefits under the plan would also earn the greatest income in the work force, it seems likely that those who received the greatest benefits would pay proportionally the largest share of the costs.

Under the plan, the minimum benefit for anyone in the student population would be approximately $2,000. The maximum income would be somewhere in the neighborhood of $23,000. Both figures represent U.S. currency earnings during a four-year period. Approximately 70 percent of the total expenditure in school would coincide with current expenditures on publicly supported higher education. The remaining 30 percent would have to be financed from several sources, including enterprises operated by the school, a tax on future earnings, a tax on the present parent population, and a progressive tax with the largest burden falling on the shoulders of the wealthy parents with children attending schools using the Micro-Society approach. This last tax would in effect ask rich parents to buy their children opportunities for meaningful work. It would work correctly, however, only if affluent parents reduced their subsidies to their children in the expectation that their children would earn an amount approximating the reduction through work in school.

Effects on Parents

The plan, in its current form, would help rich parents release their children from the private dole and poor children to obtain income they might otherwise not have. In doing so, the measure would support, in the case of rich or poor, a decrease in economic dependency between children and their parents. Affluent parents would buy their children experience that was less insulated from educative hardship. Poor parents would not have to bear the full burden of passing poverty on to their children. To say it more cryptically, the plan would provide sons and daughters of the wealthy with access to something money has until now been able to buy in only a limited way: the possibility that if one didn't work, that one might not eat.

There would be another, somewhat less tangible benefit to parents, rich or poor. A great deal has been written and a lot more said about the gap between adults and students. Some of the misunderstandings between these two groups can be traced to differences in life style. Many parents, after all, work. Most students perform little labor of the income-producing and necessity-supplying variety. The differences that arise out of these distinct orientations aren't easily extinguished. After all, one provides the other with unlimited leisure time. It is this parasitic relation that supports a neurotic game in which parents play "after all I've done for you," and students play back "it's on your own head." In fact, students have a point. Parents are to blame if they position their children to disappoint them. If students refuse to acknowledge parent sacrifices and the martyrdom implied, who can blame them? In giving students more leisure time than they can profitably use, affluent parents unwittingly conspire against the best interests of their children. Putting children on the private dole can be every bit as spiritually debilitating as putting them on welfare. In either situation, they are made consumers without also becoming producers, and in either case this inculcates the habits of the parasite. Putting children to work and making sure work had meaning as it related both to self-identity and to necessity might help to correct a class war that, in the Marxist sense, pits working parents against their own creations: leisure-class children. The plan proposes to narrow the differences between the two so that parents and children would work and play in roughly equal proportion.

Effects on School Systems and School Personnel

The Children's Income Plan would provide schools with an effective system of extrinsic rewards. This provision speaks to the problem of motivation. Extrinsic-reward systems have imperfections: no reward system on earth can induce bright children to put up with massive doses of drudgery. Still, if utilized properly, incentive programs could be helpful. In cases where students are turned off about school, extrinsic rewards might in the short run interest individuals in making one last try at the school curriculum. However, unless school activity was interesting and compelling in its own right, extrinsic rewards simply wouldn't sustain student interest. In general, those children who now respond to school would continue to respond, and probably with an increase in their activity. Students who had a marginal interest in school might be drawn into the game of acquiring income and see the drudgery of the everyday as something they must put up with to obtain other things they want. A small group of middle-class children would openly rebel against the use of extrinsic compensations on ideological grounds: i.e., they believe in responding only to their own definitions of intrinsic rewards. Another small group of children would not respond to any reward system because their alienation is so extreme. They neither want nor need what scrip would buy. Considerable effort would have to be invested in the development of a reinforcement program that rewarded effort, risk taking, creative or innovative work, as well as civic and academic achievement. In the final analysis, however, a scrip program might contribute more to the management of activity in the school than anything else. Be they teachers or students, its utility of scrip as an instrument for allocating student and faculty energies to priority areas would be incomparable.

On the wage side of the incentive program, one might well expect pressure to build for broadening the kinds of activity eligible for compensation. If that pressure was heeded, it might well mean the reshaping of school activity itself. Schools that began paying students for academic achievement or effort might find themselves also having to compensate students who completed civic, business, and athletic projects. If such a broadening was coupled with an effort to define educational priorities, it could lead to a clarification of the contract operating between suppliers and recipients of educational services. If community participation was the goal, it might be possible to draw parents, students, and teachers into the planning and budgetary hearings during the year. During that process, school objectives could be defined and adult and student energies rationally contributed to implementation.

In addition to the impact of the Plan on the internal affairs of a given school, it seems likely to expect an equivalent impact on the school system as a whole. For example, the plan could very well affect racial and economic imbalances within school districts. Assume, first, that the CIP administering agency would allocate scrip to each school district and each school district would in turn reallocate scrip to individual schools. If a high degree of racial and economic segregation existed within the boundaries of the school district, this simple allocation procedure could very well influence a student's choice of school. To predict just what the effects would be, we have to make several assumptions: (1) that middle-class children are better prepared to achieve in school, and (2) that scrip resources would be allocated on a per-capita basis. Yielding to these assumptions, it is immediately apparent that students of roughly the same absolute ability would earn higher incomes in schools serving low-income populations. By contrast, middle-class children would compete against each other for the economic prize, resulting in a narrower distribution of existing resources. In the low-income school, the same middle-class student would take home a greater share of the school's total scrip allocation.

To a limited degree, income distribution within any given school would be a function of the pricing patterns within each school. If these varied significantly between high- and low-income schools, the distribution could correct itself. However, if low-income schools placed a premium on academic achievement, they might at the same time attract children from middle-income families to higher scrip-earning opportunities within the low-income school. The net effect, of course, would be to reverse the current trend toward racial and economic segregation.

Effects on Public and Private Colleges

The last three decades have seen a startling multiplication in the number and growth of public colleges. In the last five years we have seen a simultaneous decline in the flow of public monies to private universities. In both private and public colleges during both periods we have also witnessed a sharp rise in the cost of a college education. In combination, these three trends threaten to drive the private college out of business and to turn higher education into a public monopoly.

Already the state college, insulated against many of the vicissitudes of belt tightening because of public subsidy, finds itself drawing students away from private colleges. That attraction has little to do with the quality of its services. The main attraction of the public college is the fact that it costs less to go there.

Over the long run, these trends may combine to eliminate all but a few excellent schools that cater mainly to the very rich. At first glance, the loss may seem bearable. At second look, however, there seems to be cause for alarm. The demise of the small private college implies the continued enlargement of impersonal mega-universities. Moreover, few obstacles remain to forestall decay fostered by the lack of competition and the insulation of guaranteed support. The higher-education-voucher feature of the CIP would provide a way to reverse both trends. CIP would confer sovereignty to the education consumer. It would give him the right to purchase the private or public higher education he wants. Parenthetically, higher-education vouchers would check the favored financial status of the public colleges by rechanneling the public-college subsidies to consumers who would then decide whether to spend them in the public or the private sector. The net result would be a fundamental change in the relation of college to its parent and student constituencies. Colleges that became obsolete would either change or go under. Conversely, new colleges could be started by those who became dissatisfied with the existing alternatives, simply by rounding up enough interested voucher-paying students. More important, colleges would have to become more sensitive to the interests of those who consumed their services.

In its operation, the higher-education-voucher feature of the Children's Income Plan has a great deal in common with an Education Voucher Proposal (EVP) authored, among others, by Christopher Jencks. Unlike EVP, the Children's Income Plan stresses the preservation of the private-college system rather than the creation and maintenance of alternative primary and secondary schools. Otherwise, similarities between the Jencks' Voucher Proposal and the Children's Income Plan prevail. For instance, both plan and proposal emphasize consumer sovereignty. Both oppose the monopolization of institutions by the state for the same reason, and both seek to provide students with a wider variety of choices than is now available to them.

Together with the Society School model, however, the plan implies something else: namely, the growth at the undergraduate level of programs in the professions. In the long run, then, the plan would foster the growth of a dual system of higher education. On one side of the dual system sits the liberal-arts college, on the other the professional colleges. There is no reason why a student who has specialized in law and who wants to continue his work in that area should not have access to advanced training in the area of his interest while in college. While a good argument exists supporting the liberal-arts contention that the best education is one that broadens the individual rather than one that narrows his possibilities, I see no reason why distribution requirements in existing liberal-arts colleges couldn't redress any imbalance.

14. The Future of the Model

During the course of the 1972–73 academic year, I succeeded in persuading the Boston School Department and the Boston University School of Education to supply auspices for the continued development of the Micro-Society approach. At this writing, a site has been chosen in Jamaica Plain; the teachers in the selected school voted unanimously to accept the program and my proposal; and an intensive fund-raising effort has been launched. If the funds arrive in time, I fully expect to begin the work of invention and training that will be needed to sustain the effort to establish the model and its practice in the public domain.

It is one thing to draw out a model of what you think should be done; it is quite another to implement it. Implementation calls for very specific thinking and for task orientation. Schools are run by people for people. Schools use materials in carrying out their education functions. Schools provide their services in buildings designed for educative purposes. And most people who have anything to do with the acceptance of a new model of primary and secondary schooling usually want to attach a research component to measure what happens when an idea attempts to be concrete. It follows from this that implementation and development must occur simultaneously in five areas: (1) staff training, (2) preparation of parents and students, (3) development of a materials support system, (4) creation of a suitable physical plant, and (5) the design and implementation of research measures that assess whether or not one accomplishes the objectives of the implementation schema.

Staff Training

A staff-training program will have to be developed. Whether a school is brand new and opens for the first time with a staff selected to implement the model, or already exists with a staff on the premises, teachers will have to change and learn a set of new skills to operate a Society School in an effective manner. This does not mean these skills have to be acquired overnight. Like everything else about the model, they can be acquired gradually.

The skills needed are not simply those required to manage a classroom or those one uses to implement available curriculum packages. The greater the depth of experience the staff has in the professions—medicine, business, social work, law, education, government—the better its preparation to operate a Society School. A staff ideal for the model would dedicate itself to its own intellectual growth. Part of that growth would entail being continually exposed to new activity, new concepts, and new organizations. Ideally, the implementors of the project would themselves have a large appetite for new experience. From this new experience the staff would fashion what it would offer to students. The richer its experience, the richer would be the offering.

A training program for staff would of necessity have to provide teachers with access to institutions other than schools. It would have to call on teachers to develop and create at least one organization. It would have to ask teachers to take responsibility for administering some portion of the implementation affecting the entire project as well as ask teachers to oversee development of much narrower areas.

Since the staff of any implementation would be likely to include a host of people from the community beyond the schoolhouse gate—parents, community businessmen, community professionals, and graduate students from nearby universities—sufficient training too would have to be made available so that such persons would become aware of students, familiar with the organizational behavior of schools, with the orientation of schools using the Micro-Society approach, and with the components of their own experience that should be related to program development.

On general principle, I favor a procedure that would allow the staff to create its own training program. Normally, that program might include experiences within institutions that were not schools, experiences with the materials that had already been developed, experiences organizing one or more of the thrusts intended for the project, studies in the theory of the Society School, and experiences with the research techniques that would be used to ascertain what happened. It would also seem valuable to allocate a reasonable amount of time to moral reasoning, since teachers and other staff would be expected to help their students reflect on the moral and ethical consequences of their actions and milieu.

Preparation of Students

It would seem a good idea to acquaint children with the history of the Society School as the preparation for implementing it. However, as with almost anything, there are two sides to this issue. Students might, in the experience of the past, find guidance for their activity in the present. Those against the proposition would probably be more interested in having students uncover the process themselves. Since the model has not been favored with a long history, taking a stand on either side of the question seems meaningless now. Any new implementation of the Society School is bound to be considerably different from previous efforts.

Materials Support System

Most teachers in present classrooms orient what students do around curriculum materials sold to boards of education by the school departments of the major publishing houses. These include books, reading laboratories, games, and other kinds of software. Once in the school, these materials, which usually offer printed information removed from actual events (secondary experience), supply the main focus for classroom intellectual activity. The support system of curriculum materials I propose to develop in connection with the Society School model will function differently in several respects from the traditional arrangement. Materials developed to support teachers interested in implementing some version of the Society School will be keyed to the unraveling of the historic process devised through the model. In other words, Society School materials will be designed to help change classroom activity and to help students and teachers obtain insights into changing patterns they encounter as the changing microcosm they call school comes closer to being the entity we call society. The Micro-Economy published by Harcourt Brace Jovanovich, for example, supplies teachers and students with materials they need to take the first step toward restructuring the classrooms. It is a set of materials designed to support changes in classroom life, and by my definition a support material, rather than collected information designed to edify students, but to leave school itself undisturbed.

Similarly, I discovered in the process of implementing the Society School, that students needed to know something about accounting and bookkeeping or the school economy would collapse. The development of these materials is currently in progress. Once again, they are being developed with an eye to changing the structure of classroom life so that the learning processes students experience offer direct primary experience rather than pre-packaged information or secondary experience.

However, the main body of support materials probably will fall into the category of raw materials. In a Society School, students need building materials, banking materials, printing materials, tie-dye materials, plants, seeds and the like. Moreover, they need them at various levels of sophistication. For instance, if a student of architecture or a builder of buildings wants to design a miniature house with plumbing in it, he will need to have on hand the equivalent of pipe, the plumber's blueprint, and tools to install pipe properly in the structure he makes. A student who wants to create a building that maximizes the use of energy for power and minimizes the waste will have to have support materials that allow him, in miniature, to choose the optimum energy system for the structure he builds. Succinctly, the materials support system of the Society School would supply the raw or finished materials that would make it possible for students first to think out and then to experience processes that come to them now, at best, in print.

For reasons of simplicity, I have decided to divide materials support-system development into five categories: (1) the Banking and Economics System, (2), the Law and Justice System, (3) the Environment and Construction-Industry System, (4) the Arts and Humanities System, and (5) the Social-Relations System. Each component of the support system would contribute a series of manuals relevant to its area to a sixth component called the Society School Support System. These manuals would recommend the steps necessary to organizing an enterprise in a Society School. For example, it might be useful to future implementors of the model to have monographs elaborating the steps necessary to organizing a postal system, a popcorn concession, a comic-book lending library, a toy-rental business, a toy-manufacturing business, a thrift shop, a crafts store, a real-estate brokerage, a tutorial service, a greeting-card company, a hairdresser, a car wash, a babysitting agency, a law firm, a day-care center, an accounting firm, an architectural firm, a sanitation department, a tax service, a credit-card business, and so on.

The support system might include materials for home use as well. Students who became acquainted with developments in, say, accounting or medicine shouldn't be expected to suppress their interests the moment they left school for home. Readings, tapes, cable TV tapes should be developed to help those who wanted to continue at home the explorations begun in school. Other materials might be designed to instruct parents about what their children were doing in school. Still other materials might be developed to supply the home with educational components that complemented the Micro-Society approach in school. A complete support system would also consist of fiction and non-fiction works related to Society Schooling, feature films and documentaries, and a television series that acquainted children with their possibilities.

Research

What kind of research suits the model? What measures should be developed to help us systematically discover whether a given implementation of the Society School model works? What techniques do we use to isolate the variables, and to conduct multi-variate analysis? A discussion of research methodology falls outside the intended scope of this book. However, a sketch of research that might be done does not.

My inclination is to divide the Micro-Society approach into four convenient categories: (1) economic research, (2) research into the political life of a Micro-Society, (3) study of the impact of the model on psycho-social development of individuals and on the climate of the school, and (4) impact of the model on measures of traditional academic performance. Each one of these categories can be approached at any one of four levels: (1) individual growth and change, (2) small-group growth and change, (3) organizational growth and change, and (4) society growth and change.

Because the Micro-Society approach advances the idea that schools produce goods and services, it would seem sensible to develop measures to assess how well schools do this. It might be useful, for instance, to know the total value of goods and services produced in schools. It might be useful to discover the optimum rate of capital formation, to assess rates of employment or unemployment, to study student consumption patterns, to measure trade between classrooms, between schools, and between schools and other institutions in the community. It would seem equally worthwhile to measure the rate of economic growth, the distribution of wealth, the distribution of leisure, the number and kind of business transactions (as an index of student activity), the distribution of career opportunities and experiences, and the long- and short-run input of elementary and secondary career-education experiences on eventual occupational choices. Together or singularly, these measures might tell us a great deal about the economic consequences of the education.

It should also be possible to assess the impact of political process on students. Researchers might wish to consider the short- and long-run effects of the Micro-Society approach on students and teacher understanding of economic and political process. It might be useful to discover whether students learn how to gain and use political power responsibly. It might be equally useful to study the impact that ideology prevalent outside the school has on the formation of political ideologies within. However interesting these questions may be, few would compare in interest with a test of the hypothesis that states the Micro-Society approach alters student affiliations in peer groups and changes the anatomy of an individual's status in his peer group.

Psycho-social research could deal with an equally wide range of human behavior. For example, some psychologists would be interested in assessing what if any changes occur in achievement motive, in moral reasoning, and in cognitive development. Some would center on the impact of the learning environment on the basic structures of human personality. Others might limit studies to learning behavior and growth.

Psychologists who focused on small groups might wish to study transactions between individuals and small groups, the impact of the Micro-Society legal process on students, peer-group climate within the school, the impact of the Micro-Social system on pre-Micro-Society group structures, etc. At the organization level, students and researchers might investigate institutional behavior and human behavior in institutions in the early, middle, and late stages of Micro-Society development. Others might study the impact of the model on the family, or on families at different ends of the socio-economic spectrum.

Sociologists might focus on the broader issues: how students cope with self-alienation, with the alienation of various subgroups, and the organization of the Micro-Society social system and its implications for individuals in the school. It would seem logical, for instance, for this group to study the role of women in the Micro-Society, and the long-term effect on women who early perform as judges, architects, contractors, lawyers, bankers, and in other professional roles. Similarly, if the Society School develops an active collection of enterprises that supply social services to the local community, it might be of interest to ascertain under what circumstances male students will explore occupational roles traditionally the preserve of women: teaching, day care, secretarial work, etc., and the effect these explorations might have on career choice.

It would be informative as well as worthwhile also to assess the achievement of Micro-Society children on the academic level. At the outset, at least, traditional educators and the public would demand it, and satisfying those demands would seem both expedient and wise.

However, the logic of this commentary should not be mistaken. I refuse to see school as a necessary way station en route to something else, or as a time for immersion in secondary experience. Schools must provide primary experience valuable to those who become active in them. Life in school must be made at least as compelling as life in society itself. It would therefore behoove the researcher to measure how well children digest such primary experience. Instead of measuring the effects of increased expenditures on reading scores leading ultimately to economic growth, measure the effect of increased expenditure on economic growth in the school Micro-Society. Instead of assessing the effects literacy has on employment and on income, measure the effects employment and income have on literacy. It might also be interesting to look at the longitudinal effect of the model on graduates' employment and income. Instead of hypothetical growth rates produced by schooling, measure the real rate of growth that schools produce in the community. Give up applying numbers to spirit and apply numbers where they fit best: on concrete countable things. More important, we must begin to question the application of factory research metaphors on areas of school life that have little or no legitimate kinship with the factory. At the same time, we should consider applying them where they do.

PART III

Theory

15. School and Society

If I dared attempt a complete exegesis of the theoretical contributions the Micro-Society model draws upon, I would divide them into three parts. The first would deal simply with education theory, relating what has been proposed to antecedent theory and practice of such figures as Dewey, Wirt, Mann, Pestalozzi, Froebel, Montessori, Rugg, and Illich. Second, such an exegesis might also tackle the whole range of middle-level theory dealing with cognitive development, behavioral psychology, organizational development, intervention theory, and general learning theory. Contributions on this level are so many that it would almost be impossible to include them all. In any case, the model owes less to middle-level theorists than it does to a third level: social philosophy. If one could set aside, just for a moment, the contribution of John Dewey, the greatest debts this model owes are to Hegel, Marx, Goethe, Kant, and Feuerbach. In somewhat lesser proportions, it owes debts to Locke, Voltaire, Adam Smith, and Hobbes.

However, the model's debt to Dewey and to other middle-level education theorists is an abiding one. Dewey first called for a marriage between schooling and experience, a call echoed in the preceding pages and in the schools in which I have worked. Dewey wanted to admit the world outside the classroom into school so that students could learn to cope with increasing dosages of life under the protection of adults trained to help children learn from their mistakes and to anticipate problems. The Micro-Society approach calls for a similar connection between school and society. At the secondary level, however, the model pushes Dewey further than Dewey went in this respect, calling for the admission of schools into the outside world.

Growth of Society in School

Echoing Dewey, the Society School model rejects the kind of schooling that is an imposition from above and from outside, in favor of a growing from within. That growth resonates with Dewey's concern for human personal growth; it sets as a coordinating goal the building of society as well as of self. Similarly, Dewey criticized schools for relying on predigested experience: secondary experience instead of concentrating on putting children in touch with primary experience. The model offered responds to that protest as well.

Dewey understood that making a true connection between education and experience depended on having a correct idea of experience. Here again we agree. However, here in my view we also disagree. For if we agree that a correct idea of experience precedes selecting those experiences that are most crucial for students and therefore to be given priority in school, we do not agree on a definition of "correct experience."

As Dewey himself put it, all experiences are not equally educative, and some experiences are even mis-educative. He defined those that were most educative as immediate "experiences that live fruitfully and creatively in subsequent experiences," and he urged educators to share the burden of deciding between experiences that were educative and those that were not. In doing so, he established two principles sacred among educational innovators. He urged educators to secure the genuine and active cooperation of the pupil in the construction of the purposes involved in his studying. And he regarded learning as a developmental and evolutionary process. Both principles have been incorporated in the Micro-Society approach, not simply at the level of personal growth but at the level of social growth as well. In other words, the Society School carries the same principle to another level. Not only must individuals grow, but also the social system that we call school must develop, grow, evolve, and become an expression of its members and hence of their collective personal growth. To be even more precise, Dewey did not recognize that the true substance of schooling and of the experiences schools offered needed to be the historical process itself—that one could create the basic threads of social process—economics, politics, social relations—and allow children to build society in a way that would be immediate and would put them in touch with the great processes, issues, and confrontations of past, present, and future.

Dewey wanted first to humanize and personalize the learning process, and then to democratize it. Unlike the Micro-Society approach, which leaves open the end result of social process, or at least leaves it in the hands of those who become involved with the Society School, Dewey chose what he considered to be the best and only outcome of the education process he affirmed; he chose democracy—not democracy as it was practiced, with its flaws and its brilliant moments, but ideal democracy. In making this choice, he violated his own principle: he accepted the imposition of knowledge from above, and rejected democracy itself. Dewey defended his commitment to a democratic ideology on the grounds that "democratic social arrangements promote a better quality of human experience, one which is more widely accessible and enjoyed, than do non-democratic and anti-democratic forms of social life." Furthermore, he held that the "principle of regard for individual freedom and for decency and kindliness of human relations comes back in the end to the conviction that these things are tributary to a higher quality of experience, on the part of a greater number, than are methods of repression and coercion." Dewey wanted people to have control of their lives in order to participate as equals in social relationships; this requirement was entirely compatible with his belief in a democratic society, but entirely incompatible with democratic ideology itself. Dewey called on educators to relinquish autocratic roles, yet he refused to be democratic about how he went about achieving democracy.

Dewey saw freedom as a means to *becoming*. Becoming required active occupation. *Doing* (work) permits children to "affiliate themselves with life." He contrasted active occupation with the education he opposed: "learning of lessons having an abstract and remote reference to some possible living to be done in the future." The occupation program he envisioned for schools formed in an embryonic community where "doing" operated as an introduction to work in society. Like that of the Society School, the aim of this work was not simply production; it was the development of social power and insight.

However, Dewey insisted that these insights could be drawn without going into the "narrow utilities" of economic reality. "It is this liberation from narrow utilities," Dewey wrote, "this openness to the possibilities of the human spirit that makes these practical activities in the school allies of art and centers of science and history." Dewey wanted "occupations in school freed of all economic stress." Affiliation with democratic ideals and hence of genuine learning could be obtained only by ignoring the "narrow utilities" that might inhibit the child's exploration of science, art, and history. It was precisely these *narrow utilities* that Dewey called mis-educative experience; and here Dewey and I differ once again. A theory of experience that omits economic stress and the social conflicts it engenders robs Dewey's theory of experience of much of its authenticity. Similarly, students who have been deprived of the experience of producing some goods or services of genuine value to someone else have been deprived of a social connection more valuable than can be measured in material terms.

We should build from the point where Dewey's vision left off. Thus, if we recognize that Dewey preaches a romanticism that can unwittingly lead to disillusionment and nihilism in those who become disappointed with existing forms of democracy, we should also recognize that Dewey saw possibilities for creating embryonic communities in school that have yet to be achieved. We should learn to see ideals for what they are in the context of what can be realized; we must learn to recognize where ideology fails us, or, alternatively, where we fail it by being less than we are.

One cannot get at a correct idea of experience by discounting the press of economic reality on other parts of the social system. To permit this discounting and then to build an idea of school on it is equivalent to allowing a false idea of experience to dictate the model of education. Such an allowance casts the school into the position of supplying students with counterfeit experiences. Ultimately, this leads idealists to relinquish the world to non-idealists, making humanists forget how to insist that the world conform to what they consider to be right and good. A truer new education requires a theory of experience that integrates the fundamental contexts, structures, and forces of actual existence and that distributes these in sufficient doses of reality so that students learn to shape themselves and the world in which they dwell.

The Dependent Community

To insist that we must arrive at a correct idea of experience that includes economic stress, social conflict, and legitimate political processes places the emphasis where it must be placed. Still, there are other priorities that deserve emphasis as well. Newmann and Oliver, in their *Harvard Educational Review* article "Education and Community," gave priority to community experience, defined as closely knit, self-sufficient, rural group life in which the extended family serves not only the function of procreation but also as the center of economic production, education, recreation, religion, care of the sick and aged, safety and defense.

The Micro-Society approach agrees with this sense of the world. Community has been missing in urban society. Mass society has generated the kind of alienation that allows neighbors to live side by side without knowing each other. It has produced a human experience that is fragmented, often ideologically and aesthetically bankrupt, an impersonal world that may be over-industrialized and over-mechanized. Together these components of modern life sum to a condition of self-alienation and estrangement from society. Echoing Newmann and Oliver, the Society School attempts to deal with this alienation by forming and building community.

In contrast to Dewey, who focused on the school and on the goals of improving schooling, Newmann and Oliver stress the fundamental priority of the contexts in which education is pursued. The Micro-Society approach attempts to integrate these two foci. It does so in its two stages, Building Society In School and Building Society From School, and posits an idea of school that essentially is activist and entrepreneurial.

The Society School holds other points of interest in common with what Newmann and Oliver offer. Both are, for example, pluralistic models that permit competing factions to exist and struggle within the same community. Both make it possible for every kind of ideological premise and practice to have its day and develop its influence, and both encourage a high level of participation and activity.

But we have differences as well. Newmann and Oliver promote a notion of withdrawal from what they call "great society" and predict its ultimate unraveling. While I agree that such withdrawal might be a good idea, I see very little hope for getting mass society to reverse the momentum it has built over the past 500 years, or for convincing Americans that they should give up consuming at the levels to which they have grown accustomed. Both conditions would have to be met before mass society could be unraveled.

The major difference between the Micro-Society approach and the tri-school model Newmann and Oliver propose in their article centers on the handling of economic activity. Like Dewey, they fail to map the economic life of the communities they propose to build. In evading responsibility for structuring the contexts, organizing the producing enterprises, and generating wealth, they in effect commit students to an extended period of idleness, and to the parasitic state of being consumers without being producers.

It becomes only a matter of time before the basic parasitic relationship between the tri-school model and the "great society" asserts itself, addicting students to feeding off those who work. The evasion of economic experience also robs the tri-school community of one of the central motives for having community in the first place—namely, shared responsibility for physical survival and for production of goods and services.

Ironically, instead of fostering community, the tri-school model fosters dependency on the very great society it claims to want to undo. Instead of generating human relationships in which no one person can appropriate the Time or Will of another, the Newmann-Oliver proposal fosters a relationship in which the tri-school appropriates the Time, Will, and Property of the "great society." The Micro-Society approach rejects this dependency. It asks its participants to produce things of economic value and to face the social issues that material needs pose in concrete as well as abstract terms. To do less is to risk turning the entire educative program into a series of endless debates and aborted attempts to do something besides talk.

De-Schooling

Ivan Illich has proposed a third model. Like Dewey, Newmann, and Oliver, he seeks a better link between education and experience. But, unlike either "new education" or the "tri-school idea," Illich sees schooling as the main obstacle to experience. He therefore proposes to abolish school, as part of an attempt to create a new style of educational relationship between man and his environment that will lead to a process of de-institutionalization. As the first step in the process, he proposes to give people the tools to change the structure of daily life, and unobstructed access to experience.

Illich's call for a new style of relationship between man and his experience in a sense does Newmann and Oliver one better in getting at the contexts of education; he seeks to abolish institutions that situate themselves between man and his experience. On the other hand, Illich all but ignores man's need for institutions and, in so doing, copes less well with the realities of human wants.

The abolition of institutions produces a different definition of education. Education, according to Illich, should have but one purpose: to make experience accessible to everyone. He believes that "we can depend on self-motivated learning instead of employing teachers to bribe or compel students to find the time to learn." The educator's job is "to provide the learner with new links to the world instead of continuing to funnel all educational programs through the teachers." This can be accomplished, Illich believes, if we do three things: (1) provide all who want to learn with access to available resources at any time in their lives; (2) empower all who want to share what they know to find those who want to learn it from them; (3) furnish all who want to present an issue to the public with the opportunity to make their challenge known. Illich is calling for both the liberation of learners from obligatory instruction, and the liberation of knowledge from those who have made professions out of appropriating it. And this is Illich's main theme: that bodies of information and skills (experience) must be made accessible to the learner.

In practical terms, Illich proposes to gain this access for the learner by issuing him an edu-card that entitles him to an allotment of public funds to be used over the first thirty-five years of life when and where he sees fit. During the years of infancy, a child's edu-card could be used by his mother so that she could learn to teach her offspring. After infancy, attendance at a learning center would be made obligatory for one or two months a year between the ages of five and thirty. The rest of the year could be spent working, traveling, reading, and experiencing with the edu-card purchasing access to parks, theaters, libraries, trips, and so on. Students who wanted to could also purchase the time of coaches, tutors, psychologists, and gurus.

The core of these suggestions, however, depends on the creation of what he calls "learning networks." These networks would insure everyone of ample access to the available resources of a good educational system at any time in their lives. Typically, "that system would be divided into four categories of resources: *things,* people who serve as *models* for skills and values, *peers* who challenge one to argue, to compete, to cooperate, and to understand, and *elders* who expose the student to criticism and to the experience of individuals from a different generation." Access to these resources could be obtained through networks that put the things and the people that the individual needs to learn within reach. Illich lists four such networks: Reference Services to Educational Objects; Skill Exchanges, Peer Matching, and Reference Services to Educators at large.

These suggestions, Illich insists, will end the practice of maintaining larger and larger segments of the population in schools for longer and longer. It would end the furious pace at which educators must sustain the continuous demand for their services especially as those services come into greater and greater disrepute. Most important, Illich sees his proposal as an attempt to abolish the institutions that situate themselves between man and knowledge.

As one would expect, the abolition of schools produces a radically different definition of education. It implies, for instance, students who out of natural curiosity pursue learning. It also implies an alteration in the educator's role, from someone who selects experiences for students to someone who forges new opportunities and new access routes to the continually changing world of experiences. Similarly, it supplies a process of education that permits all who want to share what they know to find those who have what they want in abundance. In other words, Illich calls for unimpeded access to knowledge. In making this call he knits his proposal to the same Deweyian principles that form the fabric of the Micro-Society approach.

Illich's proposal has many attractive features. Not only does it make experience accessible in some imaginative ways, but it also provides educational resources directly to consumers of learning: children. For teachers, administrators, publishers of educational materials, and others associated with schooling, this represents a radical change in the way things are being done; it gives priority to the consumer of learning instead of to the "supplier." Notwithstanding these merits, it is hard to see why we should be optimistic about the enactment of Illich's proposal.

To my mind, it is far more reasonable to expect professional educators to increase the influence of the institutions they control, rather than the reverse. For one, huge resources, jobs, salaries, facilities would be at stake if Illich's proposal were adopted. We can expect those who now control them to protect their prerogatives. Second, Illich's proposal has no compelling economic rationale (it would probably be very costly) to attract a following from any interest group that could make it happen. Without such a rationale, there is little chance of triggering a Reformation of Schooling. Like the two proposals considered earlier, "computer learning networks" inhabits a high moral plane; humanism supplies its most compelling rationale. To put it mildly, as far as America and its spheres of influence are concerned, the business of America is business, not virtue; so appeals to virtue that are badly capitalized and poorly advertised have about as much chance of success as the proverbial rich man has of getting into heaven.

Notwithstanding the unlikelihood of actualizing Illich's scheme in the United States, we should not close our ears to the prophetic cries coming from the wilderness of Cuernavaca. Illich's conception is immaculate even if the solution he offers should turn out to be renderable only through divine intervention. His vision comes from the heart, and it has illuminated things for those of us who could not see into the confusion. The power of his call resides in his protest against the institutionalization of children; he sees that institutionalization is inimical to human freedom. The alternative, he insists, is personal self-determination, and his insistence on this point recalls the passionate nationalist calling for freedom from imperial rule.

Further, Illich rails against school bureaucracies that put the impersonal goals of the institution ahead of the children whom they hold in custody. As an alternative, Illich proposes a humanism unencumbered by economics of scale, by requirements for dependency, or by mediums who, with narrow vision and excessive authority, steer their flocks to suicide through an overdose of schooling. In the Protestant tradition, Illich insists on an unmediated vision, a vision in which institutions diminish their role as mediators between Man and Knowledge. Like prophets and Protestants before him, who drove moneychangers from the temple, and clerics from situating themselves between God and Man, Illich urges us to drive academics from their classrooms and to join mankind intimately with experience. In what approaches the prose of the Protestant Reformation, he tenders our release from the secular City of God called school.

Illich is not preoccupied with a vision of institutional utopianism. In fact, it is quite the reverse. His ideal vision requires men to de-institutionalize society—a kind of anarchism. Like Dewey, Oliver, and Newmann, he is asking for a more personal style of relationships between men and other men, and between men and their experience. Unlike Newmann's and Oliver's, that personal style need not occur within the context of an organized community. It is here that Illich and I differ. For while I am perfectly sympathetic to Illich's desire to free men from their bondage to institutions, I think he has made too optimistic an assessment of what man is and wants.

We merchants of change must recognize the difficulties our proposals imply for the people inhabiting the institutions we target for "reform" or for "reconstruction." When we speak of altering institutions, we are really saying that we want to change the people in them. That's a humbling prospect. People who will not lift a finger to aid a fellow in trouble will fight tooth and nail to preserve their possessions and their prerogatives. It is one thing to advocate change to a celebrated fraction of mankind tuned into revolution, but it's quite another to raise an individual or a group to a higher stage of moral reasoning and action. If the future is anything like the past, the call for a de-schooled society in the terms Illich suggests, however potent, will be stilled by a population unconscious of servitude and deaf to moral persuasion. I think Illich is being particularly prophetic in realizing that men will uncover ways to institutionalize his message.

Illich's central assumption is that men want to be free. I am not convinced he can take that for granted. Most people regard institutions as sources of security, not as inhibitors of human freedom; most people see corporations as useful economic tools offering them employment and not as custodians of their minds and hearts; most people view socializing agencies such as schools as transmitters of man's mastery over his environment from generation to generation, and not as a pack of Frankensteins intent on the destruction of their creators. Illich appeals to men as they could be, but not to men as they are. His heroes prefer liberation to being held captive by security. Paradoxically, this is the learning-network proposal's strength and weakness: strength because it wants the best for men, weakness because it ignores men as they are. Unless I am mistaken, most men want the institutional security that Illich proposes to free them from.

I am drawn to Illich's vision, despite my doubts about its efficacy. I think it draws me because of its irreverence, because it tears down educational icons, and who nowadays wants to be caught defending icons? But its appeal does not make me optimistic about its chances for enactment. On the contrary, most people believe in school the way people once believed in the Church. That may say more about the needs of people for institutions than for their desire to be freed from institutions. Moreover, a huge school bureaucracy keeps itself busy making sure schools continue to grow, to make converts, to adapt themselves to the latest ideas, and to perpetuate the demand for schooling.

To be sure, if one looks within the elite corps of the educated, one can find doubters, even disbelievers in school. Many of these agnostics and atheists of schooling work for schools—are, in fact, in the service of the imperial vision that wants to transform the whole world into a school and the school into the whole world. It may sound cynical, but I think these atheists and agnostics of schooling could be relied on to restrain their iconoclasm should, say, the Nixon administration cut Alma Mater from the welfare rolls. After all, didn't the call to de-school society come from a school, albeit one in Cuernavaca? Can this be another case in which revolution gets turned into a commodity, to be bought and sold among a privileged elite, in which priests work their mysterious magic to turn intangibles into tangibles, and in which men end up joining a new sect—this time a sect of disbelievers?

Unlike Illich's "learning networks," the Society School is premised on an unidealized perception of men. It does not assume the self-motivated man; it begins with the average man, the man who sometimes is self-motivated and other times is not. Another Society School premise is that few men share the moral awareness of an Illich, an Oliver, a Newmann, or a Dewey. The average man hasn't given a thought to the harmful effects of the certification process and wouldn't want to do anything about it if he had. Fundamentally, Illich's desire to liberate men from institutions translates into an effort to make them reject their servitude to bread; he points us toward a spiritual reality, one that is reached after a rejection of what Newmann and Oliver call the "great society." I assume the contrary: most men would forsake the promise of freedom Illich offers for the promise of bread. Illich wants to give men the opportunity to be free; what he really wants is to make them aware that they have been enslaved by the institutions they have created. But men have been enslaved by the need for bread, and therefore, to those who control the supply of bread.

My idea of the unidealized man, the common man, agrees with the Grand Inquisitor in Dostoevsky's *Brothers Karamazov,* when he says men prefer bread "to some idea of freedom which they in their simplicity and their natural unruliness cannot even understand, which they fear and dread, for nothing has ever been more insupportable for man and human society than freedom." This by no means suggests that there aren't tens of thousands of men who liberate themselves by chosing some idea of heaven over bread (material goods). But what are they compared to the millions, the tens of millions, who cry to be fed before they are asked to be virtuous? And for their ration of bread these men turn to the institutions from which Ivan Illich would liberate them. The Society School starts from the assumption that men want bread and that education should help them obtain it, produce it, and distribute it.

The Society School begins from a second major premise: that schools will remain much as they are—resistant to changes from without and indifferent to changes from within. One need only walk into a Boston or New York high school to discover the obvious parallels between schools and penal institutions. In the above cities, uniformed police have been assigned to the schools, making them virtually societies of captives. In some categories school crime rose 7,000 percent in 1969 alone. On the other hand, while some schools have become more custodial, some have become less so: Parkway School experiments, schools without walls, free schools, progressive schools, and open classrooms emphasize innovation and liberty. These so-called "liberation schools" have developed in nearly every major metropolitan area. Some have occurred even in more rural settings. But they have served a narrow population (a small percentage of the total student population), drawn largely from the over-schooled upper middle class. As Illich would point out, the "free" institutions they have created do not challenge the idea of school; school remains the mediating influence, only the world of experience is now defined as school. All this is to say that as long as the certification process remains operable, schools as we know them will remain intact. Because they have situated themselves between childhood and adulthood, and have monopolized the passage from one to the other, schools are insulated against major alterations. They simply digest whatever new idea comes along.

Our single hope for change, it seems to me, rests with our ability to develop a process in which students begin to see men and institutions as they are. I do not think this can be done simply by turning children out on the world, or by making experience accessible through "learning networks," although both steps succeed in linking experience and education more intimately. Our best hope is in looking at ourselves and at each other without the falsifying vision of an ideal man or of a paradise. We may then be able to differentiate between what is possible and what we want. Fundamentally, we must come to understand that institutions are fictions; they have no personalities, no morals, no ethics other than those men give them. People are real. If we make changes, they must be changes in men. I agree with Illich that one way of getting at man is by unlocking the secrets of his institutions. But, unlike Illich, I do not think this gets done by abolishing schools. Students must gain access to the mysteries of budgets, financial statements, institutional operations, ownership, and technological practices. We can help them. Together we can learn to develop strategies and methods for altering institutions and the people in them. But one of the few places this can be done is in school.

Dewey, Newmann and Oliver, and Illich agree that schools are out of phase with experience. The Society School originates as a response to the same disorientation. If it has arrived at a different solution, it is because it starts from a different concept of experience. Dewey left the *context* of education out of his concept of experience. Newmann and Oliver admit the contexts, but are unable to offer us a mechanism or a theory of institutional reconstruction that diminishes dependency on the "great society." Illich takes a different tack. He suggests that reconstruction could be accomplished by doing away with school institutions altogether. His learning networks offer a practical way of making experience accessible to everyone. My reservations about Illich's scheme are two: (1) that he begins with an ideal man, and (2) that the learning networks he proposes fail to make certain kinds of institutional experience accessible to students.

This last reservation requires elaboration. I am not suggesting that we make available to children institutional experiences of a kind with which they have been more than adequately supplied. I am suggesting that there are institutional experiences that are and continue to be inaccessible to children. If a student is lucky, he will graduate from school with a piecemeal understanding of how the major institutions in society operate. He will have obtained fractions of experience without having been exposed to the ideological networks that order that experience and make it coherent. He will look at the "great society" he enters as a larger, unmanageable, chaotic series of stimuli that will atrophy every response he makes to them. What's the alternative? To make available to a student legitimate political, social, and economic experiences that will in the end inform and form his ideology. To do this we must create a society small enough for the student to manage and large enough to breed the kind of expertise that convinces individuals that they can have some measure of control over the environment.

Students in present schools have only limited access to legitimate political experience. Since by definition children are excluded from the American electorate, this exclusion may appear natural. But systematically excluding them from any experience with an electoral process probably does more than anything else to guarantee their apathy as adults. At best, courses in history and student-council politics offer secondary exposure to a watered-down version of political experience. Few students take this rather soupy kind of experience seriously. If it is not oversimplified, then it is either too abstract or too unappealing to be bothered with. Students wherever possible should be given access to experience, not access to pre-digested experience.

Similarly, school makes only a limited kind of social experience available to students. In urban schools and in many suburban schools, peer status varies with the amount of muscle one can command. In other words, the rule of social organization is physical force; inmates of the institution vie to create and then to control reward and punishment mechanisms as a way of demonstrating their importance. Teachers and other adults contribute to this force ethic through their own behavior as punitive authorities. Totally absent is any experience in consentual relationships where legal or social contracts dictate mutual responsibilities or duties. Even rarer, if that is possible, is any experience with interpersonal behavior based on an ethical-principle orientation. More specifically, few students experience what it means to be responsible for the welfare of large groups of people participating in common enterprise. Even fewer discover the nature of the relationship the employer should maintain with the employed. Authority roles in present schools are entirely monopolized by adults. Children are systematically taught to behave as followers, to follow the plans others make for them, rather than to operate as leaders in charge of the destinies of themselves and others. The Society School would reverse this. We would insist that the docile, the obedient, and the passive student become active as a matter of survival; that he assume authority roles and learn to use authority responsibly; and that he form his self-concept by demonstrating his ability to lead or to be competent in one of the multiple institutions he and his peers create.

More important to some is the fact that graduates and dropouts enter economic settings that are totally foreign to them after more than a decade of schooling. Financial statements are as impenetrable to the average "schooled" person as an ancient alphabet; public policies made in Washington that ultimately cost millions of people their jobs and health are riddles to the average "degreed" student, let alone to graduates of our high schools. Interest rates paid to obtain things on installment plans are incomprehensible to many; the financing required to start a business venture and the ways to obtain it are beyond the reach of most students who have been schooled; the manipulations of white-collar thieves go undiscovered because few of us have the economic sophistication to detect them; students leave school without even rudimentary experience in planning their finances, becoming victims of their own fumbling, and the rich—masters of the economic process—learn to thread their way through the tax structure, leaving the burden of payment on those who can least afford it. Instead of mastering the economics of the environment, the ignorant fall back on slogans to decide important economic matters, leaving them in a position of servitude to the informed. Schooling has left the average graduate of school unprepared to select his place in the economy, unaware of how socio-economic status affects his economic chances, and unable to defend himself against those whose primary business amounts to the exploitation of his ignorance.

The Society School would make political, social, and economic experiences, heretofore unavailable to students, accessible. The secrets of men and of their institutions can be unlocked. Their revelation would be a great stride toward an informed citizenry who might become masters of an environment in which they now meander merely as victims. One reasonable way of gaining access to these experiences is by schooling students in institutions that resemble society. The setting I have proposed seeks to reveal the secrets and the difficulties inherent in all institutional and human activity. Essentially, experience in the Society School would provide the basis for insight into men, men in institutions, and institutions themselves.

To obtain this experience, it is necessary to admit the defects we associate with the human condition and with society, as well as the possibilities. Dewey omitted economic and political stress from his "new education" because he saw them as "narrow utilities" that weakened the democratic message. In doing so, he omitted some of the very experiences that are most educative. Whether one's objective is to see things as they are or to make things as they should be, it is essential that we permit students to solve real problems while they are in school. They must learn to cope with existence (including freedom and the real restrictions on it), not with some idea of existence. It might be argued that the Society School itself is a metaphor for experience, that what is needed is to throw students directly into the world and let experience be their teacher (Paul Goodman). I disagree. If we put students out in the world, they probably would have as great a chance of becoming the victims of their inexperience as present graduates of school. If constructed properly, a Society School would allow adult experience to inform the young about the institutions they will enter as adults.

There would be economic conflict in the Society School; there would be crime; there would be children who rejected their teacher's fondest notion of paradise for the promise of bread. Assume for a moment that in the process of confronting these defects, participants in a Society School elected to create a just society in their school. Students and teachers who managed to get the school community to adopt this idea of paradise as their goal might reasonably be required to accept responsibility for its enactment. When crime occurred in the school community, they would be responsible for turning what offended them into community issues and into confrontations between the offender and his community.

These economic conflicts, as stimuli, would make social responses necessary. These social responses, in whatever shape they came, would provide the basis for building a legal system. Although its exact form would vary from school to school and from community to community, it is fairly safe to predict that during the evolution of a Society School legal system, all issues—moral, immoral, and amoral—would be raised, met, and received by the community. These confrontations and the discussions they aroused would lead unavoidably toward a system of justice where legal experience would be made accessible to everyone. Such a justice system might be contrasted with the operation of existing legal institutions in society. In fact, the Society School might agree to serve as a model for judicial reform. Social responses generated by the inadequacies of economic practice would represent the first step toward the creation of a viable social system in the Society School. The peaceful resolution of differences establishes an important precedent; it represents the first real step toward an approximate definition of community.

The teacher's role in this community process should be stated clearly. I see teachers playing the dual role of moral interventionist and technical adviser. Their job on the one hand would be to make students aware of action and of its consequences, to expose the underlying principles upon which moral behavior is premised, and to make past moral experience accessible to students in the present. On the other, teachers with extensive political, economic, and social skills, background, and knowledge would be paid to share what they knew and had with students. The teacher would also help students to organize programs in the school, and to contact institutions and individuals in the community outside the school for help, information, or new experience.

If, for example, students and teachers chose as the goal of their Society School the recovery of community, then the objective of the school would become, in Newmann's and Oliver's terms, an experience of education in community. The outcome of this experience would be a feeling of integration with other people, an aesthetic experience where enduring social relationships occurred in an environment where individuals, confident of their efficacy, defined a common good that allowed them to remain individuals. However, the means to this education would not disregard the necessity of relying on macro-society for the goods and services to sustain micro-society. The Micro-Society would produce wealth and make the decisions about its distribution. Whether that distribution came to be based on need, on work, or on one's success in accumulating capital would be decided by the members of the Micro-Society.

For the present, enough has been said about the kind of experience a Society School would make generally available. The greater lesson, the so-called hidden curriculum, would be society building itself. For in society building, students would learn how to make history. Moving from this lesson in personal efficacy to its practice, not only in school but in life, would provide the overall direction of both the participants and the model. But we begin from where we are, from where schools are. If urban schools resemble prisons intent on perfecting the custodial art, then we begin there. If there are open classrooms, we begin there. An old Boston couple once found themselves lost in Maine. They stopped to ask a farmer for directions to Augusta and were told, "Well, I wouldn't start from here if I were you." Any directions might apply if one happened to be starting from someplace else; we need to forge a map from where we are.

Index

About the Author

George Richmond grew up in a Lower East Side tenement, where his interest in painting brought him to the attention of a scholarship program that helped him attend Yale University. After graduation in 1966, he taught fifth grade in Brooklyn, and there he invented his Micro-Economy game.

After a year in New York, Richmond became assistant director and then director of the Transitional Year Program in New Haven, a compensatory education program serving minority students. From 1970 to 1973, Richmond worked on his doctorate from the Harvard School of Education, and simultaneously commuted to New York to direct the Society School project at a Lower East Side school. He is now principal of the Cohasset Junior High School in Massachusetts.

73 74 75 76 77 10 9 8 7 6 5 4 3 2 1